Maroon Heart:
The Gary Mackay Story

Maroon Heart:
The Gary Mackay Story

Gary Mackay with Mark Donaldson

Fort Publishing Ltd

First published in 2008 by Fort Publishing Ltd, Old Belmont House,
12 Robsland Avenue, Ayr, KA7 2RW

Printed by Polskabook Ltd

Cover photographs courtesy of PA Photos

Graphic design by Mark Blackadder

Typesetting by 3btype.com

ISBN: 978-1-905769-13-1

Contents

Foreword

Alex MacDonald
Hearts manager 1981–1990

It's just as well Gary Mackay was good at football . . . because he was bloody useless at most other sports!

I had the misfortune to have him as my doubles partner in a pool competition at a pub near our hotel in Nairn during pre-season at the end of July 1983. There was no way I wanted any of my players to beat me in the tournament, but my quest for greatness wasn't helped when he was drawn out the hat alongside me. He was appalling and needless-to-say we were beaten in the first round.

I think there was a bit of skulduggery going on when I was then drawn against Gary in the singles competition. His teammates were giving him stick for missing simple pots, claiming he wasn't even trying to beat me, but in truth he was simply awful. The fact he ended up spitting on me instead of the chalk before one particular shot was a fair indication of his accuracy!

Joking aside, Gary was a model professional both on and off the football pitch and always gave 100 per cent in everything he did. It was total dedication from him at all times and he was always keen to learn in a bid to improve as a player. He was the type of guy that every manager would love to have in the dressing room – someone you really could hang your hat on.

Gary, like we all do, had his faults and was maybe too serious at times and possibly should have chilled out more. Although he never appeared too uptight, he could have done with relaxing a bit more than he did. However, I very much doubt that approach hindered his footballing ability, which he had in abundance.

I tried to encourage a 'work hard, play hard' mentality when I was manager of Hearts – we certainly trained like professionals, but, unfortunately, at times played like weans! As far as I was concerned as long as the boys did it for me on the park they were then free to do what they wanted away from Tynecastle. However I got the impression that Gary's lack of ability to handle his drink possibly prevented him from enjoying himself as much as he could have when he wasn't at the club . . . .

Speaking of which, there is no doubt in my mind that Gary Mackay would have graced the top flight in England in the mid-to-late Eighties – when he was playing his best football – if he had decided to follow that particular career path. In fact, he may even have been a revelation down there because he was so dedicated, at a time when there was a drinking culture at a lot of clubs.

Gary's ability, in my opinion, could have taken him anywhere he wanted to go; therefore it was a huge boost to everyone at the football club that his passion for Heart of Midlothian kept him at Tynecastle during the best years of his career.

He may not have been the sharpest tool in the box (my nickname for him was poultice . . .) but Gary Mackay was always up for a laugh, even if it was at his expense, and without him actually realising it! As first-year professionals at the football club, Davie Bowman and Gary were assigned to look after my gear when I arrived at Tynecastle from Rangers in 1980. It didn't take me long to realise it wasn't too difficult to wind up the latter, but Gary never knew if I was being serious or not and his way out was simply to laugh at anything I said – then he would ask Bow to explain!

Apart from not being very bright, there wasn't really much else to slag Gary off about. When it came to his football he didn't mess about and it was a joy to be his manager for so many years. There's no doubt his ability was the main reason that Gary was able to play football at a high level, but I believe the support from his parents was also invaluable in helping him progress – two brilliant people who did everything they could for their son. Gary was also like their best friend; they got on so well together, which was absolutely brilliant.

He probably deserved to win more than four caps for Scotland but I think what let him down was his tackling. That wasn't one of his strong points – in fact he was fucking hopeless at it!

If I was to describe Gary Mackay in just one sentence:

'A fantastic football player with a tremendous attitude'

It was just a pity he had me as a manager!

Alex MacDonald
August 2008

Acknowledgements

Thanks to . . .

The author, Mark Donaldson, for helping make what could have been a tough task writing this book an easy one, and also listening for hours on end to my incessant and, at times, seemingly endless ramblings while recollecting my career in a maroon jersey.

My family, who have all played a huge part in my life; from my mum and dad to Vicky, Ryan and Nicholas, and in particular my granddad Munro who introduced me to the wonderful (yet frequently incredibly irritating) life as a supporter of Heart of Midlothian, and for this I am eternally grateful.

I would not be who I am today without my friends, particularly the Group of Five – Alan, Alex, Gary, Kenny and Michael (Bread) – whose friendship I have had the pleasure of since childhood.

Heart of Midlothian has also brought a lot of friends into my life, too many to list them all, however specific mentions to Gordon Lockerbie (Rest In Peace), Billy Ramsay, Iain Macleod, Ken Stott, George Foulkes, Colin Sime, Jimmy Dunn, John Borthwick and Wee Fergie.

There are several guys who also pulled on the famous maroon jersey whom I still regard as close mates: Walter Kidd, Kenny Black, John Robertson, Scott Crabbe, Davie Bowman and Jimmy Sandison.

For all these friendships I will always be grateful, but I am not naïve enough to think my career came about by luck only. Without the guidance I received from Bert Logan, George McNeill, Sandy Jardine and my ultimate mentor (both on and off the park), The Gaffer, Alex MacDonald, I would not be in a position to tell this story.

Thank you all.

Gary
July 2008

1

Jambo Till I Die

*'You can change your job, your wife, your car, your religion – but **never** your football team.'*

I was paid a basic salary of £39,000 for season 1996/97, my seventeenth and last at Hearts. It was the highest during my time at Tynecastle. Not an inconsequential amount of cash – £750 per week – although it still made me one of the lowest-paid, experienced players in the first-team squad when I left the club to join Airdrieonians in March 1997. These days our sport is awash with money. The English Premiership is a billion-pound industry with millionaire players two-a-penny. In Scotland the most talented lads in the SPL can earn enough to ensure they never have to worry about working again, but good on each and every one of them. Cash was not the main reason I played football. I was happy with every salary offered by the club over the years although, with hindsight, I could have earned a fair bit more if I had bothered to negotiate properly. Cynics might find it hard to believe but the biggest buzz was pulling on that maroon jersey. Quite simply I played the game for the love of Heart of Midlothian Football Club.

* * *

When Hearts announced at the start of 2006 they were planning to set up a Hall of Fame I was delighted, although I felt the idea was long overdue. I have always been of the opinion that the club was slightly out of touch when it came to developing a relationship with those who have graced Tynecastle. There was another positive development when the Federation of Hearts

Supporters Clubs decided to invite former players to be their guests for matches at Tynecastle and I'm also encouraged that the current regime is actively seeking to do more for players who have achieved so much for the club in the past.

From the day when the fourteen nominees were first announced for the inaugural Hall of Fame I never once thought I was guaranteed to be among the first group of inductees. I certainly hoped this would be the case but at no point was I conceited enough to think that just because I had played 640 competitive matches for Hearts – more than anyone else – and scored sixty-four goals that I would be a shoo-in for induction. In my opinion the likes of Dave Mackay, Willie Bauld, Alfie Conn, Jimmy Wardhaugh, John Cumming, Freddie Glidden and John Robertson – seven great players – all had stronger cases.

I'm not daft enough to think my inclusion was due to my skills as a player. If it was all about pure football ability then not only would guys like Alex Young and Donald Ford have been included, but also they would have been well in front of me in the pecking order. There is no doubt my long association with Hearts and my undivided loyalty to the football club was more than helpful in the nomination process.

Including friendly matches I pulled on a Hearts jersey 737 times. However, I can honestly say that not once did I feel as nervous, either before or during a game, as I was at Prestonfield House in Edinburgh prior to the inaugural ceremony in November 2006. The guests at my table would testify to that. It was an honour for me to be present as a former Hearts player and as a supporter and to be in the same venue as so many legends was a wonderful experience.

I was made aware shortly before sitting down for dinner that seven players from the following list would be inducted, so there was a 50 per cent chance of recognition:

Stephane Adam, Willie Bauld, Alfie Conn, John Cumming, Freddie Glidden, Craig Levein, Craig Gordon, Paul Hartley, Dave Mackay, Gary Mackay, Robbie Neilson, Steven Pressley, John Robertson, Jimmy Wardhaugh.

I have never been someone who is comfortable with showing my emotions in public. However, that was the last thing on my mind when my name was eventually read out as one of the first batch of inductees into the Heart of Midlothian Hall of Fame. Although football is a team game to be recognised for individual achievement is special. After taking such a public role in the Save Our Hearts campaign I was well aware there may have been some supporters who disagreed with my stance, but, rightly or wrongly, I strongly felt that the club was going in the wrong direction under the stewardship of Chris Robinson and that something had to be done. I am thankful that my forthright opinions did not prevent supporters voting for me as one of the first seven inductees.

Receiving that honour, and witnessing the heartfelt response from my fellow Jambos in the room, almost made me crumble and it was gratifying that so many people were appreciative of my efforts. Standing on stage at Prestonfield House with my award was the greatest moment of my life in relation to Hearts. The reception I received from the body of the hall was similar to the one I got from our fans at Pittodrie in November 1987, shortly after I had become the first Hearts player to be capped since Donald Ford in May 1974. It will live with me forever. It was a humbling experience to be surrounded by people I watched as a youngster and acclaimed as I got older. It was also the right time to pause for a brief moment to remember the players who are no longer with us yet who gave us, as fans, so many wonderful memories.

Prior to the dinner I was surrounded by people enjoying themselves and drinking champagne in the back of the limousine I had ordered to take us to Prestonfield House. But I was too nervous to even contemplate excess alcohol at that stage. Thankfully, a few hours later, I was able to relax after receiving my award and it was an evening I will never forget. Nevertheless there was one disappointment: the conspicuous absence from the awards ceremony of any Hearts director from Eastern Europe. I understand that Hearts is one of many business ventures for Vladimir Romanov, and that can excuse his non-attendance, but that does not extend to the rest of the directors. I felt it was disrespectful that no other member of the board made the effort to turn up. I appreciate there are stark differences in our respective cultures but people must realise how important the history of any institution is. The future is vital but our past is what shaped us as and must never be forgotten.

I'm convinced everything in my career happened for a reason. I played more times for my boyhood heroes, Heart of Midlothian, than anyone else in the club's history. That would not have been possible if I'd moved on to another club. Regrets? I've had a few but on the whole I can't complain. Not winning the league that day at Dens Park in 1986 will live with me forever, as will my failure to add to the medal collection I accumulated during my time in juvenile football. I missed out on the triumph that Robbo experienced with the 1998 Scottish Cup win and, while delighted for him, I have to admit to a tinge of jealousy. But what's done is done and while I may have an empty trophy cabinet from my time with Hearts I have many wonderful memories to cherish for the rest of my life. There is also a plaque in my house that reminds me every day that I am fortunate enough to be one of the first inductees into the Heart of Midlothian Hall of Fame – the culmination of my love affair with the football club.

* * *

I was always going to support Hearts. My granddad, Jimmy, has been a life-long fan of the club and was determined I would be a Jambo from the day I was born: 23 January 1964. As soon as I was old enough to understand he would regale me with tales of Tynecastle greats Alfie Conn, Willie Bauld and Jimmy Wardhaugh, and also of Alex Young and Dave Mackay. He was my personal club historian and he educated me in the traditions of our famous club. It was the best football education a youngster could wish for, although I am not sure if I can yet forgive him for introducing me to such a masochistic hobby!

It's certainly not a vivid memory but I do have a genuine recollection of being at the Scottish Cup final in 1968 when Hearts were beaten 3–1 by Dunfermline at Hampden, although I've been told I was lucky to get there. Travelling to the game, with my nana and granddad in the front, this four-year-old was squashed between an aunt and uncle in the back seat, when, out of the blue, a stone flew off the road and shattered the windscreen. We got the fright of our lives. The immediate concern of the adults was the condition of the car but granddad Jimmy tells me all I was worried about was getting to the match on time. Maybe this was an early warning about what following Hearts could do to people. We were relieved when the AA quickly arrived and provided us with a plastic windscreen until new glass could be fitted. My nana and aunt wanted to head back home, but a certain screaming child got his way and we continued on the Road to Hampden.

It was the first time I had ever been taken to a football match and I sat on the wall right at the front of the giant terraces with my legs draped over onto the ash track. It was the only way to get a decent view other than sitting on granddad's shoulders. Having been to my first game it was now official: I was a Hearts supporter.

As a youngster a lot of kids at school also had an allegiance to Hearts, even although Hibs were considered top dogs in Edinburgh at that time. I remember another day, in 1969 when I was five, being taken to a midweek game at Easter Road, where I sat on Ken Buchanan's knee. He was a friend of dad's and also happened to be the reigning British lightweight boxing champion, before going on to win the world title in September of the following year. However, pugilism was not his only skill and he managed to keep me still for the entire ninety minutes, far longer than dad ever managed at a game.

It was disappointing when Hearts began to stagnate during the Seventies – culminating in that dreadful defeat at the hands of our Edinburgh rivals on New Year's Day in 1973 – but my family, all of a maroon persuasion, never changed their allegiance whenever our team went through a sticky spell. I followed their example; I became a Hearts fan at Hampden in 1968, and, despite the disappointments over the next few years, there was no way that was going to change. I was a Jambo forever.

I suppose I was destined to have a long-term association with Hearts when my upbringing is considered. I went to Balgreen primary school, less than a mile from Tynecastle, before attending Tynecastle High, next door to the stadium. As a youngster I had trials with Rangers, Celtic and Hibernian and opportunities arose to join the likes of Manchester United, Arsenal and Burnley. But the day Hearts chairman Archie Martin expressed an interest in signing me was the day my mind was made up; I wanted to join the team I had supported since granddad first regaled me with his wonderful maroon-tinted tales. I was very fortunate I got the chance to play for my boyhood heroes, unlike a certain John Robertson who ended up as a player at Tynecastle, despite following Hibernian as a kid . . . .

* * *

I may have pulled on the famous Heart of Midlothian jersey 737 times, but, although I was living out a boyhood dream, I won no silverware as a result of my efforts over seventeen years. The closest we came was in season 1985/86, culminating in that fateful afternoon at Dens Park followed by heartache at Hampden in the Scottish Cup final seven days later. Even though money was not the object of our desire, that year was the most lucrative of all thanks to generous bonuses. The bonus scheme negotiated at the start of the 85/86 season was split into sequences of four games. We called it 'the accumulator'. The first-team players received very little additional cash unless we took at least six points out of the eight available. For seven points we got even more and with eight we hit the jackpot. I think with the benefit of hindsight our chairman, Wallace Mercer, would probably not have gone down that road because, during that season, six, seven or eight points were attained on a regular basis in those four-game chunks. It was a lucrative year but every single player in that squad would have swapped the money for a championship medal.

There may have been a lack of silverware during my time with Hearts but that does not mean that personal highlights were in short supply. I played fifty-four games against Hibernian, forty-eight unbeaten, ensuring that I have countless memories of the Edinburgh derby to take to my grave. Our 3–1 victory at Easter Road in September 1986 was my personal favourite, ramming taunts from their supporters about us missing out on the league title right back down their throats. The 3–0 win at Easter Road in September 1990, in our first match against them following Wallace Mercer's ill-fated takeover, was also extremely sweet amidst a poisonous atmosphere in the Leith San Siro.

Representing my country on four occasions was another highlight, but my Edinburgh derby record means even more to me than playing for Scotland and with bonuses of up to £1,000 per man for beating Hibernian I have to thank the likes of Paul Kane, Micky Weir and Gordon Hunter for paying for many of my summer holidays over the years. Cheers lads!

* * *

Seventeen years is a heck of a long time to stay with one club. In fact it's practically unheard of these days due to the Bosman ruling and the desire of players to earn as much money as they can in a relatively short career. There were one or two opportunities during my career to move elsewhere. Nottingham Forest showed an interest, as did Newcastle United, but neither team followed up with a concrete bid. Dundee United, on the other hand, offered Hearts half a million pounds for me in 1987. Vicky – my fiancée at the time – and I were in Portugal for a week's holiday prior to our wedding and the club secretary, Les Porteous, called to inform me of the offer. He told me the board considered it a reasonable bid and would grant me permission to open talks at Tannadice, but was adamant the club would not put pressure on me to go. However, I immediately explained to him that, due to the love I had for Hearts, I did not want to leave. I neither took into account Jim McLean's ability as a manager – he had just led United to the UEFA Cup final against Gothenburg, after beating Barcelona in the quarter-final – nor the quality of players at Tannadice. I simply had no interest in moving to another club at that stage of my career. I signed a new four-year contract with Hearts shortly after getting married and it was gratifying that my loyalty was rewarded with an improved deal. I would have earned a lot more money had I joined Dundee United – I was even accused of lacking ambition by some – but I was comfortable with my surroundings in Edinburgh and felt no need for change.

Whether it was down to fate I don't know but I spent my entire football life in Scotland's central belt, nearly all of it in Edinburgh, although the high-light of my career came almost ten years *after* I kicked my last ball in earnest at Tynecastle at that Hall of Fame dinner. It is more important to me than any money I may or may not have made during my career as a professional foot-baller, more important even than the four times I represented my country. Something no-one can ever put a price on.

* * *

My lifelong love affair with Heart of Midlothian, and my at-times over-the-top passion for the club, probably cost me my marriage, something I will always live to regret. It also led to me falling out with the likes of Chris Robinson (although I don't lose any sleep over that) and Craig Levein among others.

I have led most of my adult life with my heart worn not just on my sleeve but also on my right breast and there is no doubt in my mind that I have let that same heart, and my feelings for the football club, rule my head on too many occasions. Of course, given the opportunity, there are things I would change, but, even if that were possible, it would not alter the fact that the one constant for the rest of my life, rightly or wrongly, is the ongoing relationship with my football team.

A Jambo till I die.

2

The Early Years and Five-in-a-Row

'Tears for souvenirs . . .'

I was sitting in the back seat of dad's car at Seafield in north Edinburgh with tears streaming down my face after being left out of the squad once again.
I was only eleven but I'd already had enough of football.

* * *

I always thought I was quite skilful as a child. I was not, however, the tallest kid and it was clear to observers that I was playing outwith my age group when, as an eleven year-old, I joined the under-twelve setup at Salvesen Boys Club. I had belief in my own ability, although trying to persuade the coaches of my talents was a lot harder. In that age group it's common in teams with limited ability for a big, strong lad with a little talent to get chosen ahead of a smaller, yet more technically proficient kid. It's the way it was in those days and, indeed, this trend is still evident at playing fields up and down the country on a Saturday or Sunday morning. So I was grateful that, despite my size, the coaches at Salvesen selected me for their squad. I would loved to have played with and against boys from my own age group but juvenile football in Edinburgh did not become competitive until under-twelve so I was left with no choice.

At the start of the juvenile season in late summer 1975 the Salvesen coaches gave everyone in the squad an opportunity to stake a claim for a regular spot in the team. I felt I played reasonably well in a few matches, but it didn't take long before it became obvious who the 'favourites' were;

the same boys were selected week in, week out and quickly became the nucleus of the side. Results followed so there was no need to make changes, but that wasn't ideal for boys like me, who spent a lot of the time on the outside looking in. It was especially frustrating because when I played for Balgreen primary school we picked up a number of winners medals. I was also selected to play for Edinburgh in a tournament for primary schools and again was successful. I was used to playing and winning, and, to be left out without having the chance to show what I could do, hurt. To make matters worse only two substitutes were permitted in each game. We had a squad of fourteen and I was periodically selected to be on the bench but was regularly the odd man left out. I loved football and I loved training but most of all I loved playing and that wasn't happening enough for my liking. I tried not to get disillusioned and kept telling myself that I was just as good as the older boys, but it wasn't easy. It even crossed my mind to give up football and look for a new hobby – hence the waterworks in the car that day – but I'm glad I didn't throw in the towel because what happened in the years that followed was the stuff that dreams were made of.

* * *

I used to spend a lot of time playing football in the hall of my grandparents' ground-floor flat in Hutchison. The back of the front door was one goal and the entrance to the kitchen was the other. I detested losing to the extent that granddad always let me win just to prevent me from moaning. If a friend came in and beat me I used to slam the door and go in a huff. I was only four.

When I wasn't practising my skills in their hallway I would sometimes play in the swing park at Hutchison Cross, but more often than not I'd be out in their garden playing football and competing against boys of various ages, although most were a year or two older than me. I suppose it prepared me for my first full season with Salvesen.

I started kicking a football as soon as I could walk and that was all I did after school for quite a few years. Watching the 1970 World Cup on television, on the other hand, boosted my football education, and we were one of the fortunate families to have a colour television. I wanted England to win, as they were the only country that had players I recognised, having seen them on *Match of the Day*. But Brazil was the team that really caught my imagination. It was an eye-opener watching the likes of Pele, Gerson, Rivelinho, Jairzinho and Carlos Alberto, whom I actually met in 2004 on a fact-finding trip to Jamaica. I even got my picture taken with him and remember thinking that for all he achieved in football his humility was a huge lesson for me, even at the age of forty. Alberto was a man who had reached the very top of his profession, representing his country on fifty-three occasions and winning that World Cup in 1970, yet he remained so accessible.

Of course Brazil were wonderful to watch as they elegantly made their way to victory in 1970, but I got just as much of a thrill going to Tynecastle every second Saturday with granddad to watch *our* team. Granted, the quality of football was not exactly comparable with the Brazilians, but it gave me the opportunity to see real-life footballers close-up; men like Jim Brown, Ian Sneddon, Donald Ford and Tommy Murray. For an impressionable youngster this was on a par with watching Brazil and I quickly decided that I wanted to become a professional.

I enjoyed my education but don't mind admitting it was of secondary importance compared to football. Primary four was a landmark year because we were allowed into the big playground at Balgreen and were able to play football during breaks. All I focused on was getting through the morning lessons until the bell went at half-past ten, signalling a kickabout for fifteen minutes, and then it was a case of waiting for the lunch break at half-twelve. I used to sprint home to Eltringham Terrace – six minutes was my record – and quickly demolish the food mum had prepared before sprinting back in order to get fifteen more minutes of football before afternoon lessons. After school finished I should have used the time to do my homework, but more often than not there was a game of 'sidey' taking place on the grassy area at the bottom of the road, which was later bulldozed to allow access to the Fruitmarket at Chesser. The jotter remained in the bag until the morning, when the work was hastily done before school, while I tried manfully to eat breakfast at the same time.

* * *

My playing career began in earnest in 1973 when I was in primary five and got chosen for the Balgreen B team. The fact that the side was picked by my dad may have helped my chances of selection. One of my teammates was a lad called Kenny Morrison, who went on to play for Salvesen, and he was as good a player as there was in that age cohort. He was the sweeper and later had the opportunity to join Hearts as a fifteen-year-old. Hibs were also interested, but Kenny, who was heavily involved in science projects, was more interested in completing his education than playing football. When Bobby Moncur found this out he offered a part-time contract to enable him to continue his studies, but Kenny said he didn't fancy becoming a pro and that was the end of the chase.

Another of my teammates was a wee lad called Davie Grant, who, like me, was Hearts daft. Another thing we had in common was our desire to play for the Balgreen A team, in which we'd have the opportunity to play alongside Scott Maxwell. He was a year older, one of the best players in the school and captain of the A team. Scott was the guy we all looked up to. Thankfully, both Davie and I were selected for the A's in primary six so at least we managed to play alongside Scott for a year before he went off to high school.

I built up a decent medal collection in my youth – my parents still have most of them – but there will always be a special place in that collection for the first silverware I ever won. I was part of the Balgreen team that won the Calder Shield in 1974 – a primary-six tournament for schools in the east of Edinburgh. That was the first time I ever won anything and I am thankful it was not the last. I only had to wait another twelve months to add to the collection; we won the Edinburgh Primary School Association Cup at Warriston and also the Saughton League, a six-a-side tournament, beating Stenhouse in the final. That Stenhouse team included three future teammates and friends – Alan McPherson, Gary Birrell and Kenny Munro – and needless-to-say they are reminded of that defeat on a regular basis.

Our success led to greater attention for the school team and it was a privilege to be chosen to play for the Edinburgh primary select, especially when we went on to beat Glasgow RC 3–1 in the final of a regional tournament in Glasgow. Alex Peden and Mr Roseburgh were the two teachers who took the team but their presence was all that we required because the players did the rest. In fact, the biggest problem they had was explaining the 'RC' part of the opposing team's name when one of the boys asked why there were two teams from Glasgow in the competition and only one from Edinburgh. Of course Glasgow being Glasgow there was a team for kids who attended non-denominational schools and a completely separate one for those who went to Catholic schools. At that age none of us knew anything about religion and while the explanation helped broaden our horizons it remains to this day a topic I have no real interest in.

* * *

My decision not to give up football at the age of eleven – despite regularly being omitted from the under-twelve team – was vindicated in 1976 for two reasons. Firstly, I got the chance to play with and against boys of the same age at Salvesen, and, secondly, we had a new coach, Davie Landells, who had spent the previous twelve months recruiting the best talent in Edinburgh. Davie, who had previously been with Hutchison Vale Boys Club, had been scouting for Salvesen in Warriston, Saughton and Sighthill for nearly a year and had put together a very talented group. In came the likes of Davie Bowman, Ian Westwater and Carlo Croalla; they joined me and a certain John Robertson, who was a year younger than us and the only member of the team playing outwith his age group. There had always been rivalry between Hutchison Vale and Salvesen Boys Club and we were surprised our new coach had jumped the divide. His father had been a coach at Hutchie Vale as well, so there was a strong family connection with the club, but the chance to recruit virtually a whole new team to compete in the Edinburgh Juvenile League was too good an opportunity to turn down. In addition, Salvesen, then based at St Joseph's primary in Broomhouse, was one of the leading juvenile clubs in Scotland and as well as the players mentioned in this chapter it had also produced outstanding young talents like Peter Marinello.

Davie Landells was the first coach I ever came across who was hugely enthusiastic about football; most of the others were schoolteachers first and coaches second. He was also desperate to help boys improve, while at the same time ensuring that they enjoyed themselves. He instilled a great team spirit on the pitch, while we developed a great camaraderie off it. It didn't take long for me to realise that the players he brought in, when combined with those already at the club, made for a potent combination. That was proved when we remained unbeaten in competitive matches throughout our first season and capped things off by winning the Scottish Juvenile Cup.

They say success breeds success, but it can also breed complacency and for that reason Davie decided to strengthen the squad in the summer of 1977 in a bid to provide more competition for places. In came Stuart Gauld – who later went on to play twenty-two games for Hearts – and a lad called Alan McPherson, who quickly became my best mate and has remained so to this day. The first time I came into contact with Alan was during the previous season when I was in direct opposition to him during a game between Salvesen and Tynecastle. We beat them, but he played well enough in defence to catch Davie's eye and when the coach decided he could do with another centre half he remembered Alan's performance and promptly signed him up. John Robertson was the only departure from the squad; he was still eligible for another season at under-twelve and decided he preferred to play against boys of his own age.

An unbeaten season was always going to be hard to match, but, with the two new additions proving very useful, we went on another successful run at under-thirteen level and once again remained unbeaten while adding a second Scottish Juvenile Cup to the trophy room. By this stage I felt we had a quality that no other team could touch and that was proved correct over the next year or so when we remained unbeaten in all competitions, all the way through to our under-fifteen campaign. I can relate that inner confidence to how I later felt about playing for Hearts against Hibs; there was an air of invincibility about both teams and more often than not we were triumphant.

The Scottish Juvenile Cup proved to be a lucky competition for us. We won it five years in a row – from under-twelve to under-sixteen – and that was no mean feat considering that opposition players included the likes of Kenny Black at Gairdoch and Brian Rice with Whitburn. Although the Scottish Juvenile Cup did not at that time include teams from all over Scotland, I remain convinced that even if clubs from Glasgow, Tayside and Aberdeen had been involved it would have taken an exceptional side to have beaten us.

Our success did not go unnoticed by scouts and every one of our players at under-fifteen level got the chance to go on trial with a senior side. To this day I am unaware of another juvenile team in Edinburgh whose entire squad got the chance to do likewise and that is something Salvesen Boys Club remains rightly proud of. Don't get me wrong, winning was thoroughly enjoyable but later I learnt that losing the odd game here and there was actually quite healthy. So playing for Salvesen was probably unhealthy, because we were always successful. Defeat was something we didn't experience very often and so I was very blasé about the whole thing and became a bad loser. That was evident to the rest of the Tynecastle school team when we lost and I must have been dreadful company at times like that; so belated apologies to my former teammates.

I was very fortunate during my formative years to have had so many wonderful people helping me. My dad was one of the biggest influences, at Balgreen, while John Sutherland looked after us when I went to Tynecastle High. John was our physical-education teacher and also coached the school football team; he was another shrewd mentor. And of course I pay tribute to Davie Landells at Salvesen, and, when he moved on, to Ronnie McCall, who coached the team on a Sunday and also took training. I can also count two former professional footballers as influences, George Stewart and Eric Schaedler, who were still playing with Hibs but gave up their Thursday nights to help train us at under-thirteen. Very few boys clubs have the benefit of professionals coaching them and that's why I've always been keen to give something back to the game. Today I am delighted to be coaching one of the teams at Tynecastle Boys Club.

* * *

Playing juvenile football for Salvesen was thoroughly enjoyable but turning out for Tynecastle High School also had its moments. At the ages of thirteen and fourteen I trained once a week with Salvesen, played for the school team on a Saturday morning then played for Salvesen in the afternoon. That changed slightly over the following two years when Salvesen games were played on a Sunday. My record with Tynecastle was pretty decent and that allowed me to come across future teammates and adversaries in the latter stages of tournaments. We reached the Scottish Schools Cup final at under-thirteen, somehow beating Holy Cross from Hamilton 1–0 in the semi-final at Linlithgow despite taking an absolute battering for the entire game. Their tormentor-in-chief was a young lad by the name of Paul McStay, but, despite his stunning performance, Holy Cross failed to find the net. We secured our place in the final courtesy of a wonder goal from our left-winger, Davie McConville, who later went on to become a professional sprinter. Our luck ran out in the final at Prestonfield – home of Linlithgow Rose – where we were beaten 1–0 by a Larbert side that included my future buddy Kenny Black. The only positive from that day was getting the chance to play at a Junior ground; it was the first time I'd played at a real stadium with terracing and a covered enclosure.

The Scottish Schools Cup was much harder to win than its juvenile equivalent because the teams involved were from all over the country. It was also considered more prestigious and attracted a lot more interest, especially in the latter stages of the competition. Tynecastle High regularly performed well and that brought our players to the attention of the Scottish Schoolboys selectors. There were two age groups for Scottish Schoolboys – under-fifteen and under eighteen – and I was fortunate enough to be part of the under-fifteen squad after successfully coming through trials with the likes of Neale Cooper and Paul McStay. Paul – a year younger than me – was a prodigious talent and was chosen on three separate occasions: at the ages of thirteen, fourteen and fifteen. His class was evident on and off the pitch – in fact his whole family had class – and it was no surprise to me when he went on to join Celtic and later played for Scotland.

The year I played for Scottish Schoolboys coincided with the centenary match against our English counterparts. It was a privilege to represent my country but that match received nothing like as much publicity as the corresponding fixture twelve months later. I was a year too old, but, in his third and final year for the under-fifteens, Paul McStay was inspirational in the England–Scotland match at Wembley; he scored twice in a 5–4 victory in front of 70,000 paying spectators and several million more watching live on television, with the legendary Brian Moore commentating. John Robertson also played that day and never tires of telling people about his goal underneath the Twin Towers. However, newspaper reports credited the winner as an own goal by England's David Byram, although the wee man is adamant his shot was going in before being deflected!

I often look back and think what might have been during the year I was selected for the Scottish Schoolboys squad. Ten games were arranged over the twelve months – including the centenary match against England – but I only started once and to this day I do not know why. In charge of our squad was George Brough, a schoolteacher at Holyrood High School in Edinburgh, and a gentleman who was a teacher in Hamilton (but whose name I cannot recall). Before the first match they arranged a get-together in Stirling and I was in a room with Bowman, Westwater and Jimmy Doig from Salvesen when I was overhead swearing by the coach from Hamilton. I still wonder if that had anything to do with the fact I only played one game from the start – at Broomfield in Airdrie – but no reason was ever given for my omission. It could also have had something to do with an argument between my dad and George Brough, not to do with me, but regarding a football issue with Holyrood School and a youngster from Salvesen. There might, of course, have been another reason; maybe I just wasn't good enough.

Nevertheless it was an honour to be selected to represent Scottish Schoolboys and it was also a privilege to be chosen for the Edinburgh and Lothians select at under-fifteen. John Sutherland was the familiar face in charge – he was our coach at Tynecastle High – and he worked alongside Jim Dobney, who was a scout for Rangers as well as a schoolteacher at Liberton High. John was the main man when it came to coaching while Jim had superb football knowledge and was a motivational expert; together they made an excellent management team. I was fortunate to be around at the same time as a lot of other really good players who were equally, if not more, talented, but none of us would have progressed without our enthusiastic and knowledgeable coaches, and for that I will always be grateful. I am pleased that we were able to reward John and Jim with some success; we won the Inter-Region Schools Cup with the likes of Ian Westwater, Gordon Marshall, Davie Bowman and Robbo all playing a significant part not only in our victory, but also in the win against Lanarkshire – and Paul McStay – on the way to the final.

School-representative sides, on the whole, were usually either for under-fifteens or under-eighteens so for most young footballers there was a three-year wait between being selected to play for your city, your region or your country. The other representative team I had my eye on was Lothian Schools, but, unfortunately, that was only for under-eighteens so, having just played for Edinburgh and Lothians, I thought I would have to wait three years before getting the chance to play regional football once again. Not so. One day, out of the blue, came a call from Terry Christie; he wanted Davie Bowman, Ian Westwater and me, among others, to play for Lothian Schools, despite the fact that we were all just sixteen. Terry was one of the nicest people you could meet; a headmaster by trade but also a part-time manager with several lower-division Scottish league clubs over the years. He had the Midas touch when it came to producing cup shocks in the Eighties and Nineties; maybe he learned that from the unlikely successes he engineered with our group of young kids.

There really should only have been one outcome when Lothian Schools played North of Scotland at Heriot Watt University in 1980. We were a team almost entirely made up of inexperienced sixteen-year-olds, with only the faith of our coach and youthful exuberance in our favour. Their line-up included several players who had been selected to represent Scotland Schools under-eighteens; we had none at that time. The team from the north was also full of big, strapping lads, mostly from sixth forms, and they were very physical, none-more-so than Neil Fyvie and Gordon Robertson. Our team talk that day, however, was one of the most inspirational I've ever heard and from lambs to the slaughter we went out onto that pitch thinking we could beat anyone. It was the first time I can recall the hairs on the back of my neck standing upright, and that was just from Terry's team talk. He got us so fired up. He told us how good we were, that we were better footballers and that they were just physical sluggers. It worked. Despite the age difference we beat North of Scotland by five goals to nil and went on to win the Scottish Schools Select trophy. Not bad for a team of kids and a coach who put his faith in a group of fourth-year students from juvenile football.

I cherish all the medals I won as a kid; they are doubly special having failed to win anything with Hearts. Maybe if I had known then that success was far from inevitable I would have enjoyed them a little more than I did.

3

Fate Plays its Hand

'Everything happens for a reason. And when fate happens look for the good in it as it is there.'

Catherine Pulsifer – *Inspirational Words of Wisdom*

In the summer of 1979 I had a decision to make that would shape my career in football. I was desperate to serve an apprenticeship with a professional club and, with my exit from Tynecastle High School looming in May 1980 at the end of fourth year, I had to get something sorted out before education and I went our separate ways. I had been a Hearts supporter since early childhood but they were not one of three clubs in for me. There was concrete interest from Burnley, Arsenal and Manchester United – all three teams were keen for me to sign and had made offers after I had trained with them – while not long after that Celtic, Rangers and Hibs expressed a desire to take me on trial.

At that time Burnley was still a reasonably large club having spent the early years of the Seventies playing in the English top flight until they were relegated to the second division in 1976. As part of their quest to get me to put pen to paper, I was invited to a match at Turf Moor as a guest of the club, near the end of season 1978/79. My seat, in the Bob Lord stand, was on one of the wooden benches housing season-ticket holders. It was also heated! The stand had been built in 1974 – funded by the sale of star player Martin Dobson to Everton – and this impressionable fifteen-year-old remembers being very impressed by the gimmick.

Bob Lord was chairman of Burnley between 1955 and 1981 and a legendary figure in the game; I remember being in awe of him every time we met. He was a visionary and the way he conducted business was reminiscent of the late Wallace Mercer. Lord, however, never went out of his way to curry favour. He was similar to Vladimir Romanov with his ability to attract publicity for his club, although, unfortunately for Bob, a lot of it was negative and his comments were frequently ill thought out, resulting in plenty of flak flying his way.

Mr Lord was also involved with Lowerhouse cricket club, where he also had a spell as chairman. I may have been in awe of him, but he did not frighten me like he did a cub reporter covering a Lancashire League knock-out competition one sunny summer's day. When approached for a comment after a Lowerhouse victory, Lord simply turned to the youngster and told him to 'piss off'. That journalist, working for the local newspaper, was David Davies, the former executive director of the Football Association.

Lancashire has always been considered a rather unfashionable area, something that has never applied to another of my possible destinations: London. People talk about the number of nationalities in the Arsenal team under Arsene Wenger, but even at the tail end of the 1970s they had a very cosmopolitan group of players. A teammate of mine at Salvesen, Randy Smith, was the only black boy I had played with prior to my trip to England's capital, but I encountered many more people from ethnic minorities during my brief spell with the Gunners. It helped open my eyes to life outside Edinburgh.

Arsenal was the only English team I did not get the chance to witness in action, although I did get the opportunity to train with the youth players at the club's magnificent training ground. Several top-flight teams in England at that time either had purpose-built training facilities, or were in the process of constructing them; a quarter of a century later many professional clubs north of the border still don't have them. Even Burnley also had their own training ground, and they were in the second division. Training with them was the first time I had ever seen the metal object that football clubs use to replicate walls for defending free-kicks. It had been specifically made to simulate opposition players; I had no idea what it was at first and had to ask.

However, the first club I went on trial with was Manchester United after being spotted playing for Salvesen by Jimmy Dickie, the club's chief scout in Scotland. Jimmy also identified Billy Davies as a possible signing, and he used to accompany both Billy and myself on the train down to training at the Cliff. That was the first purpose-built complex I had ever seen. It had changing rooms, several grass pitches, viewing areas and a restaurant. It also had a canteen where nutritional meals, cold milk and fruit were the staple diet for players. This was all very innovative, considering it was still the Seventies.

In stark contrast to the Cliff, Salvesen did not have anywhere it could call home. We trained at Forrester high school but were not guaranteed the same venue every week for matches. There were even times when we had to wait for confirmation from the league secretary to find out which spare pitch we had been allocated for our home game that week. When I first joined the Boys Club in 1976 we would play at St Joseph's primary school. Unfortunately, that pitch no longer exists and the school now shares a campus with Broomhouse primary. We also played at Sighthill and Saughton, but the facilities in Edinburgh at that time were pretty poor (it can be argued that not much has changed).

After watching me in a few training sessions, Manchester United invited me to their FA Cup semi-final against Liverpool at Maine Road, Manchester on the last day of March 1979, and also to the replay at Goodison Park in Liverpool four days later, when Jimmy Greenhoff scored the only goal of the game to secure their place in the FA Cup final. I spent a fair amount of time travelling to England to train with Manchester United, Arsenal and Burnley, but United really pushed the boat out to impress me. Jimmy Dickie was great at helping me settle when I was in Manchester, even though I was only away from home for a few days at a time. He was United's main scout in Scotland, but had also previously worked for Hearts, and was pleasantly surprised that my favourites had not been in touch with the offer of a trial.

Jimmy's immediate boss was a guy called Joe Brown, who was on the United payroll and was in overall charge of scouting. He had been a coach at Burnley for fifteen years between 1961 and 1976 before replacing Jimmy Adamson as boss at Turf Moor. Joe's first game in charge was at Norwich in January 1976. A banner in the visiting end at Carrow Road read, 'We won't go down . . . we've got Joe Brown'. Burnley were relegated. Joe Brown remained the manager at Burnley for just over a year, until 20 February 1977, when – with the team failing to mount a promotion challenge in the second division and having won only nine of his forty-five games – his thirteen-month tenure came to an end. Despite being offered another post at the club, Brown left Turf Moor after getting the chance to head the youth set-up at Manchester United.

Joe was the man who would decide which youngsters cut the mustard and should be offered a contract so, knowing you don't get too many chances to make an impression at such a massive club, it was vitally important I tried my hardest every time I was down there. Thankfully, the training was easy and I was surrounded by very talented young lads from all over the United Kingdom. They included Norman Whiteside – who went on to accept an offer from the club and played 273 times for the Reds – and also Clayton Blackmore, another future United star.

After being identified as someone the club wanted to sign, my details were passed on by Joe Brown to manager Dave Sexton. In a bid to persuade me that Manchester United was the club where my professional career should begin, Sexton took me on a tour of the dressing room at Old Trafford when the squad was out warming-up prior to the goalless draw against Coventry in April 1979. I was then introduced to the players when they came back in. Getting the chance to meet and shake hands with Joe Jordan, Martin Buchan, Lou Macari, Gordon McQueen and Arthur Albiston – five Scots who were making a name for themselves at one of the biggest clubs in the world – was a great thrill. I had watched these players on television – plus the likes of Steve Coppell and the Greenhoff brothers, Brian and Jimmy – and was star-struck to meet them in person. Getting invited to three games – against Liverpool (twice) and Coventry – then viewing the FA Cup final on television and being able to identify with the Manchester United players I had shaken hands with was a big thing for an impressionable lad.

The people I dealt with at Arsenal and Burnley were great – there was real warmth about both clubs and they could not have been nicer – but there was something special about United. There was the fantastic training complex at the Cliff; the Old Trafford theatre of dreams, as Sir Bobby Charlton memorably described it; the glorious past, unfortunately mixed with tragedy; the global fan base that had not only fallen in love with the wonderful Busby Babes but also the flawed genius that was Georgie Best. I was a home bird, but the pull of Manchester United was massive. It was a special club, it was a magical club. I wanted to be part of it and to find out everything I could about it.

Those were the main reasons for choosing United but there was also security to take into account and, once again, they came out on top. Arsenal, managed by Terry Neill, had offered a signing-on fee of £20,000 that, at the age of just fifteen, was money I had never even dreamed about before. However, Manchester United had offered a longer contract – four years – with the first two served as an apprentice followed by professional terms when I turned eighteen. The signing-on fee was not as large as that offered by the Gunners, but I knew by accepting the offer from the Reds that I didn't have to worry about where I would be playing my football for the next four years.

I loved Hearts; I was a supporter. Hearts was always going to be *my* team, but the allure of Manchester United was almost irresistible.

* * *

I enjoyed a very successful period playing football as a youngster, winning many medals and trophies, but never got the chance to play abroad until we were invited to the Hicksville tournament in New York in the summer of 1979. It was the first time a team from Salvesen would represent the club in a competition outwith the United Kingdom. Our under-fifteen team contained a host of names that went on to make the grade as professionals. As well as me, Ian Westwater, Dave Bowman, Gordon Byrne and Carlo Croalla also made a living from the game and we were all on that flight across the Atlantic. Former Hibs midfielder Paul Kane came with us to gain experience – he was a year younger than us – although he didn't play any games in New York.

All the boys were excited at getting the chance to play football on the other side of the world, although a few of us did get homesick. I was grateful that dad was on the Salvesen committee at that time so he and mum accompanied us, meaning there was no chance I would be missing home.

Our trip to the United States was, I suppose, a reward for our success over the previous few years. The Hicksville tournament was widely regarded as one of the most prestigious in juvenile football across the globe, and only the most successful teams received an invite.

I couldn't have been happier. I was not only playing for one of the most successful youth teams around but also was due to sign for the biggest club in the world. But they say life is what happens when you are making plans. We had been back from New York for nearly three months when my younger brother, Grant, developed whooping cough. Mum took him to see the family doctor, and also used that opportunity to get him to check a small growth that had developed on one of her breasts when she was in Long Island. Grant was issued with a prescription and told to come back in three weeks for a check-up. That second trip to the doctor saw him get the all clear while mum underwent a series of tests on her breast and was told she'd eventually get the results back, but not to worry in the meantime.

Another fortnight passed. The whole family was sitting together in our house in Eltringham Terrace when the doctor knocked on the door. Mum's test results had arrived and a cancerous growth had been identified; she was just thirty-eight. Prior to that, we hadn't heard anything back from the surgery and took the view that no news was good news. So it came as a huge shock for the family, not least mum.

From that day we found it quite difficult to cope and I put my football career on hold until everything got back to normal. Of course I kept Manchester United informed of the situation and they were fully supportive of my decision. When somebody is diagnosed with cancer you never stop having concerns. I was especially close to mum and spent a lot of my childhood with her. Dad worked with the gas board and a lot of his spare time was taken up with helping out at Salvesen Boys Club, so I saw a lot more of mum. Cancer is a terrible illness and you never think it will affect anyone in your family.

It was very unusual for mum, dad, Grant or I to go to the doctor – we were generally a pretty healthy family – and my brother's whooping cough was one of those rare occasions. However, it turned out to be a blessing in disguise. If there hadn't have been a concern about Grant catching his breath then it's highly unlikely mum would have bothered going to see a doctor and then who knows what would have happened. I'm not religious – although I have many Protestant and Catholic friends and my ex-wife and both my sons are Roman Catholic – but I do believe fate plays a big part in life and that what's for you won't go by you. If something is meant to be, I believe it will happen.

The old Longmore hospital off Minto Street in Edinburgh was a woman's facility specialising in the treatment of breast cancer, so mum was very well looked after. Fortunately for her, and the rest of the family, the cancer was all in one area, although she eventually had to have a mastectomy in 1980.

Things had changed for me as well. I started to deliberate about which club I was going to join, even though Manchester United had been a certainty just a few months before. I wanted to be closer to home following mum's illness and the possibility of training with a Scottish club was suddenly much more appealing. After informing United of my decision to stay in Scotland following my short sabbatical from football, Joe Brown travelled up to my house in Eltringham Terrace to persuade me not to change my mind. He said the club was willing to let me train in Scotland and then fly me down to Manchester for games until mum made a full recovery. I can't speak highly enough of the Old Trafford backroom staff; they were all such genuine people. That's the great thing about my early career; I was lucky all the way through, from my earliest days at Salvesen until going on trial with clubs that had so many thoroughly decent people.

I certainly considered United's offer to train in Edinburgh and fly south for matches, but something just didn't sit right because of what was happening with mum. It didn't take long for clubs in Scotland to be alerted to my situation, with Rangers, Celtic and Hibs all quickly expressing an interest.

Having been a striker with Balgreen then a midfielder with Salvesen, the decision of Rangers boss John Greig to play me at right back in a trial match at the Albion training ground (where the large car park behind the Broomloan stand at Ibrox is now situated) did me no favours. That disappointed me. The club had scouted me and knew I was a midfielder so I have no idea why they played me in defence. I had no defensive qualities whatsoever, and, in fact, was bad enough in that position when I was twenty-five, never mind fifteen. So the trial with Rangers was over before it began.

It made me think even less of the Ibrox club, if that was possible. I had attended the Scottish Cup final in 1976 when Hearts lost 3–1 to Rangers at

Hampden, a result that did nothing to endear them to me. I had a severe dislike of several of their players, especially one Alex MacDonald. He scored regularly against Hearts when he was at Ibrox and was someone who had a great passion for the game. He was the equivalent of a present-day Neil Lennon: a player who gave everything for his team, but a player that opposition supporters loved to hate. It seemed to me he always tried harder against Hearts, even although I'd never seen him in action against any other team!

Celtic's trial match was at Barrowfield, just along the road from Celtic Park. I played in midfield, although maybe I would have made more impact at right-back, despite my dislike of the position. My failure to win a contract was down to one youngster: Paul McStay. He was considered the top prospect in the country and had played for Scotland schoolboys for three consecutive years. It was unfortunate for me that he played in my position and there was only going to be one winner when it came to a choice between the two of us. McStay signed for Celtic and I never heard back from them.

My Salvesen teammate Davie Bowman and I went to Hibs on trial, under the expert eye of Stan Vincent and John Fraser, who had both played for the club. We were fortunate enough to get the chance to train at Easter Road every Monday evening, usually alongside the club's part-time players, while our work in the small gymnasium brought us into contact with the likes of Gordon Rae. Hibs were very keen to sign both of us and were a progressive club, unlike Hearts on the other side of the city.

If mum had not been diagnosed with cancer then the outcome of a choice between United and Hibs would have been a no-brainer – the Reds every time – but I had to take into account my desire to remain as close to Edinburgh as possible. That's why, although I enjoyed getting the chance to train regularly with a professional club, I was slightly frustrated that no concrete offer was ever forthcoming from Easter Road, despite the fact that they were kind enough to pay the bus fares from my home in Stevenson Drive to Easter Road. People still ask me today if I would have signed for the club at the other end of the city. And given some of the less-than-charitable things I say about Hibs in this book some readers may be surprised that it is something I would even have contemplated. But I was desperate to play professional football and that may have taken precedence over my hatred of the men from the east. Let me put it this way; I am glad it is a decision I never had to make.

But my frustrations were short-lived. Fate – in the shape of a gentleman known affectionately as 'Boobsy' – struck again.

Hearts at the time employed an ex-Salvesen coach by the name of Ian 'Boobsy' Brown to work with the part-timers at Tynecastle. He had suggested to new chairman Archie Martin that there were a lot of promising local youngsters at juvenile clubs that would be worth taking a chance on, having worked with several at Salvesen. With money too tight to mention at Tynecastle, Archie believed that putting his faith in talented kids might just turn the club around. It would instil a youthful determination that had been sorely lacking as the club had bounced back and forth between the Premier Division and the first division. The chairman was more than happy to accept Boobsy's suggestion and the rest, as they say, is history. Nevertheless I have since found out there was a moment in which the history of football in Edinburgh could have taken a completely different turn. Boobsy takes up the story:

> I put forward a list of all the best youngsters in Edinburgh to Mr Martin to put before the board, although one of the directors did not think John Robertson was tall enough to make the grade and suggested Hearts maybe sign the other kids but drop their interest in Robbo. I was furious with the director and told him the 'wee, lazy, fat lad' was absolutely prolific in front of goal and unless he changed his mind he would regret his decision for the rest of his life. Thankfully, my persistence paid off!

By the way, Ian Brown instructed me he wishes it to be made clear his nickname has nothing to do with breasts. He claims he used to climb lampposts as a child in order to steal light bulbs to sell, but was always getting caught by the local constabulary and told off. His mates used to say he boobed again, hence the moniker 'Boobsy'. A likely story, if you ask me.

* * *

There was only going to be one outcome if Hearts ever came in for me. With the club, *my* club, slowly turning the corner under the guidance of Mr Martin, the day it expressed an interest in signing me was the day I decided to sign on at Tynecastle. Chairman Archie Martin was trying to put the pride back into the club and thought that signing four Scotland schoolboy internationals – John Robertson, Dave Bowman, Ian Westwater and me – was a gamble worth taking. His was right and the risk paid off big time.

When the club stepped up their attempts to sign me, the chairman took mum – now, thankfully, on the road to recovery – and dad for a meal at Cosmo's to inform them of the terms on offer. My parents were delighted with the interest shown by Hearts because they were aware of how happy it made me. They knew I would sign for the club, and that dinner at Hearts' expense was not required to persuade me to put pen-to-paper, but they didn't let on to Archie to ensure they got their free meal!

Mum and dad came back to the house that night and outlined the details of their conversation with Archie Martin. They explained the terms and conditions of the contract, and also told me that the chairman wanted to take me on a tour of Tynecastle the following day after school. I was usually quite good at getting to sleep, but as you can imagine I hardly slept a wink that night.

After attending Tynecastle high school the following day, it didn't take long to jog the distance of a Robbie Neilson throw-in to reach my destination. It was the first time I'd ever had the opportunity to enter Tynecastle stadium via the front door. There had been occasions when some of my friends had jumped over the wall and played football on the Tynecastle pitch before being chased away by groundsman Willie Montgomery. I was never very good at either climbing or running so there was no way I would ever climb the wall. Even if I did, I was so slow that Willie would have caught me. This time, however, I was getting the opportunity to enter the stadium the correct way and it was a great feeling walking through the main entrance for the first time.

Archie Martin also informed me of his intention to let me train with the reserves at Brown's gymnasium, a rather basic facility deep in the bowels of the main stand. But, despite the poor facilities, putting on that maroon kit and playing three-a-side games was a big thing for me. The chairman knew the opportunity to sign several schoolboy internationals at one fell swoop would not come along very often and so it didn't take him long to get the rest of the boys to agree terms. Having given the club my word that I would join, it was agreed that I would sign my contract at the start of July to coincide with pre-season training.

Before I had even officially signed – but after terms had been agreed – I played as a trialist in a reserve game against Arbroath at Gayfield at the tail end of season 1979/80; it was my first match in a maroon jersey and a much-needed run out. We won 2–0. I did all right, though I was really just a boy among men. I remember being conceited enough to think that if Manchester United had wanted to sign me then a reserve match in the north-east of Scotland would be a walk in the park. It wasn't and that experience showed me the standards I would have to achieve.

I finally put pen-to-paper on 16 June 1980 – around the same time as Davie Bowman, Stuart Gauld and Ian Westwater – and it was one of the proudest moments of my life. John Robertson signed on shortly after that. Colin Plenderleith, who played with Robbo, among others, for Scotland Schoolboys in the famous 5–4 victory against England in June 1980, also signed that month. We were living a dream the moment our contracts were inked, and it was also some achievement for Salvesen Boys Club to provide five players for professional clubs. Bo, Westy and I all joined Hearts while Carlo Croalla and Gordon Byrne signed for Hibs around the same time.

Our subsequent success persuaded Hearts that signing promising young-sters could be extremely beneficial, as well as being cost-effective. Therefore, shortly after putting pen to paper, I played in a mixed match at Saughton enclosure involving young trialists and reserve players from Hearts; it gave the club the chance to assess other potential signings. As a result of that game, a few more talented kids were snapped up. We all realised that if we continued to improve then there was a decent chance of getting an early opportunity to make an impact at Tynecastle. That philosophy of giving youth a chance became an integral part of the club's progress in the early Eighties.

If mum had not had her illness then Old Trafford, not Tynecastle, would have been my home. But I will forever be thankful that everything worked out so well. She ended up making a full recovery while Hearts chairman Archie Martin, literally, opened the front door and allowed me to fulfil my boyhood dream. Not many players, never mind callow youths of fifteen, turn down the chance to sign for one of the biggest clubs in the world and end up having no regrets. However, not many players have the same feelings for Heart of Midlothian as me. Fate decreed that a major part of my life was spent at the club I love and I will always be grateful for that.

4

Champions of Europe

'On top of the world (well nearly . . .)'

The highlight of my teenage years, apart from making my debut for Hearts, was representing my country at youth level. I pulled on the dark-blue shirt of Scotland for the first time in 1981 when I was selected for the under-seventeen squad for a tournament in Cannes. We played four games in six days, eventually finishing fifth in the competition.

Italy was first up in our four-team group, followed by a crack at Brazil and then, finally, East Germany. Things didn't get off to the best possible start when we were beaten 2–0 by the Italians; Giuseppe Incocciati and Alberto Di Chiara were on target for them and both went on to make their mark in Serie A.

Scotland 0–2 Italy: 15 April 1981

Marshall, Crawford, Philliben, Cooper, Black (K.), Bowman, Mackay, McStay, Rice, Black (E.), Sludden. (Subs: Hendrie, Byrne)

Two days later, however, saw us come from behind to earn a thoroughly impressive one-all draw against Brazil. A goal from Miranda gave the young samba stars the lead, but an equaliser from my former teammate in the Salvesen under-fifteen side, Gordon Byrne, on as a substitute, earned us a richly deserved point. That Brazilian side might not have had the same quality as the one that caught my imagination eleven years earlier when I watched my first World Cup on television, but it did contain the likes of Jorginho, Dunga and Bebeto and it was a pleasure to be on the same pitch as these wonderful talents. The fact they failed to beat us made it even more special.

Scotland 1–1 Brazil: 17 April 1981

Westwater, Crawford, Philliben, Cooper, Black (K.), Bowman, Mackay, McStay, Rice, Black (E.), Sludden. (Subs: Hendrie, Byrne)

Our final group game was against East Germany two days later and goals from Eric Black and Paul McStay secured a 2–1 victory, although I was disappointed to be replaced in the first half by John Hendrie. I hadn't been playing well, but it's never nice to come off before half-time when you're not injured. As a result of my performance against the East Germans I was left on the bench for the fifth/sixth play-off against Poland, but I came on for my good friend Davie Bowman and was involved in the build-up when Eric Black scored the only goal of the game to ensure our tournament ended on a high note.

There were many highlights from Cannes, including an opportunity to pit our wits against Brazil and managing to draw against them. We also came up against an Italian side that included future World Cup-winner Giuseppe Bergomi, who, even at that stage of his career, was a first-team regular at Inter Milan, having made his debut the previous year at the age of just seventeen.

Davie Bowman, however, was responsible for the funniest moment of the trip. He decided one night after a few lager shandies that urinating on a double bed would amuse him more than doing so in the toilet. Now Bow has always been a couple of sandwiches short of a picnic, but it wasn't until he sobered up and complained about his wet duvet that he realised he had pissed on the wrong bed!

* * *

After getting my first taste of international action with the Scotland under-seventeen side I was desperate for more, and my next target was to be selected for the 1982 European under-eighteen championships in Finland. Bizarrely, UEFA, in their infinite wisdom, decided that the qualification phase of the tournament would consist of fifteen groups, each with two teams. Simply put, it was a two-leg, head-to-head contest to determine who was going to Finland and who was not. We didn't know whether to laugh or cry when Scotland and England were drawn together!

The first leg was at Ibrox on 23 February 1982; we played extremely well and Paul McStay's goal secured a precious 1–0 lead to take down to Coventry for the second leg the following month. The scenario was simple: avoid defeat and we would be heading for Finland. Things, however, did not go according to plan at Highfield Road on 23 March and we found ourselves 2–0 down at the break courtesy of goals from English pair John Pearson and Martin Singleton just before half-time. Thankfully, Paul McStay grabbed a vital away goal seven minutes after the interval before Jim Dobbin's strike with twelve minutes to go secured a 2–2 draw – and a 3–2 aggregate win – and our place at the European Championships later that year. I watched most of the second leg from the bench after failing to win a starting jersey, but there was no time for moping around and I was as pleased as anyone when the referee blew his whistle to signal full-time. We were going to Finland.

England	2–2	Scotland
Pearson 35		McStay 52
Singleton 39		Dobbin 78

England: Steve Francis (Chelsea), Paul Parker (Fulham), Nick Pickering (Sunderland), Martin Duffield (QPR), Paul Elliot (Charlton), Stewart Robson (Arsenal), Martin Singleton (Coventry), Trevor Steven (Burnley), John Pearson (Sheffield Wednesday), Mark Walters (Aston Villa), Gary Childs (West Bromwich Albion)

Scotland: Bryan Gunn (Aberdeen), Jim McInally (Celtic), Dave Beaumont (Dundee United), John Philliben (Stirling Albion), Kenny Black (Rangers), Paul McStay (Celtic), Neale Cooper (Aberdeen), Jim Dobbin (Celtic), Samuel McGivern (Kilmarnock), Eric Black (Aberdeen), David Bowman (Hearts)

Subs: Robin Rae (Hibernian), Gary Mackay (Hearts), Billy Davies (Rangers), Derek Ferguson (Rangers), Dave McPherson (Rangers)

After failing to win a place in the starting line-up for the second leg against England there was a slight doubt in my mind about being selected for Finland, but my fears were unfounded and Andy Roxburgh and Walter Smith included me in the sixteen-man squad. Bryan Gunn and Eric Black, however, were soon withdrawn from the group when Aberdeen secured a place in the Scottish Cup final and they were required for the end-of-season showdown against Rangers at Hampden. Gary McGinnis and my Tynecastle teammate, Ian Westwater, replaced them.

Scotland squad for 1982 European Championships:

Robin Rae, Ian Westwater, Jim McInally, David Rennie, David Beaumont, Samuel McGivern, Alistair Dick, Pat Nevin, David Bowman, Paul McStay, Gary Mackay, John Philliben, Gary McGinnis, Brian Rice, Jim Dobbin, William Livingstone

The draw saw us placed in group four, along with Albania, Turkey and the Netherlands. Certainly not the worst outcome considering we avoided the likes of Spain, Portugal, Germany and the USSR. I wasn't selected to start the opening match against Albania, a game we won 3–0, but I did come on in the second half for Billy Livingstone and managed to score the third and final goal.

The experience of being away from home – mingling with boys from poorer countries like Turkey, Poland and Czechoslovakia – was a real eye-opener. But none were more unfortunate than the Albanian boys, who wore the same gear to train and eat in because they were so poor. They also used the water hole on the floor of the shower room when they needed the toilet, simply because that was what they were used to. It was humbling to witness just how poverty-stricken some of their players were and it made me appreciate how lucky I was.

Andy Roxburgh was a firm believer in rewarding players who had rewarded him and my goal in the opening game earned me a place in the starting line-up for our second group match against Turkey. At that time Mr Roxburgh saw me as more of a striker than a midfielder and it was great to get the chance to push forward, instead of having to concern myself with defensive duties. The Turks failed to put up much of a fight and we ran out comfortable 2–0 winners to set up a group decider against Holland.

The Dutch were able to field the nucleus of the senior European Championship-winning team of 1988, including the likes of Marco van Basten, Gerald Vanenburg, John Bosman and Johnny van T'Schip. They had also won their opening two games, but, crucially, could only manage 3–1 victories against Albania and Poland. So we had a better goal difference and knew that a point in our final game would be enough to secure a place in the semi-final.

The match took place at the Anjalankoski stadium, home of Finnish team My-Pa, just a couple of miles from our base in Kotka, near the Russian border. So, while travelling was not an issue, the opposition most decidedly was and we feared the worst when van Basten fired the Dutch ahead in just four minutes after good work from Mario Been. It would have been easy to let our heads go down but we knew we still had eighty-six minutes to get back on level terms. Both the number and quality of chances we created was unbelievable, but poor finishing and good goalkeeping prevented us from snatching the vital goal. That is, until ten minutes from time. Gary McGinnis, starting his first full game for Scotland, latched on to a cute back heel from Ally Dick to fire home from twelve yards. We managed to hold on until the final whistle to secure our place in the last four, amid jubilant scenes on and off the pitch. Players and coaching staff hugged each other while on the sparsely populated terracing one hundred or so Scotland supporters – mainly offshore oil workers from Aberdeen – danced in delight.

Scotland	1–1	Holland
McGinnis 80		van Basten 4

Scotland: Rae, Beaumont, Philliben, Rennie, McInally, Dobbin, McGinnis, Bowman, Nevin, Mackay, Dick.

Holland: Laurs, Koot, Duut, Bosman, Teuben, Snoei, van T'Schip, Vanenburg, van Basten, Roord, Been.

There were quite a few nervous players in the build-up to the semi-final against Poland. Due to our inexperience we had no idea what to expect so Andy Roxburgh and his assistant, Walter Smith, decided to take matters into their own hands. They ordered several dozen bottles of Finnish beer to accompany dinner the night before the big game. Andy told us when we sat down to eat that the alcohol, although a treat, was not a reward for reaching the last four. We were all very excited and he thought it would take the edge off us and enable us to get a good sleep, as well as aiding the recovery process from three tough group games. Every player was given two bottles of beer and while it tasted horrific it was a means to an end so I duly finished both. That meant I didn't remember much about the meal. I was pretty much teetotal into my twenties, not through choice, but because I knew I couldn't handle my drink.

The legendary Dundee-based broadcaster Dick Donnelly was one of only three Scottish journalists reporting on the tournament and I'll always remember the look on his face moments after SFA chief executive Ernie Walker asked for a quick word as we drove to Lathi, the venue for the semi-final. There was no live commentary for any of the matches in the tournament prior to the final and that was a problem for Scotland boss Jock Stein, who was his at home in Glasgow preparing his players for the annual match against England. He wanted to know what was going on during the semi and instructed Ernie to tell Dick that he had to provide a commentary down the phone. Now Dick was no stranger to the commentary game, but spending an entire ninety minutes describing proceedings to the Scotland manager from a public phone box was a new one on him.

Whether it was the effects of the alcohol from the night before, I'm not sure, but, whatever it was, it worked. Ally Dick produced a man-of-the-match performance and scored two wonderful goals to help us beat the Poles 2–0. The only downside was that Jim McInally picked up his second booking of the competition and with it a suspension for the final. Only Czechoslovakia – who had beaten the Soviet Union in the other semi – stood between Scotland and a most unlikely triumph.

We spent our last evening in Lahti celebrating before getting up early the next morning and travelling the one hundred kilometres to Helsinki, the venue for our match against Czechoslovakia. Normally there's a bit of banter on the team bus, but, on this occasion, there was a muted atmosphere due to an extremely unusual situation: two of our players were studying for exams at the back of the bus! Due to their absence from school, Pat Nevin and David Beaumont – both very clever individuals – ended up sitting their Highers on arrival in the Finnish capital under the watchful eye of David Will, the SFA youth-committee president, who doubled up as an invigilator.

At the team meeting the night before the final Andy and Walter told us of the wonderful opportunity we had to restore pride to a wounded nation, with the national team losing 1–0 to England at Hampden earlier that day. Not only would we become heroes if we won, but also we would also lift the gloom after the defeat in Glasgow.

Having taken my chance in the opening game and scored one of our goals against Albania my form remained pretty decent in subsequent matches and I was rewarded with a place in the starting eleven. Andy Roxburgh had found a niche for me and, once again, I played as a deep-lying-attacker-cum-midfielder with instructions to support the front two – Ally Dick and Pat Nevin – as often as possible. Andy was an astute tactician and believed that particular formation was be the best way to get at the Czech defence. He rated the opposition in the air, but felt they could be exploited at the back if we kept the ball on the deck. What followed was the highlight of my fledgling career.

The Czechs were more technically gifted than us, but the longer the game wore on the more confident we became. John Philliben's goal late in the first half was timed to perfection, enabling Andy Roxburgh to use it as a motivational tool at half-time. Within four minutes of the restart we doubled our advantage, courtesy of Pat Nevin. I was able to find him in space about twenty-five yards from goal and he produced an exquisite chip to leave their goalkeeper without a prayer.

Unfortunately for us, however, we had just two minutes to savour our two-goal lead, at which time Karel Kula pulled one back. Now we really had a game on our hands. Thankfully, we were able to withstand pressure and I grabbed a goal after sixty-four minutes to restore our two-goal cushion. It wasn't the best I've ever scored – a dipping shot from sixteen yards – but it was certainly one of the most important. There was no more scoring and we were crowned European champions. An achievement to be proud of, but even more so when you consider that Andy Roxburgh only had fourteen players to choose from for the final due to an injury to Jim Dobbin and Jim McInally's one-match suspension.

Incidentally, that trophy in Finland remains Scotland's only major football honour at international level.

European Under-Eighteen Championship final

Olympic Stadium, Helsinki: Attendance: 2,500

30 May 1982	Scotland	3–1	Czechoslovakia
	John Philliben 44		Karel Kula 51
	Pat Nevin 49		
	Gary Mackay 64		

Scotland: Rae, Beaumont, Bowman, Dick, McGinnis, McStay, Mackay, Nevin, Philliben, Rennie, Rice.

Czechoslovakia: Pribyl, Hasek, Vrba, Kopca, Bazant, Kubil, V. Kula, Karoch, K. Kula, Miskuf, Hirko.

We returned to a heroes' reception in Scotland, with hundreds of tartan-clad supporters greeting us at Glasgow airport. The players gave numerous interviews to newspapers as well as appearing on television and radio; the media just couldn't get enough of us. The *Daily Record* of 31 May 1982 summed up our exploits well, pointing out that, 'There has never been a braver Scotland side than this one.'

There was also a bizarre experience in Paisley shortly after our return from Finland when a little-known Italian coach took training one afternoon. His name was Fabio Capello. He was one of a batch of rookie coaches sent to Scotland that summer on a three-week study programme, as former Scotland boss Craig Brown explained to *Four Four Two* magazine in March 2008:

The visit was organised by Andy Roxburgh, who was then technical director at the SFA and also head youth coach having just led the squad to victory in Finland. There was a lot of interest in what was happening in Scotland at the time after the boys' success in Helsinki and the Italians were keen to find out more about how we had managed to conquer Europe. Andy was on very close terms with Arrigo Sacchi, who had previously come over to give some Scottish coaches a talk on the four-four-two formation, of which he was the pioneer. Through that relationship a lot of our promising young coaches went to Italy and their guys came over here – as did some big names in Italian football such as Giovanni Trapattoni and Marcello Lippi. As part of their programme the young Italian coaches were sent to observe training at various clubs in Scotland and I ended up with Capello at Clyde.

It was also Andy Roxburgh who arranged for Fabio Capello to take charge of our training session in Paisley. At one point, in the mud, the ball came to him and he just flicked it up in the air and caught it on the back of his neck. It was a great piece of skill and something that few players would have the nerve to try, let alone coaches. I certainly did not have the ability to attempt it for fear of making a fool of myself. The fact that Capello was dressed in immaculate designer gear made it all the more memorable.

Once the mayhem died down the players spent the rest of the summer basking in the glory. We also knew that we had secured our place at the world youth championships in Mexico the following year.

* * *

To give us the best possible preparation for the FIFA world youth championships, the SFA decided to fund a trip to the United States in May 1983 to help us acclimatise to the heat and high altitude of Mexico City and Toluca. We spent seven days at the US air-force academy in Colorado a week before the championships, giving us the chance to train in facilities at a comparable altitude.

The enhanced preparation seemed to work in the early stages as we beat Korea – who went on to finish fourth – in our opening match. The trip halfway around the world was certainly a wonderful experience for our group of nineteen-year-olds, but, from a personal perspective, it wasn't the most memorable tournament for me, although there was one notable exception. After our victory against the Koreans we were then beaten by Australia by two goals to one (I was an unused substitute for the two opening matches). Those results meant a crucial final group game against the hosts, Mexico, with the winners going through to the last eight and the losers either going home, us, or staying at home, them!

An incredibly passionate crowd of 86,582 – remarkably, still 50,000 short of capacity – turned up at the magnificent Azteca stadium in Mexico City in a bid to help their nation secure qualification for the knockout stages. There was just one small problem for their fans: we failed to read the script. Steve Clarke scored the only goal of the game just before half-time to guarantee a place in the last eight. I was even selected by Andy Roxburgh for a cameo six-minute appearance when I came on to replace Ally Dick. Getting the chance to play at the Azteca is something I have never forgotten, but a series of incredible events after the game made the day yet more memorable.

The host nation, Mexico, had failed to qualify for the knockout stage of its own tournament, in fact they finished bottom of the section. Needless-to-say their supporters did not take kindly to the results, although the consequences were something you might expect to see on the 'What happened next?' round of *A Question of Sport*.

In the immediate aftermath the Mexican fans tried desperately to get on to the pitch with the intention of attacking their youngsters. It was fortunate that fencing and a perimeter moat prevented that from happening. Unperturbed, they then decided to wreck part of the stadium by removing seats from the concrete bowl. They used the seats as missiles, launching them in the direction of several green-and-white-clad youngsters, who were desperately trying to make their way to the relative safety of the dressing room. Incredibly, we were applauded as we scuttled back to the bowels of the stadium as their anger turned to appreciation for our performance. But their good mood lasted only a couple of minutes before they got back to the business of venting their frustration at their former favourites.

At that point the players thought the drama was over and so we began to celebrate our place in the quarter-final. Then we heard a knock on the door. The chief of police of Mexico City appeared and told us it wasn't safe to venture outside to our waiting bus for at least an hour, until they were able to disperse the angry fans. That was easier said than done because the supporters had turned their attention to three of the four flags flying outside the main entrance: the Mexican green, white and red, the FIFA and the Central American Confederation flags were reduced to ashes, while they left the Scottish Saltire intact as a way of showing their respect for our performance.

An hour later and another knock at the door. *Senor* chief of police again . . .

> I'm afraid you will need to give us another thirty minutes before we can provide you with a police escort. The angry crowd outside still shows no sign of dispersing. We have therefore decided to help the Mexican players get out of the stadium undercover . . . by ambulance.

Needless-to-say that was an experience never repeated in all my years in football.

* * *

With Davie Bowman and Ian Westwater also involved in the Azteca stadium that night Hearts had three players taking part in a prestigious tournament; a great achievement for the club. Unfortunately, we lost 1–0 to Poland in the quarter-final and that was hard to take given that we had beaten them 2–0 in the European semi-final less than twelve months previously. Once again I was as an unused substitute and flew back to Scotland a very disappointed young man having managed only six minutes of action in four matches. I'm not saying I would have made a huge difference if I had been given more of a chance in Mexico, but it did leave a bad taste in my mouth after playing well in Finland and scoring twice. Looking back I let my disappointment cloud the fact I was representing my country at one of the biggest tournaments in the world. I regret not savouring more of the experience; I was sharing a global platform with the likes of Bebeto, Dunga, Jorginho, Ruben Sosa, Oleg Protasov and Marco van Basten and I wish I could have that time again.

I must also pay a special tribute to Andy Roxburgh, a man often derided by some in the media and in the professional game as a schoolteacher type who had never performed at a high level as a player. I have the utmost respect for the man, even if he didn't give me as much game time as I would have liked in Mexico. He prepared thoroughly for matches, made players aware of their role, was a superb tactician and treated everyone firmly yet fairly. I think I can speak for everyone in the squad when I say that we could not have had a better mentor. It was the same when I played for the full-international side; the players, many of them superstars in their own right, had a hell of a lot of time for Andy. I think I am right in saying that he suffered less from call-offs than most other Scotland managers; a sure sign that they rated the man.

Although we failed to progress past the quarter-finals in Mexico, the European victory in Finland capped an astonishing rise to prominence for the squad; thirteen of the sixteen players carved out a career at a decent level in football and four of us won full caps for Scotland. It made all those days as an apprentice at Hearts cleaning boots and sweeping the terraces worthwhile. I think chores like that are a must for young footballers; they help them appreciate the good times, like being called into the top-team squad for the first time or getting the chance to represent their country. From the first day I kicked a football in earnest I never stopped learning, but that curve is steepest between the ages of sixteen and eighteen. That's when you have to do all the dirty jobs as an apprentice – cleaning the communal bath and doing the laundry amongst other horrible tasks – but that's all part of a player's development. At Tynecastle it also meant getting on your hands and knees to remove weeds from the away terracing. It may have been a bit of a come down having spent a week in Cannes and represented my country for the first time, but it made me realise the rewards on offer in return for bit of hard work.

And that's never a bad lesson to learn at any age.

FIFA World Youth Championship in Mexico
2–9 June 1983

Scotland squad: D. Beaumont, E. Black, D. Bowman, S. Clarke, N. Cooper, A. Dick, J. Dobbin, B. Gunn, G. Mackay, B. McClair, G. McGinnis, J. McInally, D. McPherson, P. McStay, P. Nevin, J. Philliben, B. Rice, I. Westwater

Coaches: A Roxburgh, W Smith

Group A

| 3 June | South Korea | 0–2 | Scotland |
| | | | Dobbin 62, 78 |

Toluca stadium: attendance: 26,191

Scotland: Gunn, Beaumont, Bowman, Black (McGinnis), Cooper, Dobbin, McClair (Dick), McInally, McPherson, McStay, Nevin

Subs not used: Westwater, Clarke, Mackay, Philliben, Rice

5 June	Australia	2–1	Scotland
	Incantalupo 52		McStay 61
	Patikas 87		

Toluca stadium: attendance: 22,111

Scotland: Gunn, Beaumont, Bowman, Black, Clarke, Cooper, Dobbin (Dick), McPherson, McStay, Nevin, Rice (McGinnis)

Subs not used: Westwater, McClair, McInally, Mackay, Philliben

8 June   Mexico   0–1   Scotland
                                             Clarke 45

                Azteca stadium: attendance: 86,582

Scotland: Gunn, Bowman, Clarke, Cooper, Dick (Mackay), Dobbin, McGinnis, McInally, McStay, Nevin (Black), Philliben

Subs not used: Westwater, Beaumont, McClair, McPherson, Rice

Group A table	P	W	D	L	F	A	Pts
1 Scotland	3	2	0	1	4	2	4
2 South Korea	3	2	0	1	4	4	4
3 Australia	3	1	1	1	4	4	3
4 Mexico	3	0	1	2	2	4	1

Quarter-Final

11 June   Poland   1–0   Scotland
                 Klemenz, 5

                Mexico City stadium: attendance: 11,986

Scotland: Gunn, Bowman (McClair), Clarke, Cooper, Dick, Dobbin, McGinnis, McInally (Black), McStay, Nevin, Philliben

Subs not used: Westwater, Mackay, Rice, Beaumont, McPherson

5

Martin, Moncur, Mercer, MacDonald

*'A flash penthouse is not much use if the
foundations are weak.'*

It was near the end of January 1981 and I had been a professional footballer
for just over six months. It was the day after my seventeenth birthday and I
was selected to start against Morton in a Scottish Cup tie at Cappielow, only
my third appearance in a maroon jersey. Life was good. Life was perhaps too
good because that was as good as it got that season. After a goalless draw
in Greenock we were knocked out of the Cup in front of our own supporters
at Tynecastle four days later. From that point on in season 1980/81 things
started to go wrong for Hearts. The football club was not a happy place.

The Scottish Cup exit didn't help, but even a decent cup run wouldn't
have generated enough revenue to rescue the club. Heart of Midlothian was
on its knees financially and something had to be done. Archie Martin, the
chairman at the time, had been doing his best to control costs, to the extent
that he had gambled during the previous summer by offering some of the
best young talent in Edinburgh around £50 per week to sign up. Putting his
faith in youth may or may not have worked, but at least it didn't cost him
much to find out. Unfortunately, however, Archie and the board did not have
enough finance to support the financial restructuring that was required.

The problems came to a head in the first few months of 1981 when fresh
capital was needed to pay off significant debts. Money, however, had run out
and Martin was left with no alternative but to seek additional investment. He
approached his friend, Kenny Waugh, for help and with a view to a possible
takeover. Kenny was Edinburgh born-and-bred and, despite having an allegiance to Hibernian, was a better bet in the eyes of some of the players to

take over than a flamboyant young businessman from the west of Scotland by the name of Wallace Mercer. In the very few dealings I had with both men, I found Kenny a warmer and more outgoing person than Wallace and someone who knew more about youth football in the capital than his rival. Mercer on the other hand was also a successful businessman. He had been brought up in Glasgow and played rugby at the private school he attended, which perhaps accounts for the posh voice. He had supported Rangers as a boy but had no previous experience in football.

I felt that because Kenny knew the area better than Wallace he would have been a more effective owner, although investment from any source would have been an improvement on the status quo. I became a bit more comfortable with the Mercer bid once I found out that Tynecastle legend Donald Ford – one of my heroes as a boy – was instrumental in bringing him to the negotiating table. Nevertheless it was still an unsettling period for the players. I had been at the club for less than twelve months and, having just turned seventeen, wondered if my first season in a maroon jersey would also be my last.

* * *

I got on fine with Wallace Mercer. Not great. Just fine. Other players were much closer to him. I was slightly wary when he became majority shareholder at Hearts in May 1981 simply because I knew so little about him. It wasn't until he took over that I found out that with his wife, Anne, he had bought £1,000-worth of shares several years before and that he had developed an affinity for the club after moving through to Edinburgh from Glasgow. That purchase was a gesture of goodwill, not a ploy to get his foot in the door. But his involvement went a lot deeper when he was approached by Donald Ford to join a consortium seeking to counter a bid from Kenny Waugh. From having no interest in getting involved, Mercer was soon knee-deep in negotiations to acquire a majority shareholding. Ever the showman, one day he went as far as introducing Olympic 100-metres gold medallist Allan Wells to Hearts fans at the Shandon snooker centre on Slateford Road to persuade the supporters he not only had contacts but also, and more importantly, that he meant business.

A power struggle ensued between Waugh and Mercer until Wallace eventually saw off the challenge of his rival in May 1981, writing a cheque for £265,000 for the privilege with an additional £85,000 coming from the consortium. His arrival spelt the end for Archie Martin as chairman and it was no surprise when – having supported the bid from Kenny Waugh – he resigned his post less than a week after Wallace swept into power.

I'll always have a special place in my heart for Archie Martin, and not just because he is also a lifelong supporter of Hearts. He took time out to give me a guided tour of Tynecastle in a bid to persuade me to sign and I'll remember him as the man who gave me the opportunity to fulfil my dream of becoming a professional footballer. You could tell by looking at him that he was smart and had money and he was always highly enthusiastic about the club. He put his faith in kids when others would not have taken that risk and was richly rewarded for his gamble. His decision to sign Davie Bowman, John Robertson and me paid off spectacularly as it brought three major benefits to the club: a financial windfall from Coventry (for Bow); the emergence of Hearts' record goal-scorer (Robbo); a midfielder who would go on to play more games for the club than anyone else in its history (me). He made all that happen and I will be eternally grateful to him.

Unfortunately for Archie he just didn't have the money to take Hearts to the next level, unlike Wallace Mercer. For all my initial misgivings about him, Wallace was able to do just that and this larger-than-life character was one of the key reasons for the turnaround in our fortunes. He continued Archie Martin's policy of giving youth a chance – which helped my career – believing it would not only save money but could also generate cash if the players developed successfully and were then sold on. He also believed that youngsters would develop more quickly by playing alongside experienced teammates.

One thing Mercer did not have in common with Archie, however, was his opinion of manager Bobby Moncur. Moncur had played for Scotland and had been a highly distinguished captain of Newcastle United, who had led the Geordies to victory in the 1969 Fairs Cup. He was both a friend and an associate of Martin but simply didn't get along with Mercer. A press conference was held a couple of days after Wallace took control in a bid to persuade people that the two men could work together but all it did was to paper over the cracks of a relationship that simply did not work. Bobby resigned two weeks later, but that wasn't the end of the matter. Mercer decided that Moncur was in breach of contract and demanded compensation from his former manager. The club ended up receiving a cheque for £13,000! 'I didn't like the cut of his jib and was delighted when he resigned,' said Mercer about Moncur. He had been in the door for less than a month but the new chairman had already shown that he did not suffer fools gladly.

It didn't take me long to realise he was not a person to be trifled with.

* * *

I had a rough idea of the level of professionalism and work rate required when I joined Hearts. This was mainly due to being trained by excellent professionals like George Stewart and Eric Schaedler during the later part of my time at Salvesen. However, a few days into my first pre-season as a pro I soon realised those Thursday nights training with George and Eric were a piece of cake compared with Bobby Moncur's much more stringent requirements. Talk about a culture shock. I was a skinny kid, rather fragile, and not as fit as I should have been. While this made the early part of my career difficult it was just what I needed if I was going to make it in the game.

I joined Hearts at what I thought was a reasonable time for the club. We had just been promoted from the first division and Moncur had put in place a squad that he believed could take us into the higher reaches of the Premier Division in season 1980/81. But many of the players he had inherited from Willie Ormond were past their prime – eight of the team he selected for his first league match against Hamilton in February 1980 were aged twenty-six or above – and he didn't have financial backing from the board to bring in new players.

Another major problem was the lack of professionalism in the squad. Bobby Moncur was a real gentleman and a legend in the game: he was the last Newcastle captain to lift a trophy and it was easy to tell he'd been a total professional as a player because of the high standards he expected. It was his misfortune that there were too many guys at Tynecastle who were set in their ways and not prepared to embrace the changes he wanted. At times it was like a holiday camp. Alfie Conn junior was a hugely talented football player and I got on well with him; but in my view he was lazy. He'd played for bigger clubs – like Rangers, Tottenham and Celtic – and perhaps viewed Hearts as beneath his dignity as he approached the end of his career. I remember the first day of pre-season 1980/81 at Saughton enclosure; the lights round the four-hundred-metre track were spaced out at fifty-metre intervals. He ran fifty metres with the rest of us then pulled up with a hamstring injury. It seemed to me he did very little else during that pre-season yet still deemed himself fit for the first game of the new campaign.

Meanwhile, Jim Docherty, who scored plenty of goals for the reserves, used to sell cans of Coke and Mars Bars after training from the boot of his car for a profit of two pence on each sale. His total return was about forty pence a day, which hardly put him in the Richard Branson class. This little business venture was accepted by many in the squad as perfectly normal but the bottom line is that sugary snacks should not be the staple diet of a professional footballer after a tough training session. It was for some players at Tynecastle and unfortunately for Bobby it was a case of old habits die hard as far as a select group were concerned. The be all and end all for a lot of players at Hearts in the early 1980s was to pick up a salary cheque at the end of the month and that was more important to them than the team winning.

An incident at training one day typified the way things were going and left me wondering what I had got myself into. There was a bust-up involving Jim Denny and centre-half Willie McVie; it was the sort of row that happens regularly at every club in the land. Moncur stopped the session and sent everyone back to Tynecastle, which was not the reaction I expected from him. But it was what happened next that illustrated the type of players he was working with: some of them were delighted by his decision because it meant finishing an hour early. Talk about a lack of commitment.

We'd not made the best of starts to the season with only two league wins in our opening six matches and Moncur was starting to feel the pressure. Some of the more experienced professionals were simply not producing so, having already given sixteen-year-old Davie Bowman his debut against Airdrieonians in the Anglo-Scottish Cup in the opening match of the season, he decided to give me my first taste of top-team football in the League Cup tie against Ayr United at Somerset Park on 24 September 1980. I made my debut as a substitute in place of Bobby Robinson.

Having already lost the first leg 3–2 at Tynecastle to our lower-league opponents, the subsequent 4–0 defeat at Somerset Park was an utter embarrassment and not exactly the game I would have selected for my first in a maroon jersey. To borrow a familiar after-match cliché, I was gutted. It was regrettable that several teammates did not share either my hurt or embarrassment. On the way back to Edinburgh some senior members of the squad laughed and joked during a game of cards and adopted an 'oh well, life goes on' attitude. Heart of Midlothian had just been humbled by a club from a lower league, crashing out of the League Cup in the process, yet there were players on our team bus who did not give a fuck. I could perhaps have understood that behaviour, only just I may add, if world-class opposition had beaten us in a meaningless pre-season friendly but this was Ayr United for goodness sake. A few hundred Hearts fans had paid good money to travel through to Somerset Park, and had probably taken a half-day off work as well, and in return we put on a pathetic display. The whole side was abysmal. It was the first time I had been on the team bus after playing in a match and I was shocked by the behaviour of the experienced members of the squad. It was as if the defeat meant nothing and it was no coincidence that most of them did not last much longer at Tynecastle.

Neither, as it turned out, did Bobby Moncur. Being used to the utmost professionalism at Newcastle, his methods failed to win over the senior players in the dressing room and he could not comprehend why some Hearts players treated their job like a hobby and not a vocation. He won only four games that season after the debacle at Somerset Park, ensuring relegation to division one, and even if Wallace Mercer had not come in I don't think he would

have lasted much longer than the 480 days he spent in charge. In the full-
ness of time I think Moncur could have done all right as manager of Hearts
– he certainly had plenty of decent ideas – but his hands were tied because
of the financial position and I don't think he was too disappointed when he
finally moved on.

There was a vacancy to fill and both Alex Rennie and Willie McLean
were tipped by the press to replace Moncur. Wallace Mercer wanted either
Jim McLean or Jock Wallace; unfortunately for our chairman big Jock said no
while the Dundee United board refused him permission to speak to McLean
even although Wallace met Jim privately on a couple of occasions to sound
him out. I later learned that Mercer even considered Tommy Docherty, until
he was quickly talked out of it by club director Alex Naylor. Mercer was
aiming high but no matter who was brought in he knew that change was
required. 'I might not know all that much about football,' he said, 'but
what I do know is that the Hearts team that were relegated are not capable
mentally of lifting themselves up to win promotion. The team must be torn
apart – it's a ruthless task both on and off the park.' Strong words, but
Wallace Mercer was spot on. It was time for change.

Assistant manager Tony Ford took charge of the first team on an interim
basis in the summer of 1981 until a permanent appointment was made. As
a player he had plied his trade in the lower reaches of the English game but
his career ground to a halt at the age of twenty-six because of injury. He
was hardly a big name and did little to inspire either the players or the fans.
Nor did the chairman have much faith in Ford's judgement in the transfer
market; Wallace Mercer decided he would sign the players (he was twenty-
five years ahead of his time given recent events at Hearts!) Stuart MacLaren
joined from Dundee for £25,000 and was one of six signings along with Derek
Strickland, Gerry McCoy, Pat Byrne, Henry Smith and Roddy MacDonald.
Despite his lack of charisma I never had a problem with Tony Ford but poor
early results suggested we were once again moving in the wrong direction.
It wasn't long before the fans started questioning his tactics and the board
soon came to the same conclusion; after just nine wins in twenty-four
matches (and one victory in his last seven games) Ford lost his job before a
permanent replacement for Bobby Moncur had even been identified.

But this time Wallace Mercer had a ready-made solution in mind. After
finally admitting defeat in his quest to find a big name he appointed team
captain Alex MacDonald as player-manager of Hearts in December 1981.
The chairman had been persuaded of MacDonald's qualities by Bobby
Parker, who had served the club as a player and a coach as well as in the
boardroom as a director and chairman. Mercer, by his own admission, was
a risk taker. Speculate to accumulate was his philosophy but this was an

appointment from left field and probably one of the biggest gambles he had taken in either business or football.

* * *

I had a naive dislike of Alex MacDonald when he first came to Hearts in 1980. It was exactly one month after I put pen to paper that the club paid Rangers around £35,000 for the midfielder, who had spent twelve years at Ibrox. He was the type of player opposing fans loved to hate and as a young supporter watching Hearts I detested him when he was in opposition. For one reason or another he had always been a thorn in the flesh of my team. Unfortunately, my immaturity meant I was unable to separate being a supporter from being his teammate and it didn't take him long to realise I didn't like him. Things came to a head one Monday morning at Tynecastle after I had been left out for a game on the Saturday. I was in a huff with everyone and stormed past him in the corridor before training. He immediately shouted at me to stop and there was a menacing tone in his voice that suggested I had better do exactly that.

'I don't want you to like me,' he said, 'but I sure as hell want you to respect me. Saying good morning is not beyond anyone.'

I was a cocky so-and-so in the embryonic period of my Hearts career but I am glad Alex taught me vital lessons at a young age and helped me realise that it's important to have a bit of humility. His status as a European trophy winner at Ibrox, plus the 503 games he played for Rangers under great managers like Willie Waddell and Jock Wallace, meant he should have had instant respect from me and he wasn't slow to let me know that. It wasn't arrogance on his part; he was simply trying to point me in the right direction. It was part of my learning curve in being not just a pro but a good pro. I like to think his good habits rubbed off and that I became a better player, and, more importantly, a better man. One thing is certain: I had more respect for him than anyone I ever worked with.

I'm glad that incident happened early on in our working relationship because he ended up taking me under his wing and taught me important lessons, lessons in how to treat others with respect, no matter their background. Alex MacDonald also told me to look people in the eye at all times – I always used to shy away from doing that – and that was an important lesson. In fact it was only one of hundreds he taught me. I told him I didn't feel intimidated by some of the senior players during my first few months at Hearts because the club was yo-yoing between the Premier League and the first division and I felt, like confident youngsters do I suppose, that I was just as good as my new teammates. He told me that wasn't a problem as long as I showed those guys the respect they deserved, whether it was on the football pitch or in the dressing room. I had some wonderful help in the reserves from Graham Shaw and Bobby Masterton during the times I wasn't selected for the first team and I made sure I thanked them for their help, something I would not have done prior to Alex MacDonald's arrival at the club. He was like a big brother and a life coach rolled into one and for that I will always be grateful. I may have detested him as a player, but he was by far the biggest influence on my career and I have no doubt that his guidance helped prolong the time I spent playing football. Taking all these things into account it was highly fortuitous for me when he was chosen by Wallace Mercer to be the first player-manager of a football club in Britain.

It's often funny the way football pans out. The Gaffer's appointment as player-boss was only possible after an injury prevented him completing a move to St Mirren a couple of months earlier, in exchange for Lex Richardson and a hefty sum of money to help balance our books. His appointment may have been a gamble but it gave us something that had been missing for many years: leadership. Bobby Moncur and Tony Ford, both lovely men, tried hard to provide that but in the end both were unsuccessful. Alex MacDonald on the other hand was able to hit the ground running due to the support he received from Wallace Mercer. Alex was Wallace's first major managerial appointment and the chairman, determined to give him every chance to succeed, backed him to the hilt. As a result the bond between the two men was strong. The purse strings were loosened slightly, allowing the new manager to add to his squad. He had identified that the squad lacked both quality and experience and so he made former Ibrox teammate Sandy Jardine his first signing during the summer of 1982. Willie Johnston, Donald Park and Jimmy Bone arrived soon after, with the Gaffer deciding a mixture of youth and experience was the short-term solution for a club that had been in decline for too long.

In the intervening period between his appointment as player-manager and the arrival of his new signings, Alex MacDonald steadied the ship and our results picked up. We went on a run at the start of 1982 that saw the team win fourteen and lose only four of eighteen matches. Unfortunately the damage had been done at the start of the season and, despite a late charge, we missed out on promotion to the Premier League by a solitary point. At one stage our place back in the top flight looked assured. However, a collapse at home to Dumbarton (2–5) and a goalless draw at Kilmarnock left us needing to beat Motherwell at Tynecastle on the final day to go up. This was a tough task considering the Fir Park side had secured the title nearly four weeks previously, but we hoped they would take their foot off the gas and be in party mode by the time they arrived in Gorgie. Wrong. They beat us 1–0 and we faced another twelve months in the first division.

Although Alex had taken me under his wing when he was a player I failed to become a regular starter and it was disappointing that I didn't feature more in the early part of his tenure, starting on the bench on seventeen occasions during season 1981/82. I made my mind up to knuckle down over the summer and prove to him that I was deserving of more opportunities.

The Gaffer had come from a disciplined background at Rangers where every player had to wear a shirt and tie to training, courtesy of Jock Wallace. While not quite going to those extremes at Hearts, Jim Docherty's tuck shop became the first casualty of the new regime. Fitness levels improved dramatically thanks to a new pre-season training routine. Alex knew it was vitally important for him as an older member of the squad to maintain a high level of personal fitness and he wanted the same for everyone so he entrusted that side of things to former sprinter George McNeill and fitness coach Bert Logan. Both say they have a football background, but, having seen their first touch, I'm not so sure. Bert, now my business partner, was at Motherwell for a period while George was with Hibs as a youngster, but of course that doesn't count! The pair had complete autonomy over the fitness schedule and more often than not during pre-season George and Bert took the physical part of training and Alex, despite being the boss, took part along with everyone else. It wasn't long before there was a noticeable improvement and fitness levels increased tenfold. While 99.9 per cent of players moan about pre-season if the manager and his assistant also take part it's hard to complain and is in many ways inspirational. No one likes having to get fit after the summer break but George and Bert, while making us work hard, made sure we had fun at the same time.

Six months previously the club had been in chaos, run like a holiday camp with nowhere near the level of professionalism required to be successful, despite the best efforts of Bobby Moncur and Tony Ford. I thought I was living *la vida loca*, being handed my debut at the age of sixteen and convinced my career would continue to go from strength to strength. I was so insular that I thought only of myself but the arrival of Alex MacDonald was exactly what was required, both from a personal and professional perspective.

We got off to a good start in season 1982/83 with just a single defeat in our opening fourteen matches. The decision by Wallace Mercer to give the Gaffer complete control of the playing side had worked a treat. The introduction of Sandy Jardine and Willie 'Bud' Johnston – men with experience of playing in World Cups – was a masterstroke and they set standards for us youngsters and provided guidance on and off the pitch. The apathy in and around Tynecastle, evident for many years, had disappeared and the dressing room was a fun place to be again. Every morning Bow, Robbo and myself were all desperate to make a cup of tea for Bud, Sandy and later

Jimmy Bone in return for hearing about how they had made it in football and the many great characters they had encountered. We used to wait until the tea ladies, Mary and Ella, were cleaning and had their backs turned before sneaking into the tearoom for teabags. They knew we were there but never let on because they knew we were not getting up to any mischief. It was like a postgraduate seminar in how to maximise your potential in the modern game and something for which we were eternally grateful. Of course Bud Johnston had other tales but I'm not sure if practising what he preached would have been the best idea for prolonging my career . . . .

Our good start to the league season was maintained pretty much throughout the whole campaign and our level of consistency drove another strong promotion challenge. As we approached the final bend this time it was St Johnstone, Partick Thistle and ourselves fighting it out for the two available spots in the Premier League. Our 2–1 defeat by Saints at Muirton Park in April 1983 put them in the driving seat for the title; they never relinquished their lead and were crowned champions. But we managed to put together a run of five matches unbeaten at the end of the campaign, form that was too good for Partick to cope with and promotion was secured in the penultimate match when I scored in our 4–0 win at Dumbarton as Thistle lost 1–0 at home to Airdrieonians. We still had an outside chance of winning the title but needed to beat Hamilton at Tynecastle and hope that St Johnstone failed to win at home against Dunfermline. We did our job – Willie Johnston and Derek O'Connor scored for us – but Saints secured the championship with a 1–0 victory over Dunfermline. It might not have been a league-winners medal, but it was still my first taste of success as a professional footballer. We were back in Scottish football's top flight with the likes of Rangers, Celtic, Aberdeen and Dundee United and this time we would stay there. It might not have seemed like a huge achievement to some people – I believed Heart of Midlothian were as big, if not bigger, than the likes of the Dons and United – but at that stage everyone at Tynecastle was simply relieved to be back where we belonged.

I never knew what to expect from Alex MacDonald. There were times we'd go in on a Monday morning after a good win on the Saturday but he'd run us really hard. He knew the players would have been out on Saturday night and maybe on Sunday as well – with his permission of course – and he wanted us refocused. Other times we'd go expecting the worst following a defeat and he'd take us for a swim and sauna at the Commonwealth pool or have some cream cakes for us after a light training session. There were never two days the same in nearly nine years of his management. The mixture of youth and experience worked a treat although I was slightly concerned one Monday morning after a defeat when Willie Johnston squared up to me and told me to slap him, watched by Alex MacDonald. He then retaliated, with gentle force I may add, and we had a pretend fight. Bud was aware there was disappointment in the camp after losing but knew that kind of thing would lift spirits. Just as well he was only playing because one slap from him would have knocked me out!

* * *

The whole atmosphere around the club was completely different with Wallace Mercer in the boardroom and the Gaffer in charge of team affairs. Morale could not have been higher; it was a million miles away from that bus journey back from Somerset Park when I made my debut. While Alex MacDonald was busy instigating change both on and off the pitch – with an incredible thirty players either arriving or departing in the two-and-a-half year period following his appointment as manager – Wallace Mercer was doing his bit to develop the business side of the club. We did not get on that well on a personal level; he knew my feelings for Hearts and I felt that when it came to contract negotiations he realised that an extra £50 per week and a bit of lunch would be enough to persuade me to re-sign. You might say he manipulated me, albeit in an innocent way. But I recognise the tremendous job he did for the club, which was possibly at the lowest ebb in its long history when he took over. I also pay testament to his courage; it is well documented that he gave the bank a personal guarantee for a six-figure sum that was ploughed into the club, a move that could have seen him lose not only his business but also his house.

Mercer was a marketing and public-relations genius. His highly innovative approach was typified by the production of a souvenir programme for the second leg of the League Cup semi-final against Rangers at Tynecastle in November 1982, which doubled as a prize-draw entry for a £35,000 Miller house and a Ford Sierra. Needless-to-say a stunt like that got the undivided attention of the public and Hearts' biggest home crowd for four years – nearly 19,000 – was in attendance that evening. Unfortunately for the players the stunt may have made back-page headlines but our performance didn't as we were beaten 2–1 and lost the tie 4–1 on aggregate.

Speaking of stunts, a broken bone in my foot may have kept me out of action for twenty-one games in season 1984/85 but that didn't prevent me getting involved in some of the high jinks in the dressing room. Shoes were regularly nailed to the floor while jackets were stitched up at the sleeves. Chief culprits were Messrs Johnston and Bone, while Bowman was regularly up to no good as well. If you dished it out you had to be prepared to take it but silly stunts like that helped team bonding. Kenny Black was never far from trouble either but he got the shock of his life one day after training. He had arrived at Tynecastle that morning with a lovely pair of new trousers that had been made to measure. A couple of hours later when he put them back on they had, shall we say, been altered and were halfway up his shins, like the three-quarter shorts or pirate pants that are all the rage now. He wasn't happy but he would have been if he'd known he was in fashion twenty years before anybody else.

I also remember the day in April 1985 that Willie Johnston left the club. He used to wear a suit and a parka jacket to training because that's what he had been used to at Rangers, where collar-and-tie was compulsory. On his last day at Tynecastle eight of us climbed into the bath after training, each wearing an item of Willie's clothing. He took it well but insisted that the parka didn't go into the water. It was fortunate for him that no one was brave enough to try; he was a tough cookie and would have battered every one of us.

The change in the football club in just a few short years was incredible. We had gone from a team yo-yoing between the Premier Division and the first division to one that was firmly on an upward trajectory. At the start of my career with Hearts there were times when I was unsure if my wages would be paid. So we had a lot to thank Wallace Mercer and the Gaffer for. Even after a couple of defeats Alex MacDonald still allowed us out for a couple of beers as long as he reckoned we had given our best, a far cry from the dark days of the late Seventies and early Eighties when finding something to cheer about was rare. The Gaffer introduced team lunches and players ended up staying – by choice – until mid-afternoon to work on important aspects of the game like crossing and finishing. Eating habits became a lot better and the team spirit improved dramatically as everyone trained, played and ate together.

The front door at Tynecastle may have been revolving in the early Eighties, with so many players coming and going, but one man who survived – and I'm glad he did because he's a good mate of mine – was Walter Kidd. And it was all down to a change in his eating habits. In fact, at the start of the 1985/86 season he was the only player still at Tynecastle since I had joined five years previously. He had cut out the junk food and started to eat properly, lost weight as a result, trained hard and it wasn't long before he was a first-team regular. He even ended up with a wonderful nickname, when a particularly mazy run up the right flank resulted in a cry of 'Zico' from the terracing. At least being compared to a flamboyant Brazilian World Cup star is better than his nickname for me: fanny!

I've never been completely aware just how much the disappointment at Dens Park on the final day of the season in May 1986 subsequently affected my form, but it must have been significant enough for Hearts to consider selling me to Dundee United for £500,000 the following summer. I could have taken the easy way out and left Tynecastle when the going got tough but that wasn't my style. I told Alex and Sandy Jardine (who'd been promoted to co-manager) that I was prepared to fight for my place. I explained to them that playing for Hearts was all I ever wanted to do and I had gone too far down the road simply to give up everything I'd worked for. I ended up signing a new contract that would keep me at the club until the summer of 1990, exactly ten years after first putting pen-to-paper at Tynecastle.

There were many highlights during the Mercer and MacDonald era, too many to mention, but I do recall with a smile every time someone brings up the UEFA Cup quarter final against Bayern Munich in February 1989. We hadn't been playing particularly well in domestic football during the first half of season 1988/89 – resulting in Sandy Jardine being dismissed as joint manager – but for some reason we found a bit of form in the European arena. St Patrick's Athletic were comfortably eliminated in the opening round before Zico (with the benefit of the most dubious onside decision in history) went flying down the wing in Vienna before producing the perfect cross for Mike Galloway to score the goal that eliminated Austria Vienna in round two. Velez Mostar were knocked out in round three to set up the glamour tie against the German giants.

So the stage was set for one of the biggest European nights in the club's history. We were facing a side that had been runners-up in the Bundesliga in the previous season and would go one better in 88/89 by winning the German title. Bayern being Bayern they had the usual array of superstars: Stefan Reuter, Klaus Augenthaler, Roland Wohlfarth, Johnny Eckstrom and many more. So it was hardly surprising that, following a 3–0 defeat at the hands of Aberdeen on the Saturday, we went into the first leg at Tynecastle as distinct underdogs. Nevertheless, a crowd of 26,924 rolled up with great anticipation and they created one of the most atmospheric nights I can ever remember in the old stadium. The Hearts players were anything but intimidated and how we celebrated when Iain Ferguson's blistering strike from twenty-five yards give us a 1–0 lead to take to Munich. It was all the more creditable considering our domestic form and the fact Alan McLaren, who had just turned eighteen, made his European debut that night.

It was a different story in the return as the men from Munich took the game to us and I for one found it hard to find my feet, although, in my defence, I was played out of position wide on the right. While we were beaten 2–0 in the Olympic Stadium, going out 2–1 on aggregate, the trip provided some amusing moments. None-more-so than at the official reception the night before the match, which was attended by the Lord Provost of Edinburgh,

Eleanor McLaughlin, as well as various German dignitaries to celebrate not only the forthcoming game but also the fact that Munich is twinned with Edinburgh. Jimmy Caldwell, a friend of Hearts director Pilmar Smith, asked permission to borrow the Provost's chains and put them around the neck of Wallace Mercer. A stunt like that would embarrass most people but our effervescent chairman looked to the manner born in his temporary incarnation as Edinburgh's first citizen.

* * *

All good things eventually come to an end and I was extremely disappointed the day the Gaffer, my mentor, got the sack at the start of September 1990. He had been in charge for 418 games, winning 197. Unfortunately, he failed to win any of the opening three league matches that season and that was enough for Wallace Mercer to show him the door after more than ten years' service as player and manager. Robbo and I both spoke out in the press the following morning about how terrible it was to lose a man who had almost single-handedly lifted the club from near oblivion.

In the wake of the sacking, the chairman called a team meeting in the old executive club at Tynecastle, with everyone under orders to attend. As I was entering the room I got a wink from Les Porteous, who told me to stay calm. In front of everyone Mercer had a right go at me, and to a lesser extent at Robbo, and made it clear that the decision had nothing to do with us and that it was not our place to go to the papers. The board had taken a decision and he argued strongly that we should not have got involved. We were standing at the back of the room and afterwards he called us both into the boardroom and explained why he had let the Gaffer go. He wanted everyone to realise that no-one was going to undermine the decision, even although we had our own feelings for Alex. He was letting us know he was the boss and I can appreciate where he was coming from, but I'm still not sure if there was any need publicly to embarrass Robbo and me.

Despite this spat it did not affect my relationship with Mercer. He was never one to bear a grudge, which shows the mark of the man. When, twenty or so years later, in January 2006, I learned of his death I was genuinely saddened. He may not have been born a Jambo but be became as big a Hearts fan as anyone who was raised in Gorgie. Due to prior business commitments I was unable to attend the funeral but I did phone his son, Ian, and asked him to pass on my condolences to his mother and sister, Anne and Helen. They are a great family.

I'll never know if the decision to get rid of the Gaffer stemmed from a meeting between Wallace Mercer and Joe Jordan at the World Cup in Italy in 1990. Joe was in attendance as an ambassador and an interpreter while Wallace was there to support Scotland. One thing led to another and it just seemed a little too coincidental that Jordan was in place at Tynecastle before the managerial hot seat was allowed to get cold. However, it is not for me to question why.

I won't hear a bad word said about any of the men who helped shape my career in professional football. I had a great grounding at Hearts – first under Bobby Moncur and Tony Ford then from Alex MacDonald and Sandy Jardine. Moncur and Ford got us fit, but Alex (with help from Bert and George) got us fitter. Wallace Mercer, meanwhile, got Hearts beating again and is sadly missed by us all.

I worked with a lot of very good people over the years but the Gaffer is the only one I would describe as exceptional. Scottish football is desperate for people with his experience and I think it's a crying shame that his association with the beautiful game ended following his departure from Airdrie in 1999 and is now limited to a Saturday afternoon where he is a match-day host at Ibrox.

He gave so much to football. It is now time for him to get something back.

6

1985/86

'Too *numb* for tears'

The Gaffer briefly uttered something. I have no recollection what it was. I could picture in great detail the move that led to my goal against Clydebank the previous week but I have no idea what he said to us in the immediate aftermath of the defeat at Dens Park. Nothing else was said after that. There was nothing anybody could say. No words that would have lifted the mood. From that point on you could hear a pin drop. In that dressing room I sat and showed very little emotion. I was numb; too numb for tears.

Seven days on, preparing for the Scottish Cup final against Aberdeen, and the pain of Dens Park was still tangible. Twenty-two years on and the pain of Dens Park is still tangible. In physical terms we were prepared to end the season on a high at Hampden and to bring silverware back to Tynecastle. Our psychological state was a different story. We were like zombies. Ghosts from the previous week loomed large throughout the build-up. The defeat at Dens Park was a fatal blow not just to our chances of winning the league championship but also to our hopes of lifting the Scottish Cup for the first time since 1956. Sitting in the dressing room at Hampden after the match I experienced a horrible case of déjà vu. Once again I showed very little emotion. Once again I was numb; too numb for tears.

They say time is a healer. Not in this case. What happened at either end of those seven days still hurts. That summer in 1986, as a naïve twenty-two-year-old, I thought that challenging for league titles and being in Scottish Cup finals would be a regular occurrence. I could not have been more wrong. I did not realise it at the time, but that was the most momentous season of my career, one that still haunts me to this day.

* * *

Hearts supporters had few grounds for optimism during the summer of 1985. We had lost eight of our last ten games the previous season, resulting in a seventh-place finish, and only two new signings arrived during the close season. £50,000 was spent to acquire winger John Colquhoun from Celtic while Ayrshire lad Iain Jardine joined us on a free transfer from that little-known Junior team near Cumnock by the name of Anorthosis Famagusta!

Alex MacDonald was and always will be a winner. The poor results at the end of 1984/85 hurt him. He was determined that, as manager of Hearts, he would never again suffer that kind of embarrassment. To that end the Gaffer arranged a five-game, two-week, pre-season trip to Germany in July 1985, funded by Wallace Mercer. We had toured the Highlands the previous summer but were only away from our homes for nine days. This time Alex wanted to take us abroad. He thought it would help with team bonding, give the two new lads a chance to integrate as well as boosting morale for the new campaign.

Pre-season training gets harder as you get older. As an eager 21-year-old I found the prospect of running up and down the sand dunes at Gullane far easier to stomach than a veteran footballer approaching the end of his career. It was the usual start for us after returning from our summer break. We worked on strength and conditioning at Heriot Watt University (just across the road from the current Hearts Academy) under the watchful eyes of Bert Logan and George McNeill. That was followed by cross-country running in the city centre and the collective breathing-out of our backsides as each player attempted to reach the summit of Arthur's Seat before anyone else. Although tough, that climb was nothing compared to the next stage in our training programme: the dunes at Gullane beach, which came close to flouting the Geneva Convention's rules on torture! Those same sand dunes were a particular favourite of Jock Wallace when he was at Rangers, but what is not as widely known is that our predecessors in maroon jerseys at the end of the 1960s were also subjected to the same routine when Jock was a coach at Tynecastle. With his Rangers background, and his respect for his former boss, the Gaffer was of the opinion that if Gullane was good enough for Jock Wallace then it was good enough for him. Needless-to-say the two weeks in Germany were eagerly awaited as we pounded our way up and down the dunes; anything would have been better than the cruel and unusual punishment we endured in East Lothian.

With Whitley Bay probably the furthest I'd travelled for a pre-season fixture, the trip to the Rheinland-Pfalz region of West Germany was a new experience for me and most of the other boys. All credit to Alex and Sandy because the facilities at our complex were fantastic and more than made up for the remoteness of the location. We were out in the wilds but that's what the Gaffer wanted; this was a time to focus on the season ahead and he was determined that we were going to make the most of the adventure. There is always a danger of boredom when professional footballers go away for a prolonged period, but that was simply not possible with five games in fourteen days in addition to training most mornings and afternoons. The regional opposition – FSV Saarwellingen, SV Wiesbaden, Spvgg Ingelheim, Eintracht Bad Kreuznach and SC Birkenfeld – were not exactly world-beaters, but nonetheless our confidence was boosted by four victories and a draw.

Rest and relaxation are vitally important for the wellbeing of professional athletes and I didn't realise at the time just how much a tour like that can take out of you. I was young and naïve and pushed my body to the limit without thinking too much about the consequences. Thankfully, some fun was also on the curriculum, including social evenings and visits to a go-kart centre. The trip was a great success; we were already a close-knit squad but being together for this length of time further strengthened team spirit.

It was often the case on pre-season tours that the last night was reserved for frivolity, giving the jokers in the pack the chance to take centre-stage one last time before everyone headed home. That was our plan for the final evening in Germany, but, unfortunately, our plans were sabotaged from the most unlikely source. The Gaffer was a stickler for good behaviour when we were in his company. So when news reached the squad that every player had to attend a meeting with the management team in one of the hotel's conference rooms we feared the worst. We were convinced our last night was about to be ruined due to the misdemeanours of an individual or a small group, but every one of the players was adamant they had done nothing wrong. Confusion reigned as we filed into the conference room in regimental fashion, where, to our astonishment, we were met by the sight of Alex and Sandy standing beside a dozen bottles of wine. The local agent, who had organised the tour on the club's behalf, had got the alcohol at a heavily discounted price and the Gaffer decided that booze for all would be the best accompaniment for the speech he had planned.

When we were seated with a full glass in hand he informed us there was only one rule that evening: no-one was allowed to leave the room at any time. He had gathered us together to tell us what he wanted from the team in the season ahead and what he expected from each and every individual. That was the first time I had witnessed him opening up and putting his cards on the table and he didn't miss with the verbal bullets. We knew exactly where we stood with him, although everything was said in a light-hearted manner.

Kenny Black was one of the first to be targeted. Now Kenny is a great lad, and one of the first people I'd invite to dinner, but Alex had a right go at him for wanting to be everyone's buddy. He was more than happy with Kenny being friendly with his teammates, but didn't want him to be friends with the opposition as well – especially during games! The Gaffer had a go at many other players and there were few in the squad who escaped. I came under fire when I got up to go to the toilet at the back of the room. Bad mistake! Every player targeted was 'punished' with more wine and it even got to the stage that when supplies ran low members of the backroom staff were dispatched to find the bottles we had planned to take home.

Even the prospect of a very early flight back to Edinburgh the following morning failed to dampen either our spirits or enthusiasm. It was a great way to end a brilliant trip and I doubt there would have been another set of players anywhere in Scotland at the time that was so close-knit. The fact the players bonded so well was even more remarkable because of the age range in the squad: Clark, Kidd, MacDonald and Sandy Jardine in the older group while Robbo, Levein, Black, Colquhoun and I were just kids. But everyone got on so well and the more mature players looked after the inexperienced ones. We had days out during the season – going out as a team after a victory on a Saturday or meeting up on a Sunday – but the real bonding took place on that tour of Germany.

Alex and Sandy had assembled a group of lads whom, they believed, could not only play but also gel on and off the park. There were those who could drink, those who couldn't and also those who didn't want to, while some socialised and some chose not to. The Gaffer, though, never put pressure on players who decided not to take part in social events. He believed what happened on the park was the most important thing and felt that was aided by happy players off the park. The management duo had a way with them that earned the respect of players, and our respect for them increased following that last night in Germany. There is no doubt in my mind: that trip set the standard for what we went on to achieve during the season. One or two alcoholic beverages may have been consumed on that final evening if we had been left to our own devices, but it was much more fun with the Gaffer around. I wonder where Hearts would be today if we had someone like him in charge.

* * *

Coming into a changing room as a new signing is daunting for most players although I'd like to think that wasn't the case for John Colquhoun, because we tried hard to make him feel welcome. He integrated well with the squad in Germany and was selected to make his debut against his old club, Celtic, at Tynecastle in our opening match of the season. The Parkhead side had finished second in the Premier League the previous year and were one of the favourites to win their first championship since 1982. However, an upset looked on the cards when JC gave us a first-half lead. It was the perfect start for him in a Hearts jersey until Paul McStay equalised with a deflected shot right at the end of the match to earn Celtic a draw and deny us an opening-day victory. It was a result that would prove very costly come the end of the season.

Given the way the team had finished the previous season, with eight defeats in the last ten games, it can be argued that a point against one of the Old Firm was a good result, even if it felt like a defeat when they equalised so late on. That was hard to take, but not nearly as demoralising as what happened the following week. A team like St Mirren should never to able to beat Hearts 6–2, but they did; we were abysmal at Love Street that day, even though we took the lead. On a personal front my performances started to dip and, after playing poorly in the midweek League Cup win at Montrose, I was dropped for the league match at Ibrox as the Gaffer tried to freshen things up. It didn't work. We were beaten 3–1 by Rangers and to compound our misery Sandy Clark and Walter Kidd were both sent off. Alex decided to make more changes for the visit of Stirling Albion in the Skol Cup and I thought there was a chance of a recall, but once again I was left out of the squad.

My form in pre-season had been reasonable but I didn't play well when the competitive action got under way and had no complaints when I started only one of the following six matches, even though I worked as hard as I could in training. I found it especially difficult when I was left out of the starting line-up for the first Edinburgh derby of the season, against Hibernian at Tynecastle at the end of August. I had to be content with a place on the bench although I did come on for Andy Watson in a 2–1 win. The biggest slap in the face, however, came at Kilbowie Park – home of Clydebank – at the end of September 1985. With only two substitutes allowed back then the Gaffer selected himself and me for bench duty, although that is where I remained for the entire match as he chose himself instead of me to replace Kenny Black. It didn't make much difference as we lost the match by a single goal and as a result were languishing in the bottom half of the table following five defeats in eight games. For that to happen to someone who thought he was the dog's bollocks was hard to take, but it also proved to be another huge kick up the arse. Of course, I took the snub personally, which was another mistake. Alex explained that he selected himself ahead of me because that was to be his last action in a maroon jersey. Our player-manager was losing the 'player' part of his title to concentrate on his job as boss and help us climb the table. He felt he had his general on the pitch in the shape of Sandy Jardine and was happy to direct proceedings from afar. Results were to vindicate that decision.

Whether it's a coincidence or not, I don't know, but the game following the Gaffer's decision to hang up his boots was also the first in an amazing unbeaten run. I was recalled to the side for the visit of Dundee at the start of October and never missed another game that season. Our run of form leading up to that match was indifferent to say the least and it looked a familiar tale when Derek McWilliams gave the Dark Blues an early lead at Tynecastle. However, Iain Jardine's goal in the second half earned us a draw and proved to be the turning point in a remarkable campaign.

* * *

The trip to face Celtic at Parkhead on 12 October 1985 was significant on two counts. Our 1–0 victory put an end to their unbeaten record and also proved to us that, on our day, we could compete against the best teams in the league. It was also the first time that season the Gaffer named an unchanged line-up and I believe the significance of that decision cannot be underestimated. The Old Firm don't lose many games at home and any opposition team has to be at its best to come away with a victory. We nullified their threat and showed the reliability our manager was looking for. Everyone played their part and Robbo's goal was the reward for an excellent performance.

We then put together a run of results that would be considered impressive in anyone's book. Aberdeen had beaten us twice in quick succession at the start of September – in the league and in the Skol Cup quarter-final – yet we turned that form on its head only seven weeks later when Craig Levein's early goal was the difference between the two teams in our 1–0 win at Tynecastle. That Dons team – managed by Alex Ferguson – were the reigning champions and had several players who had won the European Cup Winners Cup two years previously, so it was great for our confidence. Since losing twice at Pittodrie in the space of four days we had gradually found some form, beating Celtic away and St Mirren at home in the fortnight prior to winning that game against Aberdeen at Tynecastle. The one-all draw against Dundee United at Tannadice the following week was also a decent result, considering their team contained the likes of Sturrock and Hegarty, although it was nearly maximum points for us until Richard Gough grabbed an equaliser in the final minute.

The turnaround in our fortunes also vindicated Wallace Mercer's decision not to sack the management team. He realised that Alex MacDonald and

Sandy Jardine had revived the club in just a few seasons and was happy to give them more time. To remain unbeaten in the space of a month against the best four teams in the country – Celtic, Aberdeen, Dundee United and Rangers – was a real shot in the arm. That renewed sense of purpose was all too evident when we hammered Clydebank 4–1 at Tynecastle in November just two months after losing to them at Kilbowie, taking our goal tally to ten in three games.

It wasn't all plain sailing and there were times when, although remaining unbeaten, we didn't play well. But we had the ideal man for these tricky moments. We never knew what to expect at training with Alex MacDonald and that kept us both mentally and physically attuned. His use of psychology was excellent. Some Monday mornings we trooped in for training expecting to be hammered for a below-par performance on the Saturday but he would take us for a swim and sauna at the Commonwealth pool to help us relax. On the other hand we learned not to expect an easy time at training if we had won, because more often that not he would lead us around several laps of Tynecastle on the Monday before running us into the ground on Tuesday; the football was nowhere to be seen until later in the week. He knew there was a strong possibility that a lot of us would have been out on the Saturday evening or Sunday afternoon celebrating victory – he didn't have a problem with that – but was just making sure the 'enjoyment' was sweated out of our system. His philosophy was simple: he demanded maximum effort during the week and was convinced that meant we would be spot on for match days. He wasn't often wrong.

Our 3–0 victory against Rangers at Tynecastle in November was an excellent result but we knew it would be a different story when we went through to Ibrox at the end of December, a busy period for all clubs. The victory against St Mirren the previous weekend, coupled with Aberdeen's defeat at Tannadice, ensured we leapfrogged the Dons at the summit and travelled to Glasgow as league leaders. That position, though, was in jeopardy when we learned there was a chance the match at Ibrox would not go ahead. The pitch was flat but it was also rock-hard and the game only got the go-ahead an hour before kick-off. In normal circumstances players use the warm-up to do fitness routines and ball-work, but a lot of us spent the time trying out different kinds of footwear for the slippery surface. One player who actually benefited from the conditions, being smaller and more mobile than most of his teammates, was John Colquhoun. He was magnificent, scoring both our goals and tormenting a Rangers defence that included Dave McPherson who, and I'm sure he won't mind me saying this, looked rather uncomfortable as his gigantic frame chased little John around on an awkward, icy surface. Once again in Glasgow there was not a failure in our line-up and the 2–0 win set us up perfectly for the New Year derby against Hibernian at Tynecastle.

We'd already taken three points out of a possible four from our Edinburgh rivals when they made the short trip across the city on Ne'er Day, hoping to become the first team since Clydebank at the end of September to inflict defeat on a Hearts side that was riding high at the top of the league. Things were going well, with goals from Iain Jardine and Robbo giving us a two-goal cushion, when Colin Harris forgot to read the script and pulled one back. If that match had been played at the start of the season I'm convinced there would have been a much greater chance of them getting back on level terms, but we now had such a belief that it was no surprise to me when we went straight back up to the other end of the park and Sandy Clark scored our third to wrap up the points.

It was no coincidence that our run of form after the early-October victory at Parkhead – nine wins and four draws – coincided with just one change to the starting line-up (Kenny Black for Brian Whittaker against Motherwell at Tynecastle in November). The Gaffer chopped and changed at the start of the season because some of us did not show the consistency he was hoping for, but that ceased when he found his first-choice team and the results duly followed. As our unbeaten run continued nobody wanted to lose their place in the side, as they knew it was highly unlikely they would get back in.

Another reason players were desperate to stay in the team was the bonus structure. Our basic salaries were reasonable but they were supplemented by decent appearance money and excellent win bonuses and there is no doubt in my mind that guys carried on playing even if they had niggling injuries. Players even asked if those bumps and bruises could be strapped up to enable them to train, because, if you hadn't taken part in a session by Thursday, it was unlikely you'd be selected to start on the Saturday. The basic wage for a lot of players in the Eighties was not much more than the salary earned by the average man in the street and the additional money was hugely important to guys who wanted a good lifestyle in addition to paying their mortgages. We were on an accumulator bonus at that time – calculated after every four games – so if you were able to play in a quartet of wins it really was happy days. Even getting six or seven points from the four games (remember it was two points for a win) ensured a bumper pay packet at the end of the month. I'm sure Wallace Mercer didn't mind the additional expense because our positive results saw the attendances increase at Tynecastle: more than 19,000 were at the game against Dundee United in January when I was on target in a one-all draw (compared with 7,600 for the corresponding fixture in September), so the extra revenue from higher gate money more than helped cover bonus costs.

* * *

By the turn of the year we had gathered a lot of momentum. We were unbeaten since the end of September yet no one really had the opportunity to stop and consider the implications of our excellent run. That changed, however, following a third-round victory in the Scottish Cup against Rangers at Tynecastle at the end of January 1986, two days after my twenty-second birthday. I started to feel something special was happening. The cup-tie was a topsy-turvy affair that ended 3–2 in our favour; I even managed to get on the score sheet with a scrappy goal at the back post, but they all count. All that mattered was getting through to the next round and knocking out one of the favourites for the competition. Speaking of knockouts, a sickening clash of heads between Sandy Clark and Craig Paterson meant an abrupt end to their respective afternoons and it's ironic that Sandy's replacement, Colin McAdam, scored one of the goals that secured our place in the fourth-round draw. A good day all round, except for Sandy and Craig of course, and the result really kicked us on for the remainder of the season.

On doctor's orders concussion renders most players unavailable for a couple of weeks, but Sandy Clark was not most players. He was the kind of guy you wanted on your side when the going got tough and he simply brushed aside the damage to his skull and declared himself fit for the match the following week, which was our second trip of the season to Kilbowie to face Clydebank. This time I was pleased to be selected for the starting eleven but things didn't go according to plan and we found ourselves a goal down with time running out. Sandy's decision to play may not have pleased the club doctor, but it certainly pleased us when he equalised with only four minutes left to preserve our unbeaten record. Before the match we were desperate for the win, but with the clock ticking down we were happy to take the point and the damage to our title challenge was not as bad as we feared with nearest challengers Dundee United also failing to win as they were held by St Mirren at Love Street. Rangers and Aberdeen also drew, at Ibrox, so Celtic were the only beneficiaries of the weekend courtesy of their win at Dundee, which moved them level on points with Dundee United. Nevertheless we still had a four-point lead at the top with only ten games remaining.

I was never really much of a goal-scoring midfielder – averaging about one every ten games during my career – although I did manage to score some vital goals during the 85/86 campaign and it was around the turn of the year that I hit a purple patch. Four goals in seven games is not bad by anyone's standards and it certainly amazed me when I found the net against Dundee United, Rangers and Dundee in the league and at Hamilton in the fourth round of the Scottish Cup. The cup-tie at Douglas Park was due to take place the week after the league match against Dundee at Tynecastle, but bad weather meant it was delayed by more than a fortnight. In the interim we faced a vital match against Celtic at Parkhead, which, if we had lost, would have meant the gap between us narrowing to just three points. It would also have seen Aberdeen – who won at Hibs – move to within a point of us at the top of the table. Things weren't going our way when Maurice Johnston gave Celtic the lead after half an hour, but, once again, we were indebted to Robbo who scored just before the break to earn a vital point. Hearts had been top of the Premier League since the victory against St Mirren in mid-December but I never felt we received the credit we deserved from the media. That seemed to change, however, with those two results against the Old Firm; eliminating Rangers from the Scottish Cup and more than holding our own at Parkhead. All of a sudden we were being taken seriously and anyone with a betting slip from pre-season with odds of 200/1 for Hearts to win the title was taking a much greater interest in our campaign!

Because of the inclement weather it seemed that our Scottish Cup fourth-round tie against Hamilton at Douglas Park would never go ahead – the pitch had been declared unplayable on four occasions – and the delays were very frustrating. The tie was originally scheduled for Saturday, 15 February but was called off well in advance due to frost. The two teams were due to try again in the midweek following our match against Celtic, but once again no luck with that date. All the while the impending quarter-final tie against St Mirren for the winners was looming fast. The SFA informed us that we must try again the following Monday – 3 March – and we should keep trying to fulfil the fixture every day that week if the big freeze persisted. To everyone's relief the game eventually went ahead on the Monday and the atmosphere inside Douglas Park was electric. Referee Brian McGinlay even had to delay the kick-off by fifteen minutes to let the huge crowd in. Fortunately, we recovered from losing a goal to John Brogan after just fifteen seconds and I grabbed the winner after Robbo had equalised. That is only part of the story and most of the credit should have gone to Henry Smith, who produced two magnificent saves to deny John McNaught and John Brogan near the end. It was a relief because Hamilton were riding high at the top of division one at that time and the fixture was definitely in the banana-skin category.

We did not have to wait long to play our quarter-final against St Mirren – six days to be exact – although the Gaffer was concerned that the lack of time might affect our preparation. We were thankful, however, that we had an extra day to prepare as the game was put back twenty-four hours to avoid clashing with the Hibs–Celtic tie at Easter Road. We ran out comfortable 4–1 winners in front of a decent crowd of more than 20,000. For one reason or another at that time, games against St Mirren ended up being very physical and more often than not their goalkeeper, Campbell Money, was the subject of 'treatment' from Sandy Clark. Challenges on keepers were part and parcel of the game and a good old-fashioned dunt was deemed acceptable by referees, which played right into Sandy's hands; it is a man's game after all. I'm not suggesting Campbell Money was soft, but let's just say I don't think he relished games against Hearts when the bold Sandy was in our starting eleven and the opening challenge on him went unpunished. It was no surprise, therefore, when Money went off with concussion after just three minutes of the quarter-final following a clash with Mr Clark. Our path to the last four was relatively straightforward after that because they had to play defender Neil Cooper between the sticks due to the absence of a recognised goalkeeper among their substitutes.

St Mirren actually played a pivotal role in many ways that season: there was the 6–2 defeat they inflicted upon us in August; our Scottish Cup quarter-final win; and then their result against Celtic at Love Street in the final league match of the season. Of course the Cup victory was the most pleasing and it was a great achievement for Hearts to reach a Scottish Cup semi-final for the first time in nine seasons. More importantly it was a tangible reward for our supporters. Attendances at Tynecastle nearly doubled over the course of the season as fans realised that something special was happening, so it was fitting we were able to give them something to shout about as well as a trip to Hampden. Less than six months before we had been knocked out the Skol Cup at Pittodrie, we were losing to teams like Motherwell and Clydebank and a relegation struggle was on the cards. The turnaround in our fortunes had been dramatic.

With two Scottish Cup ties in quick succession there was a danger that we would lose our momentum in the league and our position at the top of the table. Thankfully, that was not the case and our excellent form continued with a 2–0 victory against Motherwell at Tynecastle. It was a result that saw us extend our lead at the summit to three points, with title challengers Celtic and Dundee United drawing at Parkhead.

With things going well, the Gaffer quite rightly kept our feet on the ground. That wasn't too difficult, though, in mid-March when a glance at some of our forthcoming fixtures – Hibernian, Rangers, Dundee United (league and Scottish Cup) and Aberdeen – was more than enough to focus our minds. One of our regular victories at Easter Road – by two goals to one with Robbo netting his customary goal, this time from the penalty spot – equalled the Premier League record of twenty-two matches without defeat and kept us three points clear at the top. That was soon extended to five when we beat St Mirren 3–0 at Tynecastle the following midweek. There were now just five league games left and the victory against the Saints put us firmly in the driving seat for our first title since 1959/60: we had a five-point lead over Dundee United, seven points over Aberdeen while Celtic trailed us by nine, although they did have three games in hand.

It was as you were at the top of the table following our 3–1 victory against Rangers at Tynecastle in the final game in March; Robbo scored twice, the eighth consecutive game in which he had found the net. Celtic, Dundee United and Aberdeen also won that day, but it was another match played and another step closer to winning the championship.

Our league challenge took a break at the beginning of April as attention turned to the Scottish Cup semi-final against Dundee United at Hampden. The Gaffer decided to take us to the Hospitality Inn in Irvine two days before the match to give us time to prepare in relative privacy and once again he came up trumps with a fresh idea. Having had plenty of time to psyche ourselves up for the challenge ahead everyone was raring to go by kick-off. I was, if anything, too hyped-up and it was no surprise when I picked up the game's first caution for a foul on Ian Redford after only ten minutes. I had never played in a national cup final before and was a little too eager to impress. I was thankful that I was able to control both my nerves and my aggression, but it was difficult to control my emotions when John Colquhoun's right-foot volley hit the back of the net. In the second half the expected onslaught from United never materialised and we had secured a place in the Scottish Cup final for the first time in ten years. In normal circumstances this would be sufficient reason for a party, but we knew there was still plenty of work to do and so the celebrations were put on hold.

We faced Dundee United in our next match too, this time in the league. We travelled north to Tannadice realising that a backlash was a real possibility after the result at Hampden. The match was billed as a title decider by many and the 7,000 tickets for the Hearts end were snapped up in no time at all. Victory for them would have narrowed the gap with us to just one point, but we managed to increase our lead at the top to five points thanks to one of our best performances of the season. John Robertson scored one of his greatest-ever goals – a stunning half-volley from thirty yards – to give us a first-half lead, John Colquhoun added number two in the second half (with his head!) before Robbo completed the rout shortly after the hour mark to send the visiting supporters into raptures. I even had the luxury of enjoying the end of the game from the dugout after the Gaffer replaced me with Colin McAdam, who was told to sit in front of the defence and not let anything past. When Kenny Hope blew the full-time whistle I sprinted onto the pitch to celebrate with my teammates. In those days of two points for a win we had a five-point lead with only three league matches remaining – two of which were at Tynecastle – and I wouldn't have swapped our position for anything.

With the title race reaching a climax and three clubs still in with a chance, our home fixture against Aberdeen was selected for live television coverage and was put back twenty-four hours to the Sunday. This gave Celtic the chance to narrow the gap at the top to three points when they faced Hibs at Parkhead on the Saturday, which they duly took thanks to goals in the last ten minutes from Owen Archdeacon and Brian McClair. But although the men from Parkhead still had a game in hand Hearts remained odds-on to clinch the title and I was convinced it was all over bar the shouting.

Aberdeen had been eliminated from the title race a few days before coming to Tynecastle when they were beaten 1–0 at home by Dundee United, but they travelled south intent on putting down a marker ahead of the Scottish Cup final. We started nervously and were a shadow of our normal selves. To this day I struggle to fathom why nerves got the better of us for large parts of the match but I do know that I didn't have my best game that afternoon and had no complaints after being replaced by Ian Jardine just after the hour mark. It was tough viewing for the last thirty minutes and my head was in my hands when referee Bob Valentine pointed to the spot after my replacement was adjudged to have handled the ball. Peter Weir converted the penalty and suddenly our twenty-five-match unbeaten run in the league was under threat. We knew going into the game that, no matter the result, we would still have our destiny in our own hands but this was a blow we could have done without. However, to our great relief John Colquhoun popped up with the equaliser with five minutes to go and both our unbeaten record and our title challenge were preserved. It wasn't good for my health though.

Two games to go – plus the cup final – and we were on course for a glorious double. A total of 20,198 fans made their way to Tynecastle for the penultimate league fixture against Clydebank. I'm sure there were less than 198 fans supporting the visitors that day, so that meant more than 20,000 Hearts fans were in place. Every single one of them was expecting an avalanche of goals, which would have ensured that even a last-day collapse at Dens Park would be rendered immaterial unless, of course, Celtic were able to conjure up a mathematical miracle and score a barrow load of goals in their last two games. With the Premier League expanding to twelve teams from the start of the following season it meant that relegation was scrapped, allowing Clydebank to come to Tynecastle and play with a freedom not normally available to those at the foot of the table. That was an option for them, but they decided to play with caution and defended very deep, making it hard to get in behind their defence. It soon became clear that a lot of patience would be required and it took until the thirty-fourth minute for us to break the deadlock. Sandy Clark was the only Hearts player who had been able to test Jim Gallacher in the Bankies' goal, so it came as a great relief when I managed to open the scoring after picking the ball up just over the halfway line, following good work out of defence by Sandy Jardine and George Cowie. It remains one of my favourite goals, but, sadly, we were unable to add to our tally, much to the frustration of the players and thousands of very nervous fans. Nevertheless, when the dust had settled, we still had a two-point advantage over Celtic and I was convinced I had scored the goal that would see us crowned champions.

There is no doubt we were naive, both as individuals and as a team, as we approached the end of the season. Two-thirds of the group that day had no experience of being so close to major honours. All of a sudden this squad of players put together on a shoestring budget by Alex MacDonald and Sandy Jardine were just two matches from clinching both the league title and the Scottish Cup. Everyone at Tynecastle knew what we were trying to achieve but it's a bit like becoming a parent; no one can prepare you for what lies ahead. The most important thing was getting maximum points in the penultimate match and we had done that. More goals would have been nice but we knew our destiny would be in our own hands when we travelled up the A90 to Dens Park the following Saturday. Of course if Celtic failed to win their game in hand – at Motherwell in midweek – that journey would turn into a party, but as far as we were concerned Hearts had completed the eighteen league fixtures at Tynecastle without losing and were just ninety minutes away from making history.

* * *

I was sitting in my flat in Harrison Road in Edinburgh having decided to follow events at Fir Park on Ceefax and I had mixed emotions. Thirty minutes had been played and it remained goalless between Motherwell and Celtic; part of me was hoping it would stay that way and Hearts would be league champions for the first time since 1960, but, being young and naïve, I wasn't too concerned about Celtic scoring because I wanted us to win the title off our own bat. Soon after, Brian McClair scored the first of his brace as Celtic beat Motherwell 2–0. Now it was all down to what happened at Dundee that weekend. Events at Love Street, where St Mirren would face our sole challengers, did not matter as long as we avoided defeat at Dens. It was that simple. In fact even if we lost at Dens by a single goal Celtic would still have needed to win by at least a margin of three.

The Gaffer did his best to ensure a normal build-up to the biggest match of our lives; he never once went over the top and, as always, played it perfectly. There were a few minor injuries but nothing too serious. A few of the guys also complained about feeling under the weather – Kenny Black, Neil Berry, Brian Whittaker and John Colquhoun – but it didn't stop them playing a full part in training. George Cowie was the only one who seemed to be badly affected by the bug and he failed to recover in time.

A notice was pinned on the dressing-room wall; the bus to Dundee was leaving Tynecastle at 10.15 a.m. and would pick up players who lived outside of Edinburgh at the Forth Bridge half an hour later. I prepared for the big match as normal and tried not to let nerves get the better of me. I slept well the night before and was raring to go when I left my flat early on Saturday morning. Everything went according to plan; I arrived at Tynecastle fifteen minutes before the scheduled departure time and witnessed a mixture of nervous excitement and enthusiasm among the lads. Nothing untoward or unusual as the bus departed bang on time but that wasn't the case when we reached the bridge. Craig Levein was nowhere to be seen; he had been affected by the bug and spent the rest of the day after Friday training in bed. It was only the third league match of the season that Craig had missed, but we were a close-knit squad and were confident that whoever replaced him could do a job.

Alex and Sandy did not usually reveal their team until a couple of hours before kick-off, just as well on this occasion as at least one change was required following Craig's withdrawal. George Cowie played the previous week against Clydebank but the bug meant he missed out and was replaced by Walter Kidd. Kenny Black, although fit enough to travel, was not well enough to last the full ninety minutes so was named among the substitutes with Ian Jardine – despite suffering from a bad back – taking his place. Roddy MacDonald was chosen to replace Craig, meaning the Gaffer had to make three changes for that one match, where previously it had taken him eight games to do so. There may have been one or two enforced alterations from the normal starting line-up – Smith, Kidd, Whittaker, S. Jardine, Berry, Levein, Colquhoun, Black, Clark, Mackay, Robertson – but we had more than enough quality to get the job done.

The first half at Dens Park was a scrappy affair with very few clear-cut chances, although Roddy MacDonald came close with a header from one of my corners. There was also a strong shout for a penalty as Sandy Clark appeared to be fouled in the box but referee Bill Crombie – a Hearts supporter and a late replacement – deemed the infringement unworthy of a spot kick. It remains a contentious call but at the time I didn't think it was a penalty, and, having seen a replay of the incident for the first time in a BBC documentary, I still believe that. It took me twenty years to pluck up the courage to watch the footage again – when I took part in the *That Was the Team That Was* documentary on Scottish football – but I'm glad I did because it helped with the healing process.

News reached us in the dressing room at half-time that Celtic were leading 4–0 at Love Street but that was of no concern to me because I knew that score line was immaterial if we kept a clean sheet. The Gaffer was forced into making a change at the break when Kenny Black replaced Brian Whittaker, who was struggling with the effects of the bug, but KB had filled in at left back on a number of occasions during the season so it didn't disrupt our game plan. John Colquhoun engineered an opportunity shortly after the restart but elected to go himself and missed the target; with hindsight, he may have been better laying the ball off to Robbo, who was in a better position. Dundee certainly had a fair bit of pressure and created a couple of reasonable chances, but we held firm and never looked like losing a goal. Then disaster struck: with seven minutes remaining, their substitute, Albert Kidd, scored two quick goals without reply and our world caved in.

The league title is won over the course of a season and it's not down to a referee failing to point to the spot or to missed chances at Dens Park on the final day. For whatever reason our concentration went out of the window and it was too late in the game to do anything about it. Was it pressure? Was it because so many of us had not been in that pressure-pot situation before? Was it a lack of bottle? I'll never know. It should be borne in mind that Dundee were still pushing for a European spot while St Mirren had nothing to play for and this may have taken the edge off their game. Celtic kept on our coattails throughout the season so all credit to them. When there was a sign of frailty in our ranks they took advantage with that result in Paisley. However, when I heard that some of the St Mirren players who were on the receiving end of the 5–0 defeat were out celebrating with the Celtic players it certainly left a bad taste in my mouth, although maybe they were just letting their hair down at the end of a hard season. I have studied the make up of the St Mirren team that day and there is no doubt that some of them had feelings for Celtic. Did that play a part? We will probably never know. In the end it was down to us and if we had taken care of our own performance then it would have been us celebrating, not them.

Dundee	2–0	Hearts
(A. Kidd, 2)		

Dundee: Geddes, Shannon, McKinlay (A. Kidd), Glennie, Smith (McCormack), Duffy, Mennie, Brown, Harvey, Connor, Hendry

Hearts: Smith, Kidd, Whittaker (Black), S. Jardine, Berry, MacDonald, Colquhoun, I. Jardine, (W. McKay), Clark, G. Mackay, Robertson

Referee: Bill Crombie (Edinburgh)

Booking: MacDonald

People still talk about that dramatic end to the season and they will for years to come. What happened on that fateful day is not something that I often reminisce about but I have no regrets about being part of it. Of course it was a huge disappointment for everyone connected with Hearts, and it would have been wonderful to have successfully negotiated the final hurdle. But I remember what it was like as a supporter in the late Seventies and subsequently as a young player in the early Eighties: having to win at Arbroath to get promotion then win at Dumbarton to get back into the Premier League, events that occurred just a few years before Dens. The club made huge strides in a very short space of time and that must not be forgotten. Would I go through it all again? Without question, because anything is better than being part of a yo-yo club with an uncertain future.

I really believed we were going to win the league the day Robbo scored that stunning half volley at Tannadice but it wasn't to be. Hindsight is a wonderful thing but I can honestly say that I could not have done any more at Dens. Alex MacDonald had great experience as a player and the preparation was exactly right. Being forced to make three changes from the previous week was unfortunate but the players who started the match on Tayside were the best prepared and those most ready to take the game on.

Years later somebody suggested to me that Sandy Jardine had actually spoken to Dundee's Colin Hendry as they were walking off the pitch at Dens Park to ask if he would be interested in signing for us that summer and, if it's true, that sums up just how professional a management team Alex and Sandy were. They wanted to take Hearts to another level and believed the acquisition of Colin was another piece in the jigsaw. When you see how his playing career panned out it proves they also had a real eye for a player.

I am not one of those people who constantly thinks, 'If only'. Yes we dropped points at the start of the season but if we had won those matches would we have been as consistent throughout the rest of the campaign? We gave the Hearts supporters who had experienced such hard times during the Seventies something to cheer about and helped restore their pride. I would have loved to be remembered as Gary Mackay, the midfielder who was part of a championship-winning team. If I played my part in that not happening then I'm sorry, but I'd rather be positive and say I was part of a club – from Wallace Mercer down to the players – that got us so close to winning the title.

I used to think the result at Dens Park did not have an influence on our performance in the Scottish Cup final the following week but I now realise it was a fatal blow. If we had won the league then I am convinced the Cup would have taken care of itself. Without realising it, we were under huge pressure after losing to Dundee; Aberdeen took full advantage and thumped us. Sadly it was another day to forget and I felt so sorry for the 40,000 Hearts fans who suffered heartache for the second time in seven days. It was also too much for Walter Kidd, who was sent off for throwing the ball at an opponent in protest at me receiving a caution (which also meant I was suspended for the start of the following season). While I don't condone what Walter did, he was simply expressing his deeply pent-up emotions. We've now become accustomed to the roller-coaster ride that is being a Hearts supporter. It's part and parcel of following the Boys in Maroon and has happened in virtually every era. With that act, Walter probably summed up the frustration of everyone associated with the club over the years.

Scottish Cup final: 10 May 1986

Aberdeen   3–0   Hearts
(Hewitt 2, Stark)

Aberdeen: Leighton, McKimmie, McQueen, McMaster (Stark), McLeish, W. Miller, Hewitt (J. Miller), Cooper, McDougall, Bett, Weir

Hearts: Smith, Kidd, Whittaker, Jardine, Berry, Levein, Colquhoun, Black, Clark, Mackay, Robertson

Referee: Hugh Alexander (Irvine)

Bookings: Kidd, Berry, Mackay, Robertson

Sent off: Kidd

The open-top bus was waiting at the Norton House hotel to transport the victorious Hearts players through the city centre with the Scottish Cup. Unfortunately for us that ceased to become our destination at 4.45 p.m. on 10 May and instead we made our way to the Caledonian hotel, where we were met with a sensational reception from more than three thousand supporters. I don't think it's possible to put into words how disappointed they were, but every one of them wanted to show their appreciation for a group of players who had taken them on a never-to-be-forgotten journey and given them experiences that had not been seen for nearly thirty years. I found it difficult to control my emotions at the end of a quite incredible season; I tried to shake as many hands as possible but it quickly became too much for me and I retreated into the hotel. There may not have been tears in the dressing room at either Dens Park or Hampden but I made up for it once I was back indoors. I felt I had let those people down and felt uncomfortable receiving adulation at the end of a season in which I had won nothing. When the players eventually went back inside the fans stayed outside for more than an hour, cheering and clapping.

We may not have been the best team that season, but we certainly had the best supporters.

* * *

At the end of a season the squad normally breaks up for the holidays, but that year the club had arranged a seven-day trip to Trinidad and Tobago. Although most of the boys just wanted to go back to their families to reflect on what might have been, it wasn't a bad thing for us to stay together for a little while longer and to console each other. Of course a week in the Caribbean would have been perfect for celebrating if we had won either the league or the Scottish Cup, but there were worse places to drown our sorrows. Sandy Clark certainly enjoyed himself by grabbing a hat-trick in our opening match against Barbados while Walter Kidd stunned everyone, including himself, by living up to his Zico nickname and scoring two of our three goals in the second match against Trinidad and Tobago. Robbo had to be content with a solitary strike – against Tintoc in our final match – but it would be unfair in the extreme to complain about his comparative barren spell in the Caribbean, given his twenty goals during the season.

The summer had one last twist for Hearts fans. The fixture computer decided that our first match of the new season would be at Love Street. If that was someone's idea of a joke then I, for one, wasn't laughing. The only consolation was that our fans had more reason to be optimistic about the season ahead.

7

Scotland

'Luck of the Scots helps the Irish'

A journalist once asked me if I thought I was responsible for the renaissance in Irish football following a certain goal in Sofia on a dark and dreary evening in November 1987, when I became the first Hearts player to score for Scotland since Alex Young in 1960. As much as I would like to take the credit, the only people responsible for the emergence of the Republic of Ireland on the international stage were Jack Charlton and his talented group of Irish players from Barnsley, Liverpool, Glasgow, Wales, Preston, Huddersfield, London and Newquay as well, of course, as those from Dublin, Cork and Galway!

Mick McCarthy, John Aldridge, Ray Houghton, Kevin Sheedy, Mark Lawrenson, Tony Galvin, Chris Hughton and Chris Morris were all born elsewhere but they played a significant part in helping the Republic of Ireland accumulate eleven points from eight European Championship qualifying matches. Jack Charlton, the manager, and a former World Cup winner with England, had astutely used a new ruling allowing players to represent a country even if they were not born there, as long as parents or grandparents were. His gang of merry men had done their job; their qualifying campaign was over and their fate was no longer in their own hands.

Scotland's chances of qualifying had fizzled out after disappointing results early in the campaign (a draw and a defeat against Ireland, being hammered 4–1 in Belgium and a scoreless draw against Bulgaria at Hampden in our opening match). So we travelled to Eastern Europe in the knowledge, that, although we were only playing for pride, we could still do the Republic a huge favour by winning the match. My goal three minutes from time in our penultimate qualifying fixture in Sofia secured a 1–0 victory for Scotland and ensured the Republic would qualify for their first major finals at the expense of Bulgaria. That night I was a very unlikely hero in the pubs and clubs of old Dublin.

* * *

It doesn't matter where Hearts play on a Saturday, or even a Sunday, it is the duty of players and backroom staff to attend the annual remembrance service at Haymarket, where a war memorial to the club stands proudly to commemorate the seven players and many others who were killed in action during the First World War. After attending the ceremony on Sunday, 8 November 1987, the first-team squad accepted an invitation from the Ardmillan Hearts supporters club to grab a bite to eat and some refreshments before heading home. I was sitting having a sausage roll with my cup of tea and was halfway through the veritable feast when Craig Levein and I were called over by the chairman and the Gaffer. We were informed that we had been called up to the Scotland squad for the European Championship qualifier in Bulgaria three days later. There had been a few call-offs due to injuries (or possibly some players didn't fancy a trip to Eastern Europe for a fixture that meant very little) and we were asked to report for duty. We were also told that one of us would definitely be on the bench, although at that stage no decision had been taken on whether it would be cover for defence or midfield.

The possibility of representing my country was a great thrill for me. I had only been involved with the full-international squad once before and that was for a friendly against the Netherlands in Eindhoven in the midweek prior to the league decider at Dens Park in 1986. I was an unused substitute that evening but was able to sit on the bench and witness a scintillating performance from Aberdeen midfielder Robert Connor in the goalless draw. That gave me a taste of the big time and I was delighted to get another opportunity to sample the international experience. With a half-eaten sausage roll and a lukewarm cup of tea left on the table, I went back to Tynecastle to pick up my boots before heading home to pack my bags and then drove west to meet up with the rest of the Scotland players at the Gleddoch House hotel in Renfrewshire.

I've always thought it's harder for a player who's been called into an international squad to get game time ahead of someone who was named among the original group. However, on this occasion the midfield had been particularly hard hit by call-offs and I flew out to Bulgaria on the Monday afternoon in an optimistic frame of mind. After training in Sofia on the Tuesday,

Andy Roxburgh named the team and the substitutes and to my delight I was to start on the bench. Forty-eight hours before I had been munching a sausage roll and wondering how I would spend the rest of my Sunday afternoon.

Eastern Europe on a cold, November evening in 1987 is not a scene that would sell many postcards. The Vasil Levski stadium in Sofia was packed full with 60,000 passionate Bulgarians – most wearing dark clothing to match the surroundings – and just a handful of Tartan Army foot-soldiers. There was also a heavy military presence with thousands of uniforms visible throughout the stadium, although I later learned that they were off-duty and in attendance to support their team. The scenario was simple: a win or a draw would have been enough for Bulgaria to qualify for the 1988 European Championships in West Germany. An unlikely win for Scotland and the Republic of Ireland would qualify. Earning a point at home sounds easy, but I was in the same situation nineteen months previously with Hearts, and, like us at Dens Park, things did not go according to plan.

We had fought out a goalless draw with Bulgaria in the opening game of the campaign and the match in Sofia was following a similar pattern. We matched them and the game was even in the opening period but it was evident their nerves were getting the better of them and, as time went on, our confidence started to grow. Paul McStay was involved in most of our good play in the first half but an ankle injury shortly before the break curtailed his influence. At half-time our physio removed his boot and the swelling was immediate. Being the consummate professional Paul wanted to continue in spite of the pain but Andy Roxburgh decided not to risk any more damage, especially as Celtic were heavily involved in European competition and so he took the decision to give me my introduction to international football. It was kind of ironic, given that he had also been in charge of the team that won the European under-nineteen championships in 1982, as well as the squad that went to Mexico for the World Cup a year later.

The second half continued where the first half left off. Like the surroundings it was pretty dreich on the pitch as well. Needing just a point, the Bulgarian players did not know whether to attack or defend and I felt the longer the match remained goalless the more chance we had. The introduction of Gordon Durie for Graeme Sharp after seventy-two minutes was pretty much a straight swap, but it soon proved vital. Keeper Jim Leighton sent a long kick down the right-hand side and Gordon won the ball well in the air from their left back before stepping inside another defender and laying a perfect pass for me to run on to. Whether it was due to the condition of the pitch or my lack of a first touch (clue: it wasn't the first one!) I allowed the ball to run across my body beyond my favoured right foot and onto my left. For once my standing foot came up with the goods and from twenty yards

I smashed a shot into the top-right-hand corner of the net. And there were only three minutes remaining.

Despite housing sixty thousand spectators, the stadium had been relatively quiet throughout with a nervy atmosphere evident. That goal plunged it into an eerie silence, with the only noise coming from the small batch of loyal Scotland fans shoehorned into a small section of terracing plus a rather feminine shriek from the goal scorer.

My goal had the same affect on the Bulgarians as disturbing a queen bee in her hive – it triggered an immediate reaction. With time running out and their chances of qualifying for West Germany disappearing fast they threw everyone forward in a late, desperate attempt to snatch an equaliser. That gave us plenty of space to exploit in attacking areas and Brian McClair missed a glorious opportunity to score a second goal. In the end it didn't matter and we held on. The consequence was that the focus of attention was directed exclusively at me for scoring the winning goal, instead of it being shared with my more illustrious teammate. Our win ensured the Republic of Ireland had qualified for Euro '88 at the expense of Bulgaria. There wasn't even time to get back to the dressing room to celebrate when I was asked to do a live television interview along with Andy Roxburgh. It transpired those interviews were never shown as the angry Bulgarian producer was so pissed off by the result that he pulled the plug without telling anyone!

Win, lose or draw flights back to Scotland after midweek matches in Europe are usually quiet affairs with everyone desperate to get back home to bed. For me this one was different; it was my very own Roy of the Rovers tale. Scoring for your country on your debut is something that only happens in comic strips . . . .

I was chatting to Alex McLeish on the way back and he told me I'd get a wonderful reception the following Saturday, before asking me where Hearts were playing. I told him I was up against him at Pittodrie and that raised a chuckle; he was completely oblivious to his team's next fixture. Excuse the pun but the four-and-a-half-hour flight flew by, and there was more to come. On disembarking at Glasgow airport, well after midnight, I made my way to the baggage-collection area where I was met by a familiar face: Celtic and Ireland goalkeeper Pat Bonner was standing there with a bottle of champagne. He'd made the effort to come to the airport after our victory secured qualification for the Republic and he was delighted. 'A great thing you've done,' he exclaimed with a huge grin stretching from ear to ear. 'You'll probably never realise just how much this means to the people of Ireland that we now have the opportunity to compete in our first major championship.' He also mentioned that Jack Charlton, who was fishing for salmon when the news came through that Scotland had won, sent his warmest regards. It was one of those nights.

Scotland had to win that match for someone to be the hero; I was fortunate to be in the right place at the right time. Jim Leighton and his defenders keeping a clean sheet was just as important as me scoring but there was not enough champagne to share with the squad so I forced myself to keep it and I've still got it to this day.

* * *

In my rush to meet up with the Scotland squad on the Sunday prior to the match in Bulgaria I had forgotten to ask the Gaffer for the morning off after I arrived back home. As it transpired there was a message of congratulations from him on my answering machine when I got home, that ended with the words: ' . . . and I'll see you tomorrow morning, bright and early at ten o'clock for training.' That was the great thing about Alex MacDonald; I could quite easily have become the twenty-two-year-old big head after scoring for my country but he never let me get ideas above my station.

The following morning, or I suppose I should say later that morning, the reception I received before training from my teammates at Hearts was wonderful. That's where the pleasantries ended. We had a six-a-side match in the salubrious surroundings of Roseburn Park when the ball was knocked out of play. I shouted that the decision should go my way, when, quick as a flash, Neil Berry roared, 'It's not fucking Scotland you're with now Mackay.' There is nothing like your teammates to bring you back down to earth and we had a right laugh about it afterwards. I thoroughly enjoyed training that day and it was probably just what I needed after the events of the previous evening. I doubt if many of my Scotland teammates trained with their respective clubs less than seven hours after landing at Glasgow airport – they were probably enjoying a hot bath or a massage – but I think it was the right decision to get me straight back to normality with a big game at Aberdeen fast approaching.

It didn't take long upon for requests for interviews to come flooding in from Ireland and the next forty-eight hours were a bit of a blur. All credit to the Gaffer, who said he was happy for me to comply with the requests, but only after the match at Pittodrie. I received several letters from supporters in the Republic saying how grateful they were for my goal and there was even an opportunity to appear on *The Late Late Show* with Gay Byrne in Dublin that I had to reject due to time constraints. I did, however, agree to requests from Scottish Provident and Marshall's Chunky Chicken to appear in newspaper adverts they were planning for the Irish press.

As fate would have it, Hearts were drawn against St Patrick's Athletic the following year in the UEFA Cup so this time the Gaffer could have no complaints about me heading over to Ireland. Prior to flying out for the first leg in Dublin I received a West German postcard with an Irish stamp. It was simply addressed to Gary Mackay, Edinburgh, Scotland and had clearly been sent by a fan on his or her return home, having forgotten to post it during the European Championships. It said simply 'Thanks to your goal I am enjoying a wonderful time following my country here in Germany. Please find cheque enclosed.' Nice to see the Irish hadn't lost their sense of humour, despite failing to make the last four. However, I am sure the Ray Houghton goal that secured victory against England in their opening match would have made the trip worthwhile for every Irish supporter.

I did one or two interviews with the Irish media when I was in Dublin, but I was conscious of the fact that I was there to represent Hearts and was not in Ireland simply to hawk myself around radio and television stations. At least my mum and dad got some trade for their pub – Mackay's Centre Spot in Morrison Street – when St Pat's supporters used it as their base for the return leg. It was their way of saying thanks for the goal and they spent a fair bit of cash over the two days.

It was another seven years before I returned to Ireland. I had been invited to take part in a charity match between St Pat's and St Kevin's to raise funds for football teams at grassroots level. It was in October 1995, a day after Hearts lost 3–1 at Kilmarnock, so I flew across after the game from Prestwick airport and spent Saturday and Sunday night in Dublin. It was a star-studded occasion and I felt honoured to be asked. Alex Ferguson was in charge of our side while the players taking part included David Fairclough and Mark Lawrenson plus Steve Collins the boxer. The great George Best was also there to kick the match off and it was a most enjoyable afternoon.

My goal in the Vasil Levski stadium in Sofia may have proved insignificant in terms of Scotland qualifying for a major championship but I'm delighted to have played a very small part in the history of Irish football. Was I responsible for its renaissance? Maybe Packie Bonner gave some champagne to that journalist as well.

* * *

I suppose it's hard to eclipse scoring on your international debut. That's the way it panned out for me, although I was fortunate enough to win another three caps. The first was when I came on as a substitute for Derek Whyte in our final Euro qualifier in Luxembourg in December 1987. Unlike the game in Bulgaria, the match was meaningless for both sides and it was no surprise when the SFA decided against releasing a video of the ninety minutes. The only thing I can remember is taking a corner from the left that Alex McLeish got his head to, but, unfortunately, he missed the target. Had the header gone it that would have been two wins out of two for me in the dark blue but it wasn't to be. The game lived up to the occasion and finished goalless.

My third cap came against Saudi Arabia in a friendly in Riyadh in February 1988, again as a substitute, again for Paul McStay. At least that game had goals and finished 2–2 although it was notable only for the fact that three Hearts players represented their country at the same time in the second half, when Henry Smith and John Colquhoun were introduced to the action.

The fourth and final cap was won in Malta the following month and it was the only one of the four in which I started the match. Once again a friendly, it was the first meeting between the two nations and took place at the wonderfully named Ta'Qali stadium in Valletta. My first start for Scotland lasted precisely fifty-five minutes before I was replaced by Jim McInally but at least I can say that I've started a match for my country.

My form for Hearts around that time was reasonably good and I'd played in four consecutive international matches. Next up for Scotland was England at Wembley, in May 1988. My only previous experience of the Twin Towers was getting permission from Bobby Moncur shortly after joining Hearts to head down to London in May 1981 to watch us beat the Auld Enemy 1–0, thanks to a goal from John Robertson of Nottingham Forest. It was always a huge ambition of mine to play at Wembley and I was quietly confident I might get the chance if I could maintain my form at club level. The best-laid plans; I broke my jaw in a clash with Celtic's Billy Stark at Tynecastle the week after they beat us in the Scottish Cup semi-final at Hampden. I scored the winning goal that day in our 2–1 win before being replaced due to the injury. That sidelined me for the rest of the season and my dream of playing for Scotland at Wembley was over before the squad had even been announced.

For whatever reason I never pulled on the dark blue again but I'll always treasure my four international caps. Do I feel that I should have won more? Maybe, but there was a deep talent pool available to Scotland managers at the time – much deeper than it is today – and perhaps I wasn't quite up to the standard required. Nor do I feel that I would have necessarily got more caps if I had been playing for one of the Old Firm sides. Interestingly, however, it was only when Tosh McKinlay moved to Celtic that he got much-deserved international recognition, despite his outstanding performances for Hearts. He would not have won those caps had he stayed at Tynecastle.

But I have no complaints. I will forever have the memory of that goal in Bulgaria, which sparked scenes of jubilation across southern Ireland. The only slight disappointment, apart from missing the England game, is that none of my four caps were won while representing my country at our national stadium. It was simply a quirk of fate that the four matches were all overseas. I still have a tinge of regret about that.

8

Derby Days

'Who put the ball in the Hibees net?
Robbo, Robbo . . .'

I am very proud of my record in Edinburgh derbies: played fifty-four competitive matches and lost just eight, scoring four goals in the process. Only John Robertson featured more times for Hearts than I did against the men in green and white; he played on fifty-five occasions and tasted defeat only seven times, although I have to concede he scored a few more goals against them than I did. With footballers changing clubs these days nearly as often as teams change the design of their kits I think it's highly unlikely that anyone in a maroon jersey will ever come close to matching either the win/loss percentage or even play as many games as we did against our Capital rivals.

It is an excellent record and in some ways was my reward for a lot of the heartache (forgive the pun) suffered by Jambos in the 1970s. Neither I, nor any other Hearts supporter of a certain vintage, will ever be allowed to forget that day at the start of 1973. They've not had a lot to cheer about down Leith way since, oh, about 1902, and for it to be us on the receiving end of that thrashing was a double whammy. I may only have been nine at the time, but it hurt and it still does.

Unlike Robbo I've never been that good with statistics. He was even affectionately given the moniker 'Ceefax' by the boys in the dressing room on account of his incredible ability to remember facts about games he had played in. On the other hand my memory is, and has always been, dreadful and the Internet (something to do with computers, I believe . . .) was a huge help in reminding me what I actually did during my career. It was also very useful when researching my derby record, although there are many memorable matches I took part in against Hibs that I don't need the World Wide Web to remind me about.

The Edinburgh derby: it is easier for me to explain what it means as a supporter, rather than as a Hearts player. It means everything. Nobody is going to tell me that the Scottish Cup ties against Hibernian I have been involved in – as a player in 1994 (2–1 win at Easter Road) and as a supporter at Hampden in 2006 (4–0 victory in the semi-final) – didn't have extra significance. We won them both and ensured the bragging rights stayed in Gorgie. The elation I felt as a player lasted for the rest of the evening. But as a fan it hung around until the next derby.

Why is the name 'Wayne Foster' still sung at every Hearts–Hibs encounter? It is in remembrance of 1994. And Paul Hartley's hat-trick heroics of 2006 will ensure he is a Hearts legend for years to come. The Edinburgh derby? It really does mean everything.

One little anecdote reveals a lot about the feelings of my fellow Jambos for the fixture. My relationship with Billy Ramsey, who became an integral part of my testimonial committee, started before the New Year's Day derby in 1985. I was walking away from Tynecastle on the day before the match. Billy recognised me and introduced himself as we were walking under the bridge at McLeod Street. He told me he appreciated the way I played for the maroon jersey; he said it epitomised how thousands of Hearts and Hibs fans felt about their clubs and about the forthcoming game. It was pure passion. From that day Billy and I were firm friends, and we still are. Our relationship is now as much about friendship as it is about Heart of Midlothian, but that's what brought us together.

There are certain quirks of fate in football that are impossible to explain. Why, when Hearts won only four out of thirty competitive derbies during the Seventies, did we then go on an unbeaten run of seventeen games from the first time I faced Hibernian in a league match in September 1983 right through until our 2–1 defeat at Easter Road in October 1987? All footballers and teams go through spells when they have both a bogey side and a club they love playing against. Hibernian and their players relished facing Hearts in the Seventies, but hated Edinburgh derbies in the Eighties.

During my teens I stood on the terraces for most of those miserable matches, without being able to affect the outcome, and it was incredibly hard to take. I am grateful, however, that I had a part to play on the pitch in the Eighties and Nineties and some of my best memories as a footballer come from those matches against our city rivals. That Internet contraption informed me that Hearts lost only twelve of seventy-three games against Hibernian in the Eighties and Nineties; a wonderful record against any opposition.

The East of Scotland Football Association Shield (to give it its full title) used to be a prominent competition for senior clubs in the area, especially in the 1950s and 1960s when first-team squads competed on an annual basis for the splendid trophy. It is hardly surprising, that, more often than not, the final was contested by Hearts and Hibernian, but, unfortunately, the significance of the competition dwindled to the extent that these days the two capital rivals usually meet in an end-of-season clash and field their reserve line-ups in front of a couple of hundred loyal fans.

I was very fortunate when, in August 1980, aged just sixteen, it was agreed by both clubs prior to the East of Scotland encounter that the match should be an opportunity for promising youngsters to be rewarded with their first experience of a Hearts–Hibs clash. This would give the kids a chance not only to sample the ferocity of a local derby but also allow them to play alongside seasoned professionals as part of a mixed team comprising old heads and eager youths. Given my background, it was apt that the first voice I heard from the crowd just before that first-ever match against Hibernian belonged to someone who played a big part in Edinburgh juvenile football. I'd hardly made my way to the end of the tunnel at Tynecastle when a huge cry of 'C'mon Mackay, get intae them' came bellowing from the terracing in front of the main stand. Maggie Waddell was a small, and quite heavy, woman who helped run North Merchiston Boys Club. She was also Hearts daft. Maggie was very outspoken and not afraid to make herself heard. The stadium was not exactly packed to capacity that evening and her cry was easily audible all around the ground. Some young players may have been intimidated or embarrassed by Maggie's highly vocal support, but it made the hairs on the back of my neck stand to attention and proved inspirational.

It didn't take long for Hearts to build up a two-goal lead – Willie Gibson scored one of our goals – and it was on course to be the perfect derby debut until Hibs scored twice to earn a draw. It may only have been the East of Scotland Shield but, for me, any match at any level against our city rivals was, and always will be, win-at-all-costs. We weren't victorious that day after being in front, and it hurt. It hurt a lot and was an all-too-brutal reminder of what life had been like during the Seventies. I am pleased to say that in years to come hurt was not an emotion I experienced very frequently against the Leithers.

I was selected to start in another East of Scotland tie, this time a semi-final, against Hibernian in October 1981 and it gave me a first taste of victory in an Edinburgh derby. These games were not classed as competitive matches as far as the statisticians are concerned, but that didn't matter a jot to me as an own goal and a Roddy MacDonald strike earned us a 2–1 win at Easter Road, with Derek Rodier on target for the home side. A place in the final was secured, but, far more importantly, we had beaten our local rivals and we had beaten them on their own patch.

East of Scotland ties and friendly matches were the only occasions when Hearts came up against Hibernian at the start of the Eighties due to our lower-league status, and it was the latter that provided me with my first opportunity to play against their first-choice eleven. Following consultation between the boards at Easter Road and Tynecastle it was agreed that Hearts would provide the opposition for the Tom Hart trophy (Hart was the Hibernian chairman who famously persuaded George Best to sign for his club) on Monday, 9 August 1982. It had been just over three years since the two first teams had met in another friendly – in the Skol Festival Trophy, when Willie Ormond was in charge of Hearts – so the game was eagerly anticipated. However, for once it wasn't the behaviour of the players that was the problem.

Former Hibernian boss Jock Stein was due to present the trophy at the end of the match but proceedings were marred by crowd violence. Although trouble on the terraces is something I hate to see at any time, I have to admit the behaviour of a small minority of supporters that day, and the subsequent coverage it received, ensured our team got less flak in the newspapers the following morning after our 1–0 defeat.

I always admired Hibernian midfielder Ralph Callachan as a footballer. He was my boyhood hero during his spell at Hearts and was the player I tried to emulate in kickabouts as a child. (I was extremely disappointed that he opted to sign for our city rivals when he returned to Scotland following a spell with Newcastle United.) I felt privileged that day – even though it was billed as a friendly – to get the chance to compete against him as part of a Hearts side that was going through a transitional phase. Our line-up at Easter Road had an average age of nearly twenty-eight and included three thirty-somethings: Peter Marinello (playing against his old team), Sandy Jardine and player-boss Alex MacDonald. At the age of eighteen I was the youngest in our team. In fact only Peter Shields (21), Walter Kidd (24) and I were twenty-four or under. There were signs however that the Gaffer was starting to change things by slowly incorporating youngsters into the first team. Fellow teenagers Davie Bowman, John Robertson and Stuart Gauld were all given several opportunities to impress before Christmas and the pendulum was slowly swinging, giving the team a more youthful appearance.

Following our promotion to the top flight in season 1982/83, my first competitive appearance against the men in green and white occurred in a Premier League encounter in September 1983. I was nineteen and had been playing for the first team for three years but was still very raw. After Hearts had spent several years yo-yoing between the top flight and the second tier of Scottish football this was the first competitive Edinburgh derby since Hibernian inflicted a 2–1 defeat in March 1979. It was also the first major match I had been selected to play in and I don't mind admitting I was a cocky little bastard during the build-up to the game. I was of the opinion that everybody in the crowd of around twenty thousand was there to see me. As you can imagine I got precisely what I deserved: well and truly shown up.

One of the headlines in the press the day after our 3–2 victory read simply 'A Star is Born', and it was not a reference to me. John Robertson scored twice on his derby debut and quite rightly took the plaudits. I was left feeling sorry for myself after a below-par performance. The picture was being painted that would be painted many times in the future; Robbo's goals putting Hibs to the sword. Ralph Callachan (how ironic) opened the scoring for Hibernian early on and it stayed that way until half-time. Robbo got the first of his brace just before the hour mark but Willie Irvine quickly put the home side back in front. After that goal it was decided that my race was run. I was quite rightly replaced, by Alex MacDonald, and came off the park physically drained having had a nightmare. In all my years playing football it was the most exhausted I have ever felt following a match, both mentally and physically. I let the occasion get to me in a big way, expending far too much nervous energy due to my determination to make an impact, and, in the end, only succeeded in running about like a headless chicken for most of my time on the pitch. We were fortunate that, shortly after my departure, the wee man saved the day by popping up to score his second, the equaliser, before Jimmy Bone grabbed the winner with thirteen minutes remaining to maintain our 100 per cent record after two league games.

I had mixed emotions after the final whistle. First and foremost, as a fan, I was ecstatic with the win. However, I was extremely disappointed with my performance, which was nowhere near good enough to sustain a regular run in the first team. But it helped me realise that in order to get to the top in any profession, never mind football, it is advisable not to think you're the bee's knees before you have achieved anything. My performance that day was the kick up the backside I sorely needed.

We didn't know it at the time but that was the start of seventeen unbeaten competitive matches against Hibernian, stretching four years until 1987. What made the win even more pleasing was that our starting line-up that day contained a quartet of teenagers: Davie Bowman, Stuart Gauld and I were all nineteen, while Robbo was a year younger. Following his goal-scoring exploits on his derby debut the wee man made it something of a habit; the moniker 'Hammer of Hibs' was quickly bestowed upon him and he lived up to that name with twenty-seven competitive goals in fifty-five games against our rivals. That statistic makes it even more ironic that John was all set to join Hibernian until Tom Hart's 'sign now or never wear a Hibs strip ever again' ultimatum ended any chance of history being rewritten.

* * *

31 December 1984

It was unusual for me to be called into the manager's office so when the request came from Sandy Jardine, on behalf of Alex MacDonald, on the eve of the 1985 Ne'er Day game against Hibernian I wondered if something was up. What had I done wrong? All sorts of things crossed my mind, including being dropped, but I'd been playing reasonably well and thought that would be a tad harsh. There was very little conversation in his room but thankfully the things that *were* said intimated to me that nothing was amiss. The purpose of my summons was for the Gaffer to give me a little white tablet. He told me to go home and to take half the pill an hour before I planned to go to sleep. I asked no questions, did as he requested, had a wonderful sleep and was buzzing when I awoke on the morning of the match. I produced one of my better performances in a maroon jersey, scoring in our 2–1 victory and everything in the world was rosy. Except for one thing; my conscience was bothering me. Just what was in that white tablet? Before boarding the bus to leave Easter Road that evening I had a quiet word with the Gaffer and asked him if he would care to put my mind at rest. 'That, son,' he informed me, 'was half a paracetamol tablet.'

The psychology had worked brilliantly; I assumed it was a sleeping pill. Those man-management qualities were a key component of Alex and Sandy's success at Tynecastle. I was a twenty-year-old kid trying to build a reputation as a professional footballer and they knew exactly how to play the psychological card for every member of the squad. It's the same at all levels of football: whether it's the under-fourteens I coach on a Sunday morning or the seasoned pro coming to the end of his career, every single player has to be treated as an individual. The Gaffer and Sandy were experts in this field, as in so many others.

* * *

First of January Eighty-Six
Iain slammed one between the sticks
Robbo too, and Sandy Clark
We're the Gorgie Jam Tarts

Early days.

Above left: With mum.

Above right: With dad.

Below left: With my first ever trophy, Balgreen primary school 1976.

Below right: Once a Jambo . . . in my first Hearts tracksuit.

The Salvesen years.

I am proudly holding the Scottish Cup after our under-twelve side at Salvesen Boys Club won it in 1976. Salvesen was one of the most successful clubs in Scotland during the Seventies.

A fabulous haul. Salvesen's trophy presentation ceremony for 1977/78. George Stewart of Hibs is on my right.

Salvesen Boys Club with the Scottish Cup for under-sixteens. I am third from right, front row; Dave Bowman is second from right, back row. The keeper is Ian Westwater.

Champions of Europe

In 1982 I was in the team that won the under-eighteen European championships in Finland. I am fourth from the left, front row, while other notables include Paul McStay, second left front row, and, in the back row, Pat Nevin and Brian McClair, far right and second right respectively.

We returned home from Finland to a heroes welcome. It is still the only time Scotland has won a major championship and this story in the *Daily Record* was typical of the coverage we received.

... but the young Scots' dream comes true

CHAMPIONS OF EUROPE ... the triumphant Scots give a lift to team boss Andy Roxburgh after their magnificent 3-1 victory over Czechoslovakia

BOYS GET IT RIGHT

SCOTLAND 3   CZECHOSLOVAKIA 1
Scorers: Scotland — Phillben (38), Nevin (49), Mackay (64). Czechoslovakia—Miskuf (51).

From JACK ADAMS, HELSINKI

WE are the champions...that was the victory song of Scotland's Under-18 team as they paraded the European Championship trophy round the Olympic Stadium here yesterday.

And how these magnificent youngsters deserved to sing and dance their way into the dressing rooms after their historic victory.

There was no shame in their tears of happiness—the brave are allowed to cry in victory.

Heat

THERE HAS NEVER BEEN A BRAVER SCOTLAND SIDE THAN THIS ONE.

After five games in 10 days they might have been expected to wilt in the searing heat.

But out of that furnace emerged iron men, moulded to a hardness the Czechs just couldn't handle.

Even when their legs began to go their hearts wouldn't let them give up or think about defeat.

This wasn't their best performance but this time they got it right in front of goal.

The goals that earned them

Scotland's first ever European title were all gems.

In 29 minutes Gary Mackay beat a great free kick round the Czech wall only to hit the post.

Then with 30 seconds of the first half left Scotland struck a real killer blow.

Pat Nevin, the man of this tournament, sent over a perfect corner which was pushed back across goal by Alistair Dick and there was John Philliben on the spot to crash the ball home.

From then on there was only going to be one winner and in the 49th minute Scotland grabbed a truly magnificent second goal.

PAT NEVIN WILL NEVER SCORE A BETTER GOAL.

He beat five defenders inside the penalty box before calmly sidefooting the ball past the Czech 'keeper.

Maybe the Scottish

youngsters just couldn't believe the sheer brilliance of that goal because two minutes later they made their only mistake in defence to let Miskuf score.

This was the time for Scotland to show their real courage, to show that they deserved to be champions of Europe.

And how they rose to that challenge — in 64 minutes Gary Mackay of Hearts scored a third with a glorious 30-yard shot.

The championship had been won and it was time for singing and dancing as the jubilant young Scots carried manager Andy Roxburgh and the trophy round the stadium.

Then in the dressing room

they toasted victory with ice-cold milk.

This was the most magnificent performance by a Scottish youth team I have ever known. Just think, we are now going to the World Championships in Mexico as champions of Europe.

And there was more praise from Jock Stein. He said from his home: "I am absolutely delighted. This is a great tonic for everyone in the Scottish game."

Russia beat Poland 3-1 in the third-place play off.

SCOTLAND — Rae (Hibs), Beaumont (Dundee Utd.), Philliben (Stirling), Rennie (Leicester), Rice (Hibs), Bowman (Hearts), McStay (Celtic), McGinnis (Dundee Utd.), Nevin (Clyde), Mackay (Hearts), Dick (Spurs). Subs.: McGivern (Kilmarnock), Livingstone (Wolves).

Becoming a Jambo

Left: What a specimen! Here I am at the notorious Gullane sands for my first pre-season as a professional.

Right: I'd just signed for Hearts, in 1980, when I posed for this photo with the Scottish Cup.

Below: The Hearts squad in 1983/84. We had some fabulous players, including Willie Johnston (*second right*), John Robertson (*third right*) and Jimmy Bone (*eighth right*).

The master chefs. We did watch our diets in the Eighties as this photo of Robbo and I shows.

I got my fair share of goals for a midfielder, including this one against Dundee in May 1984. My teammates looking on are (*from left to right*) Walter 'Zico' Kidd, Sandy Jardine, the Gaffer and Bow.

I loved playing against the Old Firm, especially against great players like Tommy Burns (*left*) and Brian Whittaker (a future teammate) both of whom, sadly, are no longer with us.

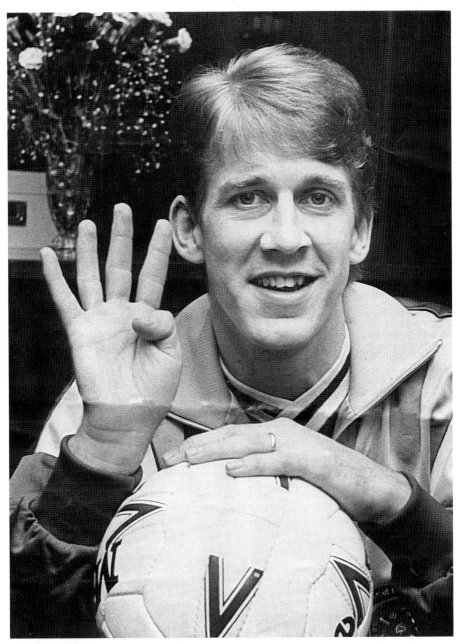

Robbo must have been jealous when I notched four goals in a
Scottish Cup tie against Inverness Caledonian in January 1985.
As is the custom I was presented with the match ball.

My wedding in 1988. Pictured with my bride, Vicky, and best man Kenny
Black and his wife.

At the grand opening of mum and dad's pub, the Centre Spot,
in Morrison Street. Note the gaffer's dodgy handshake!

Total commitment was expected in Edinburgh derby matches,
as Kevin McAllister and I demonstrate.
(Courtesy Mirrorpix)

I faced many fine midfielders in my career but few were as talented
as Paul Gascoigne of Rangers.
(Courtesy Mirrorpix)

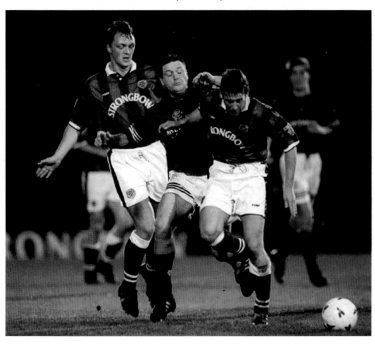

Heartbreak. Albert Kidd turns away in triumph after scoring for Dundee against Hearts at Dens Park. It was the last game of the 1985/86 season and the 2–0 defeat cost us the league championship, on goal difference. It is a day that I will never forget – for all the wrong reasons.

Chairman Wallace Mercer (*in collar and tie*) was, like all Hearts fans, bitterly disappointed by the loss of the league on that fateful day at Dens but he still found time to comfort this distraught Jambo.
(both courtesy Eric McCowat)

Just a week after Dens we had a chance to redeem ourselves in the 1986 Scottish Cup final at Hampden. But we clearly had been affected more than we realised by the title trauma and lost 3–0 to Aberdeen. In this shot I am being marshalled by Dons defender Stewart McKimmie.

(courtesy: Getty Images Ltd)

I was always proud to play for my country and I won four
Scotland caps. Here I am with one of them.

Perhaps my most dramatic moment in a Scotland jersey came against
Bulgaria in 1987, when I scored the only goal in a match in Sofia. It won
the game for Scotland but sent Ireland to the European Championships in
West Germany. I became an unlikely hero to the Irish nation and was
presented with champagne by Ireland goalkeeper, Pat Bonner.

(both courtesy Eric McCowat)

My time as manager of Airdrie was bedevilled by severe financial problems, which culminated in the club going into administration. I am pictured here with my assistant manager, Walter Kidd.

(courtesy: Mirrorpix)

I was proud to lay a wreath at this memorial in Contalmaison, northern France. It commemorates the Hearts players killed at the Battle of the Somme in 1916 (members of the legendary McCrae's battalion), and was built by public subscription. My fellow Jambo, actor Ken Stott, is also pictured, wearing the dark tie.

The co-commentator. I work each match-day at Tynecastle for radio and the official Hearts website.

It was a thrill to run out at Tynecastle again in a Hearts strip for Robbie Neilson's testimonial in May 2008. I admit however that I was putting up a few pounds overweight!

With (*from left to right*) Iain Macleod of Save Our Hearts,
Vladimir Romanov, Svetlana, Mr Romanov's wife, and me. Our owner is
wearing a Hearts kilt, which we presented to him on behalf of Hearts fans.

I spent three hours talking about Hearts and possible tactical formations in
Romanov's offices in Kaunas. His football knowledge and his passion for
the club were evident throughout.

Save Our Hearts. Along with thousands of other Hearts fans I was determined to stop the proposed move away from Tynecastle. I would like to think that this rally – involving more than three thousand supporters – helped our cause.

It's not often history repeats itself in football, but there was a major case of déjà-vu on 30 August 1986 when the 3–1 score line mirrored the result from the Ne'er Day game of that year. Even the scorers were the same, albeit in a different order (Robbo, I. Jardine, Clark). I have no idea who thought up this superb little ditty but I still remember it after all these years and it brings back fond memories. By this stage in my career – early twenties – I had yet to taste defeat in a competitive Edinburgh derby and it was a feeling I was getting used to. Every Eighties meeting with Hibs was approached with a genuine belief that we would win the match, or at least not lose. I'm convinced their players thought they would struggle in a head-to-head battle given their awful record. You could argue we were a goal to the good before a ball had been kicked. It is impossible to put a price on such a huge psychological advantage.

The Edinburgh derby is massive and to be in a position to influence the result for a period of fourteen years was beyond the wildest dreams of my childhood. I was, and always will be, passionate about the fixture, which is easy for me given my ties to the club. It must have been more difficult for an 'outsider' to have the same passion for beating Hibernian as I did. Alex MacDonald, however, took to the fixture like a duck to water. The Gaffer never showed his true emotions in public, but there were many times behind closed doors when we saw another side to him. It wasn't pleasant and it didn't happen too often, but when he inflicted his wrath on us we paid attention out of sheer respect for the man. And there were far more good times than bad.

The biggest test of character for Hearts in an Edinburgh derby came when we faced Hibernian following *that* season, 1985/86, when we almost pulled off a historic league-and-cup double. It was the end of August and emotions were still raw from the double-whammy less than four months earlier. So it was no surprise when we strolled onto the pitch shortly after arriving at Easter Road to see a lot of very confident Hibernian supporters on the terraces. They had got there early to greet us and we were met by a chorus of jeers and guffaws; how very kind of them.

Their fans, who expected to turn us over, did their best to take the piss. One of their supporters clubs even renamed itself the Albert Kidd May 1986 Supporters Club. That sums them up; they had done nothing for decades and were reduced to mocking a team that was vastly superior to their favourites. I am delighted to say that their behaviour backfired spectacularly; we had the last laugh, beating them as convincingly as I can recall any Hearts team demolishing our Edinburgh rivals, and that's happened a few times in recent history. On the pitch their players didn't say much about May, or at least I think that was the case. I was so focused on getting a result that day I hardly heard a thing from the moment I got off the bus.

Needless-to-say everyone in maroon was in buoyant mood at the final whistle and there was a skip in my step as I made my way down the tunnel after shaking hands with the opposition players then celebrating in front of our supporters. I will never forget what happened next. On our arrival in the away dressing room I was treated to the sight of the Gaffer thumping his hand against the wall and chanting at the top of his voice, 'Can you hear the Hibees sing – no, no.' It was out of character; he was a good winner and a bad, but respectful, loser.

Last in the dressing room was our physiotherapist Alan Rae – a lovely man but someone you dare not cross – and he must have got the fright of his life when a cry of 'leave that door open' bellowed from across the room. He was getting a row from Doddie for trying to close the door. The Gaffer wanted everybody in the tunnel, including the opposition and the television cameras, to hear him. He also wanted every one of the players and back-room staff to join in with the impromptu singsong. Some, like me, were more than happy to help him belt out his little ditty; others had to be coerced. I have no idea what led to his behaviour that day, although the politics in the week leading up to the game, when the character of our squad was questioned, had a lot to do with it. The Gaffer was simply making them aware we were still there and that Hearts were still beating.

That 3–1 win in September 1986 was probably my favourite victory against Hibernian, but the one immediately after Wallace Mercer's ill-fated takeover exactly four years later was also very special. Due to the tense atmosphere in the city, Lothian and Borders police suggested it would be in our best interests if we changed our usual pre-match build-up. We had lunch at the Queensferry hotel in North Queensferry on Saturday, 15 September 1990 before a convoy of police outriders escorted us to Easter Road. For an away game most players left their cars at Tynecastle before boarding the team bus, but such was the animosity from sections of the Hibs support it was agreed that everyone was to make their way over the Forth Road Bridge and that none of our vehicles were to be left in Edinburgh.

The atmosphere inside Easter Road that day was poisonous; it was above and beyond anything I had ever experienced before or since. So it was no real surprise when fights broke out on the home terracing, leading to the game being stopped for a time. I think our boys were more relaxed, whereas the pressure on their players was massive due to a combination of desperation and desire. If the shoe had been on the other foot I would have been equally determined to put one over on the opposition.

On the field, Robbo – surprise, surprise – quickly took the sting out of proceedings with the opener. Craig Levein added number two shortly after and the wee man's second goal wrapped things up in double quick time.

Those three goals were the equivalent of throwing petrol onto a raging fire but what went on that summer off the pitch had nothing to do with the players representing Heart of Midlothian. We were there to do a job and it was done with great aplomb. It was slightly ironic that Robbo should get two goals as he was vehemently opposed to the takeover and made his feelings well known at the time of Wallace's approach, siding very much with the Hands Off Hibs campaign. It wasn't something that I concerned myself with. I adopted the possibly selfish approach that all I was interested in was my own club. I was, however, pleased that the merger never took place as it meant many more happy years on the pitch at their expense. Some years later former Hibernian captain Murdo McLeod eloquently described that season as a 'shit' one (in a BBC documentary).

I'm glad we were able to play a part in their mediocrity.

* * *

I used to love the derbies at Easter Road even more than those at Tynecastle. I took great pleasure warming up in front of the east terracing, opposite the main stand, where the hardcore Hibernian boys used to congregate. I found the venom directed at me truly inspirational and such eloquence got me fired up and completely focused. It made the manager's team talk superfluous. When the match got underway I liked playing in front of the old wooden stand, where the green-and-white cravat-wearers used to sit. I had been present many times in the Seventies as a supporter and was forced to listen to that ever-so-slightly-superior brand of Hibernian fan stamp his or her feet in celebration, creating quite a din in the process. The opportunity to silence those people and give them nothing to bang about in that rickety old structure inspired me. I knew it was a good day when the only audible noise came from the away terracing and the other three-quarters of the stadium stayed silent. Hearts supporters were always in the minority when we made the short journey down to Leith but our fans, in defiance at being outnumbered, made sure they were heard and more often than not those songs were sung to celebrate victories.

One such occasion when they were able to walk back along Albion Road and over the Crawford Bridge with a smile on their faces was 2 January 1992. That Ne'er Day clash was the first Edinburgh derby selected for live transmission by BSkyB and I look back on it with fond memories. We won very comfortably by four goals to one, showcasing our dominance over our city rivals to the entire nation. I even popped up with two goals, although I try to forget one of them was into my own net! I managed to get a few of my mates some tickets for the match and after I scored – at the right end –

I ran over to the enclosure in front of the old wooden stand to celebrate in front of them. That night Scott Crabbe and I decided to toast our success so we headed to North Beachwood, just along the road from the main street in Corstorphine. We wanted to visit to a guy called Harry Mitchell, a great Jambo who later sponsored my testimonial dinner; we also met up with Billy Ramsay, who was on my testimonial committee. I was staying at Tyler's Acre at the time, not too far away, and I'll never forget walking home from Harry's house arm in arm with Crabbo, singing at the top of our voices. In our drunken state we challenged each other to make more noise than the animals at nearby Edinburgh Zoo, and, although my memory is slightly hazy, I am sure we gave them a run for their money.

* * *

The year 1994 was both memorable and forgettable for Hearts, and for me, when it came to Edinburgh derbies. Neither I, nor anyone else of a maroon persuasion will ever forget the smash-and-grab fourth-round victory in the Scottish Cup at Easter Road in February. The winning goal with just three minutes left by a substitute from Lancashire ensured that shouts of 'Wayne, Wayne, Super Wayne' were sung at the fixture for years to come. We got an absolute doing that day, to the extent that Kevin McAllister's trickery actually made me dizzy. At one-all we had not given up hope of snatching an ill-deserved winner, but I'm sure every one of the Hearts players would have taken the offer of a replay without a second thought. I was playing in an unfamiliar role at right-back, although I moved forward into midfield after manager Sandy Clark brought on Jim Weir. He slotted into the defence, allowing me to take over from Scott Leitch in the centre of midfield. I played a small part in the build-up to Wayne Foster's winning goal before watching as our Lancashire lad went one-on-one with goalkeeper Jim Leighton. Time seemed to stand still for a few seconds before the ball ended up in the back of the net. Defeating your local rivals is always special, but that was our twenty-first game unbeaten against them and I remember seeing a giant key being hoisted in celebration above someone's head on the away terraces when we rushed towards the fence to congratulate Wayne. The result may have been slightly fortuitous that Sunday afternoon, but it showed our determin-ation to maintain that unbeaten record.

Fast forward six months and the fantastic feeling we experienced fol-lowing that victory at Easter Road was replicated; only this time it was the Hibernian players enjoying it. Perhaps fate was conspiring against us that late August afternoon because we were all over them that day. It was similar to the Scottish Cup tie in which they outplayed us yet still found themselves on the losing side. The end of our unbeaten twenty-two-game record was always going to be tough, but for it to happen at Tynecastle rubbed salt into our wounds. Gordon Hunter's scrappy goal in front of the Gorgie Road terracing sent the visiting supporters into raptures and was enough to secure the points. I hit the crossbar with an effort later in the game that would have probably earned us a point. They say it never rains but it pours and this was certainly true for me when I was sent off for a second yellow card. But looking back, it was some achievement to go unbeaten against any team between 1983 and 1987 then from 1989 to 1994, never mind your local rivals, and these statistics will be etched in my brain forever.

I always took great delight when approaching the Hibernian players after we won to offer my commiserations; the same could not be said on the few occasions I tasted defeat. I know it wasn't very professional, and that I was taking the easy way out, but I tried to get down the tunnel as quickly as possible after an Edinburgh derby loss to avoid 'pleasantries' with the likes of Paul Kane and Mickey Weir. I wanted to give them dog's abuse when we won, but I only ever saw their backsides as they hastily made their way off the pitch. When the shoe was on the other foot I knew how they were feeling and I couldn't bring myself to shake their hands and view the smug looks on their faces. I'm not proud of my actions, although I think it shows that I cared passionately. The same can also be said for the likes of Kane, Weir and Gordon Hunter on the opposition side: three big Hibees with a passion for their club that has to be respected. It's funny that I now get on well with all three because we were bitter foes when we played against each other. They had the same commitment to Hibs as I had to Hearts. They were guys who had grown up in the area, supported their local team and got the chance to fulfil a boyhood dream. Where we differ is that I can look back in years to come and remember the wonderful feeling at the end of so many derbies and savour the joy of our fans. The Hibs boys had a pretty dismal time and I have no sympathy for them!

From the seven derby defeats I was unfortunate to experience I am grateful for the fact I was only on the pitch at the end of four of those matches, conveniently avoiding what would have been uncomfortable handshakes on three occasions. Frustration definitely got the better of me in the Gordon Hunter game. I was like a child throwing his toys out of the pram when the equalising goal failed to materialise and my illegal use of the shoulder deservedly resulted in a second caution. My dismissal ensured I got the chance to use the Radox before any of my teammates. Did I take the easy option and get myself deliberately sent off? I like to think not but the truth is I probably did.

The other two defeats were at Easter Road; I was replaced by John

Colquhoun in October 1994 as we went down 2–1 in the first match since the twenty-two-match unbeaten run came to an end. The other loss was on the first day of 1996 when Paul Smith was my replacement as Hibernian bounced back from a 7–0 defeat at Ibrox to beat us 2–1 and record their first Ne'er Day derby win for twenty years. That was the last time I tasted defeat in a capital clash and needless-to-say I didn't hang around the dugout area to congratulate the opposition as they made their way down the tunnel.

I am not proud of any red card I received during my playing career, as I never considered myself a malicious player or one who went onto the pitch deliberately to harm an opponent. Although anyone watching the Edinburgh derby at the start of October 1995 may have thought differently. It was the first time Jim Jefferies had taken charge of Hearts against Hibernian and came on the back of our defeat at Easter Road near the end of the previous season when we were struggling to survive in the top league. Big Dave McPherson scored five minutes before half-time to give us a one-goal lead at the interval, but they flew out of the traps at the start of the second half. It didn't take them long to score twice and take the lead. I wasn't having much of an influence and it was shortly after Hibs took the lead, that, once again out of frustration, the red mist descended and I was sent off by referee Willie Young for stamping on Gareth Evans. (In my defence I thought it was Darren Jackson I was trampling over, which would have been worth it!) Gareth and I became good friends when we played together at Airdrie and we used to share the daily journey through to Lanarkshire from Edinburgh so there were no hard feelings on his part. Robbo went on to equalise for Hearts in stoppage time before proclaiming in the post-match press conference that 'It's never over until the fat striker scores.'

Once again Robbo had rescued the team by finding the net against the team he loved to torment. I felt I had let the team down and sat in the changing room after the game with my head in my hands while my team-mates celebrated after playing the get-out-of-jail card. To this day I have never seen that goal and have no intention of watching the highlights of a game in which I stood on an opposing player. Things happen in the heat of the moment (I don't think Ivan Sproule meant to stand on Saulius Mikoliunas in the Tennent's Scottish Cup semi-final at Hampden in April 2006) and I didn't mean to stand on Gareth. It was a moment of madness. I got fined two weeks' wages as a result of my stupidity so it was costly for me in more ways than one.

* * *

Tommy McLean is a football man I have the utmost respect for, but that doesn't mean we always saw eye to eye. I had not played particularly well in the defeat to Airdrie in the Scottish Cup semi-final replay at Hampden in April 1995, and, as a result, was dropped from the starting eleven for the trip to Easter Road on 6 May in the penultimate match of a vital season. Edinburgh derbies were and are a huge part of my life but I was honest with myself and when I was named among the substitutes I couldn't complain. With only two league matches left we were struggling to survive and our cause wasn't helped that day when we slumped to an extremely disappointing 3–1 defeat. That put me in a bad mood, but not as much as Tommy's decision to embarrass me by telling me to get warmed up as we entered time added on for stoppages, then putting me on for Dave McPherson with only thirty seconds remaining. That was the only time in my entire career that I came close to refusing to obey orders and telling the manager where he could stick his decision. I felt that the immediate aftermath of such a disappointment was not the right time to vent my spleen so I waited until the Monday to ask for an explanation as to why I was selected for such a short period. There was a bad smell about the way the whole episode had been handled and I had to ask Tommy why he had made that decision. His answer, however, disappointed me greatly and was certainly not what I expected.

On the Thursday prior to the game I went up to the Woodhall Arms, located between Juniper Green and Currie and just up the road from my house, to meet the proprietor of the pub, former Hibernian defender George Stewart. George and I were good friends as he was one of the players who helped coach me when I played for Salvesen Boys Club (he was also a member of my testimonial committee, along with fervent Hibee Kenny McLean senior). I regularly frequented his premises for some good company and my usual glass of fresh orange juice. The conversation that day went along the usual lines; he asked if I was up for the match on the Saturday and we had a bit of jovial banter as it was his former club providing the opposition. I explained that I didn't think I would be playing due to my poor performance against Airdrie. George also asked if I could provide him with two tickets for the Hearts end for a friend; I told him I would deliver them the following day and, as promised, dropped them off after training. That is the true version of events. Unfortunately for me a different tale got back to Tommy.

Eamonn Bannon, on behalf of Tommy McLean, told me on the Monday after the game that word had got back to them – he wasn't forthcoming about who told them – that I had discussed details of the Hearts team with George and they thought this, if true, was scandalous. My explanation that I was completely unaware of their team selection when I was in the pub the previous Thursday and Friday, and that it was therefore impossible for me to have passed on those details, not that I would ever have done such a thing, was considered but rejected, much to my annoyance.

That was a real eye-opener for me. Tommy McLean knew I played well in the first derby that season and both he and Eamonn were aware of my passion for the club and how much Edinburgh derbies meant to me. They knew I wouldn't discuss confidential details with anyone and so I was stunned they appeared to believe a completely fabricated story. In addition, I was very disappointed they didn't seek clarification from me in the hours leading up to the derby. My professionalism and integrity were being questioned and that hurt. I made my feelings known to them in no uncertain terms.

That wasn't the only time I was left on the bench for an Edinburgh derby. I had no reason, of course, to expect to start any game and was always disappointed to be left out, but it was harder to take when Hibernian provided the opposition. Another petted lip would have been visible in March 1996; I was surprised when Jim Jefferies decided to name me among the replacements for the capital clash at Tynecastle because I felt my form at the time was quite good. The omission made me more determined to do well if I got the chance to come on. I wanted to prove to the manager he was wrong to leave me out and was fortunate enough to do so when I replaced Neil Pointon and scored in the 1–1 draw. Once again after an Edinburgh derby I had mixed feelings; pleased with my goal but disappointed that I wasn't deemed good enough to start.

* * *

My last Edinburgh derby, not that I knew it at the time, was yet another Ne'er Day clash: on 1 January 1997. I played the full match as Hearts won 4–0 to record their biggest win at Easter Road for thirty-six years, but that would be the last time I would wear a maroon jersey at the home of our biggest rivals. I was hoping to feature in the final Edinburgh derby of that season but my almost-seventeen-year association as a player with Heart of Midlothian Football Club was to end the day before Hibernian travelled across town in March 1997.

I was preparing as normal that week when Jim Jefferies called me into his office and told me an offer had come in from Airdrie and the club had given me permission to speak to them if I wanted to. I believed that was the end of the line for me at Tynecastle and it was one of the saddest days of my life. As far as I'm concerned when someone gives you permission to speak to another employer it's because they consider you surplus to requirements. Jim told me I'd still be on the bench if I turned down the move but I knew

I no longer had a significant part to play at the club so went for talks with Airdrie and put pen to paper soon after.

The first game for my new club was that weekend, the same day as Hearts faced Hibernian. I tried hard to concentrate but couldn't stop thinking about what might be happening in the derby. It was goalless at Broadwood at half-time in our game and I rushed to the changing room to find out the score from Tynecastle. It turned out I wasn't the only Airdrie player that day keen to find out what was happening in the Edinburgh derby; several teammates told me they had selected Hearts on the fixed-odds coupon and were also desperate for a home win! We scored twice in the second half to secure victory in my first game for the Diamonds and my joy was complete when the kit man informed me on the way down the tunnel at full-time that Neil McCann had scored a late winner for Hearts. At least a difficult week had ended on a high but it quickly sunk in that I would never again pull on a maroon jersey, puff out my chest, stand shoulder to shoulder with my opposite number, look straight ahead down the tunnel at either Tynecastle or Easter Road then go into battle with the green-and-white enemy. I experienced those wonderful feelings fifty-four times and was only beaten on eight occasions, something I cherish even more than representing my country four times.

That's what my Edinburgh derby record means to me.

9

Tynecastle Tales

'Boys will be boys – and footballers are the worst boys of all!'

That much-used phrase about football, 'It's a funny old game', is regularly attributed to former England striker Jimmy Greaves. However, in his autobiography *'Greavsie'* he claims he rarely used it and is unaware of its origin. Wherever it came from I'm sure the remark was intended to relate to the strange things that can happen on a pitch, and I'd be amazed if there was ever a more bizarre ending to a game than when Graham Weir, one of my former clients with Kickstart 2000, scored twice in the last sixty seconds of stoppage time at Tynecastle to earn Hearts a 4–4 draw against Hibernian on 2 January 2003. Taken literally I'm sure the phrase could also mean those jovial times associated with either being a footballer or being at the match as a supporter and I wish to share one or two of my more light-hearted memories from nearly seventeen years at Tynecastle. During that time I played in 640 competitive games, plus 97 friendlies and testimonials. Needless-to-say there were one or two funny moments along the way.

* * *

Having joined Heart of Midlothian at sixteen in the summer of 1980 I had to wait a year for my first pre-season tour as the club did not embark on a lengthy trip in the weeks following my arrival. I played in some idyllic locations during my career – none more so than the Caribbean in 1986 – but the north-east of England was not one of them. These days some clubs get ready for the new season by travelling both near and far, with Germany, the

Netherlands, the United States of America and the Far East among favoured destinations. Aberdeen even went to Alexandria in Egypt ahead of the 2007/2008 season. We were not that lucky in the summer of 1981; we prepared for the new season in Northumberland – North Shields, Whitley Bay and Blyth to be exact.

We beat North Shields 4–2 on Saturday, 25 July and manager Tony Ford allowed us a night out in Newcastle as a little treat with the next game, against Whitley Bay, not taking place until the Monday. Davie Bowman and I were especially excited by the prospect of some sightseeing (and I use that term quite literally) and a bit of ornithology in the Bigg Market until we were told that only the more experienced members of the squad – the likes of Derek O'Connor, Gary and Frank Liddell, Stewart MacLaren, Roddy MacDonald, Paddy Byrne and Henry Smith – had permission to go because they were the only ones who could be trusted! I have no idea how many of the older players decided a night out in Newcastle was better than another evening in our hotel – I suspect most of them – but while they partied and more than likely got up to no good Bow and I were stuck in our room sharing a club sandwich and watching television.

Normal service was resumed on the Monday evening with the squad back together for our match against Whitley Bay, a game that included one of the funniest incidents I have ever seen. Around three hundred Hearts fans had spent the weekend in the north-east, taking in our three fixtures and no doubt enjoying themselves slightly more than I did on the Saturday evening. By Monday more than a few were the worse for wear and I'd be interested to find out how many of those who attended our 1–1 draw against Whitley Bay remember anything about the match, especially a supporter by the name of Peter Beverage. Known to his fellow fans as 'the Cat', Peter was a great Hearts man of some renown who thought it would be amusing to sneak up behind one of the linesmen when he wasn't looking and pull the hairs on the back of his leg. He was lucky that the official took it in good spirit while the one policeman on duty, controlling a crowd of around four hundred, decided it was in his best interests not to get involved. He even managed a smile when some Hearts fans climbed over the advertising boards and started dancing round the corner flag while the play was ongoing at the other end of the pitch.

* * *

I may not have won anything significant as a player with Hearts but I did sample European football on several occasions. My first foray was against Paris St Germain in 1984, the first time for eight years we had had the chance to pit our wits against the cream of the Continent. I swapped the Tynecastle terraces – having watched the games against Lokomotiv Leipzig and Hamburg as a supporter – for the pitch in the Parc des Princes in Paris and a role in central midfield. I might just as well have been on the terraces that night such was the quality of the opposition. Of all the players I have faced Safet Susic was the pick of the bunch. The Yugoslavia international – who, at the age of twenty-nine, was at the peak of his career and had represented his country at the World Cup in Spain two years previously and would go on to do so again at Italia 90 – gave a master-class in France that night scoring two goals and creating the fourth as they put us to the sword.

The return leg at Tynecastle was pretty much incidental as there was no way our experienced opponents were going to throw away a four-goal lead. Nevertheless we prepared as thoroughly as we would for any European fixture and stayed over at the Marine hotel in North Berwick the night before the game. At training that day Bud Johnston informed some of the boys that he had been given a tip for a horse from one of the lads he used to play with in England and it was by all accounts a sure-fire winner. But then aren't they all? Now Willie wasn't much of a gambler and warned us from the start that he wanted nothing to do with the consequences if the horse had three legs and ended up at the gluepot factory. A couple of us went to the local newsagent after training and bought a copy of the *Racing Post* and to our amazement the nag had a tissue price of 33/1. Word spread like wildfire through the squad and it wasn't long before all the boys were aware of the tip. However, when hearing the price many felt the horse had no chance and gave it a body-swerve. But the rest of us were looking for something to relieve the boredom and decided to head to the local bookies. Not surprisingly the gentleman behind the counter at Morrison's bookmakers in North Berwick had not exactly been inundated by customers writing the name Springle on a betting slip and it was surprising that he did not respond to our collective submission of four or five slips with something along the lines of 'Are you sure this is the horse you want to back boys?' Kenny Black and I, and a couple of others, had £10 on the nag. Jimmy Bone was very secretive with his slip and to this day I have no idea of his stake, but, as you're about to find out, it was certainly more than any of his teammates had wagered. With the bets placed we fought our way through the smoke-filled chamber to join the elderly men in front of the television screen to view the race.

I don't know who gave Willie the tip but he sure knew what he was talking about. Springle travelled like a dream throughout the race, showing a devastating turn of foot in the final few furlongs to romp clear to the sheer amazement of Auld Jock and his mates standing next to us as well as ourselves. My first-ever bet and I was about to pick up £330 plus my stake.

With four of us due a total of £1,360 it wasn't the best day for the book-maker's profits, but that was just the opening salvo. Jimmy Bone had a huge grin on his face as he sauntered up to the collection point, calmly placed his betting slip face down and turned to us and winked. His smile quickly disappeared when the man behind the counter informed him there was a problem. Protesting vehemently that we had all been paid out, and so should he, Jimmy was informed there was nothing wrong with his bet. It was just that the bookie did not have enough money on the premises to cope with such a large pay out. He was handed as much money as the manager could lay his hands on and asked if he would mind accepting an IOU and coming back the next day for the balance. Jimmy agreed and the smile returned as wide as before. The sly old bugger . . .

I didn't know it at the time but the former Hibs chairman, Kenny Waugh, owned that chain of bookmakers and that made the win even sweeter. Not only did he have a shocking record in the Edinburgh derby, which resulted in us enjoying win bonuses at the expense of his team, he was also the one paying out bonuses to the Jambos for an off-the-field victory!

* * *

It's no coincidence that a lot of these tales concern events that either took place during pre-season or immediately after a campaign had ended. In 1986 the squad was in the Isle of Man for a four-team, pre-season tournament with Bohemians of Dublin, Wigan Athletic and Stoke City. We lost our opening game to Stoke and drew with Wigan. I'm sure it had nothing to do with my performances in the first two games that I was left out the team for our final match, a 3–0 win against Bohemians, but the Gaffer maybe thought otherwise. After the match against the Dubliners the players were given per-mission to let our hair down and go out for a couple of drinks as a reward for our hard work during pre-season. As you would expect most of the boys went out on the town, including Kenny Black and I, but for some reason we got back to the hotel quite early. We were aware of a noise coming from the basement so decided to investigate and found a tiny nightclub; there was a DJ playing tunes but no revellers, because the club had not long been open. Despite the lack of numbers the bar was open and, having managed to sink a few pints in town, the pair of us felt it would have been rude not to indulge further. By this stage it would be fair to say we were both bordering on ineb-riation; Blacky even had to start using his toes to count how many beers he'd had after running out of fingers. I, on the other hand, was on Planet Mackay after three or four lager shandies. Quickly realising it was impossible to make a fool of ourselves with no one else in the room, except the DJ,

Blacky asked him to put on 'The Stripper', a song by David Rose. Like a genie appearing from a lamp his wish was granted. Off came his shirt to reveal a bare, hairy yet strangely muscular torso. Off came my top to reveal a peely-wally, milk-bottle-coloured top half. We both took off our shoes to reveal, well, socks of course. Off came his trousers in time to the music; he swung them around his head then threw them over a chandelier. Not being a showman, like KB, I just unzipped my trousers and put them on a chair. We were both standing there in our pants with Kenny set to remove his when Sandy Jardine walked in . . . .

'I hope you've not been drinking,' he said.

We quickly put our clothes back on before anyone else came in and it was just as well because a family of four arrived shortly thereafter to check out the facilities. I hate to imagine what mummy and daddy would have said if their two young children had asked them what the silly men were doing!

* * *

My memory of when this escapade happened is cloudy but I do know we were on a mid-season trip to Portugal – I think it was January 1988 – and I can also tell you it had nothing to do with me. I found it hilarious nonetheless.

Our two fitness coaches Bert Logan and George McNeill were heading out to dinner one evening in their hired car – they didn't have the same curfews as the players – when they were stopped five hundred metres from the hotel by a group of boys returning from a leisurely walk. John Robertson, Wayne Foster and Kenny Black had flagged down the vehicle. After exchanging pleasantries and enquiring about their dinner destination Robbo (I'm sorry wee man if it wasn't you but that's what Mr Logan said) reached into the car and took the keys out of the ignition before launching them over a hedge and into a field with knee-high grass. The rest of the boys scampered for dear life leaving Bert and George with a car in the middle of the road, no keys, and, with dusk approaching, hee-haw chance of finding them. The vehicle was abandoned for the evening after being bumped off the road and the pair returned to the hotel to phone for a taxi but not before informing the Gaffer and Sandy Jardine of the mischief. Guess who was made to get up early the next morning and told not to return to the hotel without the keys? The boys eventually found the keys and returned them to Bert and George but it was no surprise when Robbo, Blacky and Fozzy were watched like hawks for the rest of the trip.

I also have vague recollections during that trip (Bert Logan wishes his recollections of the incident were vague as well instead of ingrained in his memory!) of seeing Bert sitting in a bar one evening and dropping my trousers, getting his attention then pressing my balls against the window and walking away. Let's just leave it there shall we?

* * *

Have you heard the one about the footballer getting placed in solitary confinement in his hotel during an end-of-season tour? Neither had I until the start of the Nineties. I was looking for a new sparring partner after Kenny Black left in the summer of 1989 and thought I'd found ideal replacements in Ian Baird and Tosh McKinlay. Three more different guys you could not meet. I was reasonably mild-mannered with an inability to handle more than two drinks, Bairdy loved a pint and had a bit of a temper while Tosh wouldn't harm a fly and was teetotal.

We were in Spain at the end of season 1991/92 letting our hair down after a successful season. Hearts finished second that year, splitting the Old Firm in the process, and we went to Mallorca determined to enjoy ourselves. Unfortunately, Ian Baird took things slightly too far one night, as did I. We were in Manos bar in Magaluf enjoying the hospitality not wisely but too well and in my drunken state I decided it would be quite funny to pee in an ashtray and throw the contents over Bairdy's head. I mentioned he had a temper. Well I was completely oblivious of it until that evening. He went absolutely berserk. He was in the middle of a twenty-four-hour, non-stop drinking binge and did not take kindly to it being interrupted by my piss running down the back of his neck. Yogi launched himself at me and held me down on the floor of the bar (quite rightly I suppose considering the circumstances) and the pair of us had to be separated. The incident didn't stop him continuing his bender; eventually we were forced to lock him in his room for his own safety! After seeing a side of Bairdy I didn't particularly like it wasn't long after he sobered up that I apologised to him in case he set on me again. The apology was accepted and we were still mates. I had learned my lesson.

* * *

My last Tynecastle tale is not strictly within the parameters of this chapter's guidelines; it did not take place when I was at the club, but it concerns my former Tynecastle teammates so that's good enough for me. Anyway it's my book and I make the rules!

In 2000 I was asked to help put together a squad of ten former Hearts players to take part in the Scottish Masters Football at Braehead. We reached the final but lost out to Rangers. Thankfully, we received an invite to compete in the following year's tournament and this squad was assembled:

Henry Smith, Allan Moore, Wayne Foster, Paul Cherry, Sandy Stewart, Gary Mackay, David Bowman, Eamonn Bannon, Neil Pointon, Kenny Black

We gained revenge for our defeat in the final the previous year in our opening match by hammering Rangers 5–2. That was followed by victory against Aberdeen then a 6–0 hammering of Celtic to secure our place in the final. Once again former Ibrox players provided the opposition in the showpiece game but this time we won by five goals to three to not only win the Scottish Masters for the first time but also to secure our place in the grand final later that year. We were fortunate that every member of the successful squad was available for the trip to London, and, courtesy of Andy Naylor at GNER who sorted us out with first-class rail travel, several of us made our way south hoping to add the British Masters title to its Scottish equivalent. Others, like Eamonn, flew down and missed one heck of a party.

I can honestly say I never had a drink before a game throughout my career, not even forty-eight hours beforehand, but that statistic was soon put to bed courtesy of a rowdy train journey to London. Things started well as we left Waverley; we promised to behave, act sensibly and prepare in the most professional manner possible. That plan went out the window by Wallyford! Bacon, eggs and beans for breakfast, washed down by two pints of lager shandy . . . and we'd only reached Dunbar. Let's just say we consumed enough alcohol to force GNER officials to radio ahead to ensure fresh supplies were brought onto the train at York. We wiped out every single can of beer and bottle of wine available on the trolley in less than two-and-a-half hours.

It should come as no surprise that my recollections of that day are pretty sketchy, although I do remember going to a rough London boozer in the evening and watching on the big screen as England hammered Germany 5–1 in Munich. The drink continued to flow and we somehow managed to gatecrash a card school in the pub. I knew from card games on the team bus that several of the Hearts boys – Robbo, Blacky, Henry and Sandy Stewart – were sharks so it was no surprise when we wiped the floor with the locals. Word quickly spread that several drunken footballers were taking quite a bit of money from pub regulars and it wasn't long before more hopefuls arrived and patiently waited for their turn. The path between the pub and the cash machine across the road was a well-trodden one as one by one they tried to knock us off our perch. But we won almost every pot. We thanked our lucky stars that the whole night was good-humoured because there are a few places where strangers taking money from locals would end up in a riot.

Most people when they are extremely drunk get put to bed by loving, yet annoyed, members of their family or by friends. I think I was poured to bed that night. It wasn't the most professional way to prepare for the grand final and our 'preparations' ensured we were found wanting when we faced mighty Liverpool in the opening match the following day. I may be wrong but something tells me the likes of Ian Rush, Jan Molby, John Barnes and Ray Houghton were not completely pissed the night before and were certainly not in a spit-and-sawdust pub playing cards.

Taking everything into account I suppose a 3–1 defeat was pretty good considering most of us were still drunk. It was a surprise that we were even able to score against Liverpool, but that was nothing to the incredulity when we proceeded to hammer Leeds United 6–2 in our other game. I hate to imagine what their players got up to the night before!

* * *

Needless to say there are many other stories I am aware of, either having been part of them or being told about them, but nearly all are X-certificate and not suitable for a book of this nature. I'm sure several former team-mates will be relieved that certain Tynecastle tales are not getting a public airing in this instance. However, the truth will out one day . . . .

10

Replacing the Irreplaceable

'The right man, the wrong time'

It was never going to be easy finding someone to replace Alex MacDonald in the managerial hotseat and whoever was chosen had a lot to live up to, at least as far as our squad were concerned. The show of defiance in September 1990 from John Robertson and I following Wallace Mercer's decision to relieve the Gaffer of his duties showed how difficult it would be to get the players onside. Between 1986 and 1990 we managed to split the Old Firm twice, finishing a highly creditable second in the table on two occasions. If that wasn't hard enough for the new man to emulate, Alex had signed every player at Tynecastle and so his successor would inherit players who were used to a routine that had been in place for many years. We were stubbornly set in our ways, in a comfort zone if you like, and that was to become problematic.

Wallace Mercer, however, was adamant he had identified the man to take Hearts to the next level and to bring silverware back to Tynecastle. That man was Joe Jordan. He had been part of the Scotland backroom staff at the World Cup at Italia 90 where he was used among his other roles as a translator, having learnt to speak Italian fluently during his two years with AC Milan in the early Eighties. Jordan was not directly involved with the national squad during the tournament but was seen by the SFA as the ideal ambassador for Scotland due to his relatively high profile in the host country. He also spent time in the months leading up to the World Cup scouting for suitable hotels close to Genoa and Turin. There was one memorable incident when the only way he was able to get to one of the SFA-suggested lodgings was by cable car. Now I am led to believe that Joe is not overly keen on heights – although he never let on to us – but it was something clearly not known to anyone at Park Gardens when he was designated for that particular recce. I believe he was none too pleased with certain members of the establishment when he returned to Glasgow to submit his findings.

Jordan was also given the role as press-liaison officer; he acted as a conduit between the SFA and the Scottish press, and impressed both sides. I'm led to believe that Wallace was unaware of Joe's involvement with the national team at the World Cup, but that all changed following a lunch hosted by the chairman, at his expense, for a dozen selected journalists in Portofino shortly after the defeat in the opening match at the hands of Costa Rica. The day concluded with Mercer – having enjoyed the fine Italian wine at the picturesque restaurant overlooking the harbour of the Mediterranean port – driving a boat back across the bay to the hacks' hotel, having earlier, with sober contemplation, steadfastly refused to even board it 'just in case'. In between times the football world was put to rights over some fine food, the cud was chewed and the name Joe Jordan was introduced to the conversation by the writers, impressed by the help given by the former Scotland striker as they went about their business. Alex MacDonald remained the manager of Hearts, but on that day a seed was sewn in the mind of Wallace Mercer that would ultimately signal the end for the Gaffer at Tynecastle.

* * *

Wallace Mercer was accused of being many things but he was always decisive. When we began the 1990/91 season with three consecutive defeats and a League Cup exit at Aberdeen he felt the time was right to close one chapter of the famous Heart of Midlothian book and start a fresh one. Having been impressed by Joe Jordan's record at Bristol City in his first managerial role, the man's ability to work wonders with a restricted budget and by what the journalists in Italy had said about him Mercer was determined to get his man. Wallace sought the advice of luminaries like Alex Ferguson and Kenny Dalglish and got a positive vibe, although they warned him that he would find it hard to persuade Jordan to swap life in Bristol for a return to the country of his birth. The chairman also believed the time was right to bring in foreign players and felt Jordan was the right man for this task (even though Joe never did sign anyone from the Continent). As well as being thorough and decisive, I forgot to say Wallace was also determined, and, more often than not, got what he wanted.

My 360th match for Heart of Midlothian – the 3–1 defeat at Ibrox on 8 September 1990 – was also Alex MacDonald's last game in charge.

Wallace Mercer did not waste any time in appointing Joe Jordan as the Gaffer's replacement and the former Scotland international faced a baptism of fire in his opening fixture: the first Edinburgh derby of the season and a trip to Easter Road for the first time since the chairman had tried to merge the two teams that summer. Joe made four changes to *his* team in a bid to inject some much needed impetus and youthful zest – thankfully, I kept my place – with Craig Levein and Jimmy Sandison coming into the side at the expense of Dave McPherson and Derek Ferguson while youngsters Alan McLaren and George Wright replaced the more experienced duo of Walter Kidd and Dave McCreery. It worked. Robbo scored twice and Craig Levein was also on target as the Joe Jordan era got off to a winning start.

The new manager spent the first few weeks trying to mould both team tactics and training and he was not frightened to dispense a quiet, yet firm, discipline. We lost only one of his first six games in charge – a 3–0 reverse against Celtic at Parkhead – and we also secured a place in the second round of the UEFA Cup following an impressive aggregate victory over Russian side FC Dnipro. An injury picked up in training meant I started only two of those six matches but I was pleased to be selected as a substitute for the second leg against Dnipro at Tynecastle, before regaining a starting jersey for the 1–1 draw against Motherwell at the start of October. By this time Frank Connor, Jordan's assistant manager, was also making his mark.

The appointment of Frank as his assistant was a very shrewd move by Joe Jordan. A man who was up there in honesty and integrity with Alex MacDonald – I can pay him no higher compliment – and a spitting image for the Reverend Ian Paisley! He was firmly of the old school and warned us from day one not to call him 'Rev'. We didn't, at least not to his face. Frank demanded high standards of discipline, fitness, cleanliness and, most importantly, respect for him and for everyone at the club. He had worked with Jock Wallace, as well as being his own man at Raith Rovers between 1986 and 1990, and had experience in the game that money couldn't buy. He was also an important buffer between the manager and players and excelled in that role. Joe Jordan was officially the manager and that's exactly what he did: he managed. He would take the training but we hardly saw him otherwise. If Frank ever took training we didn't see Joe at all that day. I'm not entirely sure if Jordan knew exactly how good Frank Connor was going to be when he appointed him; he would have been well aware of his qualities, but I don't know if he realised the positive impact Frank had on the players. He was the perfect foil for Joe, always in the right place at the right time and always with the perfect response in any given situation, whether it was an arm round the shoulder or a joke. Even now when I bump into Mr Connor there's a warmth that emanates from him; not a huge amount of people have that and it's due to his desire to get as much out of life as possible.

It didn't take Joe Jordan long to stamp his authority on the club. Nor did it take him long to realise we were missing a Joe Jordan type in attack. Robbo, John Colquhoun, Crabbo and Iain Ferguson were all decent goalscorers but he felt they were too similar. He wanted a presence up front so agreed to sell Ferguson in December 1990 before splashing out £350,000 for six-foot Middlesbrough striker Ian Baird the following month. That was the sum total of his signings that season as he was prepared to give those of us already at the club a chance to prove our worth. However, after a disappointing fifth-place finish it was all-change in the summer of 1991.

Dave McCreery (free transfer), John Colquhoun (£400,000) and Jimmy Sandison (£100,000) all departed while midfielder John Millar (free), Northern Irish winger Steve Penney (free) and former Manchester United defender Graeme Hogg (£200,000) were brought in, with only Hogg costing us any money. JC was certainly a loss and I had my doubts at the time if we were replacing him with players of similar quality. Those doubts were to prove correct, although the addition of John Millar certainly proved to be a masterstroke. Having added to his squad and let others leave, the pre-season in 1991 gave Joe an opportunity to really stamp his authority. It worked. His first full season in charge proved to be very successful and we managed to split the Old Firm for the third time since 1986.

Joe Jordan the manager was not at all what I expected. As a youngster I remembered watching his goals for Leeds and Manchester United and was sure he would incorporate that bustling, physical style of play when it came to management. I was doing him a disservice, of course, and my expectations could not have been further from the truth. He may have scored eleven goals for Scotland, several courtesy of his all-action approach, but when Jordan became a manager his approach to the tactical side of the game was thoughtful and methodical, with aggression way down the pecking order. Nor was he a man who sought confrontation or one who showed his anger in public. In fact he was very self-assured and confident, which no doubt came from having played at the top level for so long.

I can understand why Joe's managerial style was so successful at Bristol City. He made players far more aware of the technical and tactical side of the game and was in many ways way ahead of his time. He tried to implement a similar structure at Hearts – Alex and Sandy often spoke about tactical issues but we seldom worked on them at training – and his approach was relatively successful, although I think he would have achieved more with a group of players that hadn't been so used to the ways of the previous manager. Joe did a decent job at Tynecastle given the circumstances, although I wish we had bought more into his methods during the early part of his tenure. I can understand why we didn't; we were used to a certain routine and when a footballer is used to something and comfortable with it change is not easily embraced. Jordan was trying to implement new ideas and a new style aimed at taking us to the next level and designed to help us challenge for silverware on a regular basis. He was very close to taking us to that next stage – competing with the Old Firm, splitting them on a regular basis and possibly even mounting a significant title challenge – but we were too set in our ways to adapt. With hindsight, he was probably the right man for the job but at the wrong time.

There is no doubt Joe Jordan had many first-rate managerial qualities and an excellent tactical brain but I cannot thank him for playing me as a wing-back for so long. I'm sure he knew it wasn't my favoured position. This boy's body was not designed to spend part of his career making lung-bursting runs up and down the right touchline, blowing out of his arse in the process. My preferred position was in central midfield, supporting the strikers. However, with his chosen 3-5-2 formation, Joe knew he had the personnel to take control of games, and that team was one to be reckoned with during his first full season of 1991/92. We won twenty-seven of our forty-four league games and finished second in the Premier League, just nine points behind champions Rangers. I think part of the reason for our relative success that year, like 1985/86 in a way, was our team spirit and the fact that there were no superstars in our ranks. I became good friends with Ian Baird – the word 'bampot' was invented for him – while John Millar was a cracking player for us, playing a similar role to Colin Cameron and Paul Hartley in later years. We hadn't always had a goalscoring threat from midfield but John brought that to the team. It was certainly an achievement to split the Old Firm once again, but we failed to build on that success and less than twelve months later Wallace Mercer would have to look for another manager of Heart of Midlothian.

* * *

Joe Jordan was a single-minded and determined character. He made decisions because he believed they were in the best interests of the football club. It wasn't a popularity contest for him. That was best summed up on the first day of October 1992, one of the saddest occasions for me as a footballer. Dundee United wanted to sign Scott Crabbe and were prepared to throw in winger Allan Preston, along with just over £200,000, to persuade Hearts to part company with the popular striker. Joe had already identified a lack of width in our team and gave his blessing to the deal. Crabbo is four years younger than me but someone I became really close to, partly due to the fact that he, too, is a massive Hearts fan. He was brought up as a supporter, went on to play for the club for more than six years and scored a total of fifty-two goals, but his long association came to an abrupt end when he was forced to swap Tynecastle for Tannadice. Sentiment did not come into it as far as Joe was concerned.

He didn't know it at the time, but Scott Crabbe's appearance as a substitute (for John Robertson) in the first leg of the UEFA Cup first round tie against Slavia Prague in Czechoslovakia was to be his last European involvement with Hearts. He was transferred the day after we secured our place in the second round, courtesy of a memorable 4–2 victory at Tynecastle. I scored the second goal that night in front of one of the most raucous Gorgie atmospheres I can remember. That 4–3 aggregate victory earned us a tie against Standard Liege, but we made the trip to Belgium for the second leg with a mountain to climb – Belgian international midfielder Alain Bettagno scored the only goal of the game in the first leg at Tynecastle to put our opponents firmly in the driving seat. In the return leg at the Sclessin stadium, Joe Jordan decided to deploy me as the spare man, just off the front two of John Robertson and Ian Ferguson; it was a role I relished but one I had not played regularly since my teens. We played well that night and were unlucky to lose to a Marc Wilmots goal, going out 2–0 on aggregate.

The manager was clearly happy with our formation in Belgium, and the way we played, so it was same again for the Edinburgh derby at Tynecastle three days later, with Ian Baird returning from injury to take the place of Ian Ferguson in the only change to the side. Once again Joe wanted me to support the front two – this time Robbo and Bairdy – and it worked as the latter scored the only goal of the game after just seventeen minutes. However, not long after the goal Gordon Hunter proceeded to break my jaw with his forearm. Although he would swear to this day it was an accident, it didn't seem or feel that way to me. At half-time, although in severe pain, Dr Melvin gave me the green light to continue. He made a beeline for me at the end of the match and I wasn't even off the pitch when he said, 'I'm glad we got you through that with no more damage; it could have been quite serious.' As it turned out it was serious, the pain was excruciating and I was to be out of action for three weeks.

I went to Murrayfield hospital on the Tuesday for an operation, therefore missing that evening's Premier League match at Partick, and did not find out the result until I was woken by Joe Jordan the following morning. He had come in on his way into Tynecastle to see how I was recovering from the op. My memories of his visit remain hazy although I do remember waking up with a swollen and sore face – the effects of the painkillers I was on to numb the pain had worn off – and hearing him tell me we had drawn 1–1 at Firhill the night before. I am also convinced he said to me, 'and we would have won if you had been playing'. To this day I don't know if that part of the conversation was a dream; it's not the kind of thing I would have expected him to say, although I would love to ask him if he did say it.

* * *

There's been a lot of coverage over the last few years about the so-called darker side of football, whether it's the Italian match-fixing scandal involving the likes of Juventus, Lazio, Fiorentina and AC Milan or the report by Lord Stevens into alleged illegal payments in football. Hand on heart (excuse the pun) I can honestly say that I have never witnessed any wrongdoing during my time in the game, although I can understand if Hearts supporters felt there was something amiss at Brockville on the first day of May 1993.

It was the fourth-last game of the season and a UEFA Cup spot was still up for grabs, despite a dreadful run of form that had seen us fail to win any of the previous five league matches (there was also the small matter of a Scottish Cup semi-final defeat to Rangers) before heading for Falkirk. We had been fourth in the table and in pole position to clinch a place in Europe prior to that dreadful run but had been overtaken by Dundee United, and they were two points ahead of us going into that set of fixtures. We were up against a Falkirk side fighting for their lives at the foot of the table, while United faced Partick Thistle at Tannadice. They duly beat the Jags by three goals to one while we capitulated at Brockville on a day that was by some distance my most embarrassing as a professional.

I spent three days in bed with the cold leading up to that game but got a phone call from Frank Connor on the Friday morning asking if I would be available for selection at Brockville. I said I was struggling, but so, he said, were the team. I told him I would rest for twenty-four hours and then report for duty at lunchtime on Saturday. If I had known how the match was going to pan out I wouldn't even have answered the phone. I was about to be part of a group of players that shamed the name of Heart of Midlothian Football Club.

It doesn't matter which team provides the opposition, no Hearts side should ever lose 6–0 to anyone, never mind a club at the foot of the table. I'd love to be able to find excuses for the result but the harsh truth is that there weren't any. Were injury and illness possible reasons? Not when you see the team that Hearts fielded:

Smith, McLaren, Snodin, Levein, Mackay, van de Ven, Robertson, Ferguson, Baird, Berry, Bannon

Six players with international caps for Scotland were in our starting line-up. So what went wrong? There were rumours that some of the lads in the squad were no longer playing for Joe Jordan and were not pulling their weight. But the only two people who could answer that would be Joe and Frank Connor and if they felt that was the case then why did they select players they felt were not interested. There were a lot of good times during Joe's reign, there were also difficult times; on that afternoon, both individually and collectively, we let down not only the management team but also the supporters and everyone associated with the club.

It wasn't long before rumours abounded that we had chucked the game to get Joe sacked. I can relate to that given our performance at Brockville, but there is no evidence to support these accusations, although I was unaware of any negativity among the players leading up to the match due to my absence from training. Yes there were guys who didn't get on with the manager but I don't believe for one moment that it's possible for any professional footballer to down tools and not give his all once he steps over that white line, because it would be far too obvious. A player will never admit to 'not being interested'. However, if there are five or six who, for whatever reason, are not on form then it becomes impossible for a side to win because the others cannot lift the team on their own. Never mind five or six playing poorly at Brockville; that day, you would have found it difficult to name any of our players who performed to a satisfactory level.

I am pretty certain there was not one player in a Hearts jersey that day who didn't try, but when confidence is low and the team is not getting results, and there happens to be a bit of negativity in the changing room, then either one piece of bad luck or the concession of the opening goal can result in a swift downward spiral. As it was Falkirk led 2–0 at half-time but it wasn't until the third goal went in that some of our heads went down. Three became four, four became five and five quickly became six.

It's easy to suggest that Falkirk had more to play for than us but it's also easy to dismiss that as a factor. Yes, their victory lifted them above Airdrieonians and off the foot of the table but we also had every incentive to get maximum points: if we'd won at Brockville we would have been only two points behind Dundee United in the race for Europe, with three matches still to play, including a game in hand over them.

The 6–0 defeat at the hands of Falkirk turned out to be the one-hundred-and-forty-third and last game in charge for Jordan and there were a few relieved players when he was given his marching orders by Wallace Mercer, even although he had a very respectable 48.25 per cent win ratio. There is no doubt things were not right at the football club at that time. There was unrest in the dressing room, while the fans were becoming increasingly concerned at the sudden dip in form, to the extent that around three hundred turned their back on the match at Brockville in favour of a trip to Fir Park to watch the reserves attempt to win the league. The performance of our second string was the only shining light in a relatively uneventful season and although reserve coach Sandy Clark's side could only manage a goalless draw in Lanarkshire that afternoon, when a win would have secured the title, they only had to wait another few days to be crowned champions when nearest challengers Dundee United were beaten in a midweek fixture.

The biggest difficulty we had under Joe Jordan was in trying to adapt to his methods. There was a sea change in the way that he managed compared with Alex and Sandy. He altered the way we trained; we did a lot more tactical shadow work in the week leading up to a game and a lot of it was highly innovative. However, professional footballers are a stubborn bunch and don't like change and when we were forced to alter our habits it took that little bit longer to adapt to a new way of doing things.

Joe Jordan also brought fifteen new players to the club in two-and-a-half years, but the majority of them were no better than those already there. The likes of Ian Baird, Glynn Snodin and Peter van de Ven played more often than not, but guys like Steve Penney, Gary Williams, John Sharples and Adrian Boothroyd were bit-part players and did not turn out regularly. The nucleus of the team consisted of those who had performed well for Alex McDonald.

Don't get me wrong, there were many good times with Jordan and his methods – although not universally popular in the dressing room as time wore on – were very nearly successful, particularly in season 1991/92 when we split the Old Firm but couldn't quite catch Rangers. During that campaign, when we were pushing the Ibrox side very strongly at the top of the league, the rumour mill suggested that Joe asked Wallace Mercer for money to sign Stan Collymore. It was reported the manager felt that Stan, available from Crystal Palace for around £150,000, was the last piece in the jigsaw, but, ultimately, nothing came of it.

Season 1992/93 was up-and-down but when results took a turn for the worse a lot of pressure was shifted onto the shoulders of Frank Connor. Frank was a bubbly and effervescent character while Joe was a more studious type who, to my eye, wanted to distance himself from the players. I found that difficult because of the relationship I had had with the Gaffer. Of course it didn't stop me giving my all. I had another reason for working hard; I had to master the new role he gave me as a wing back when he changed the shape of the team and went to three at the back. The difficulties arose near the end of March 1993 after the Edinburgh derby win against Hibs when John Robertson, who else, scored the only goal of the game at Tynecastle. We then went six matches without a victory prior to the trip to Brockville and it was clear there were problems. It can be argued that we were not lifting ourselves as we should have but I think it was more a case of him not being able to lift us.

Joe Jordan had his own way of doing things. He'd picked up this vast knowledge from Scotland, England and Italy and tried to implement it on a group of players who were used to a simpler way of life. There was a lot of speculation about his future leading up to the game against Falkirk – Wallace Mercer had seen the warning signs in previous games – but any suggestion that we deliberately chucked that game to get Jordan sacked is, in my opinion, wide of the mark. I got out of my sick bed to play in the match – I wish I hadn't – so I would take offence if anyone questioned my commitment to the cause that afternoon. Were some of my other teammates giving the same effort as me that day? That's a question only they can answer.

11

Tynecastle Teammates

'Just because you work with people doesn't mean you have to like them . . .'

There were never any cliques during my time with Hearts and I think that had a significant part to play in the excellent team spirit I experienced for most of my career at Tynecastle. There were teammates I was a lot friendlier with than others but try telling me that's not the case with colleagues in any workplace.

* * *

I've been very close to Kenny Black for a long time. We became firm friends when he joined Hearts and he was even best man at my wedding. Our paths first crossed in 1977 when Salvesen Boys Club faced Gairdoch in a Scottish Juvenile Cup tie. We came up against each other on a number of other occasions, playing juvenile football as well as representing our schools in national competitions, but the friendship didn't flourish until he arrived at Tynecastle. Kenny is somebody with no agenda. What you see is what you get. He is a selfless person who always puts others first and has been a good mate to me over the years. The only testing time was when I was made manager at Airdrie – Kenny was still there as a player – and I decided to bring in Walter Kidd as my assistant. Looking back maybe I should have considered retaining my best man and offered him a player-coach role or even the job as assistant manager. But I made a hasty decision – I wouldn't necessarily say it was the wrong one – to bring Walter on board without contemplating the possibility of involving KB. My judgement that because my legs had gone then his must have gone too was perhaps ill-considered. Having quickly apologised to Kenny the matter was forgotten, although he eventually decided to try his luck as a player with Raith Rovers and went to Starks Park along with Peter Hetherston and John McVeigh, who had been the Gaffer's assistant at New Broomfield. To this day Kenny is excellent company on a night out, of which we have a few in both Scotland and England because his family live in Sheffield following his spell as coach at Leicester City. His patter has never changed from the first night I went through to Rainbow Rocks in Stirling and he welcomed me with a glass of champagne, while standing there with his trousers round his ankles!

I also consider Walter Kidd a good friend while Sandy Clark and I got on well as he was very close to Walter. I've been very fortunate that the loyalty of my close friends has never wavered and I hope that I have reciprocated. Over the years I've known 'Zico' I don't think I could have asked for a more loyal work colleague and friend. I watched him playing for Hearts in the late Seventies and he was the only member of that team that I played with for any length of time. He survived the changes at Tynecastle in the early Eighties and that was testament to his desire to succeed under Alex MacDonald and Sandy Jardine. He also gave me great protection on the pitch, and occasionally had to give me some protection off it as well. Kenny Black and Walter Kidd: great professionals and two people you would want alongside you in the trenches.

John Robertson is the best footballer I have ever played with. I can't speak about the qualities of Conn, Bauld and Wardhaugh because I never played with them; I only heard stories about how good they were from my grandfather. In my opinion the Wee Man deserves the title of Best Hearts Player of Recent Times during the last forty or so years. It was fitting he was part of the squad that lifted the Scottish Cup at Celtic Park in 1998. There's no doubt he deserved to win more than sixteen caps and be given the opportunity to add to his three goals for Scotland but Robbo was unfortunate that, at his peak, there was an abundance of quality Scottish strikers – Ally McCoist and Maurice Johnston to name but two – on the scene.

The Wee Man has an unerring ability to remember facts, stats and goals not only from his career but also from the careers of others. That is just as well because my memory is like a sieve. His memory served him well when we were in the Isle of Man on a pre-season tour at the end of July 1986. He went for a walk and when he came back to the hotel he informed us he had been assaulted and had had his money taken off him. The story goes if it was £23.56 he had in his pocket that was the exact amount he reported stolen. He was that thorough.

Robbo got on with everybody at Hearts but I wouldn't say there was one player he was closer to than anyone else. We had a great understanding and I look back with pride on the goals we engineered from a situation that may have looked pre-planned to the casual observer. Some people now call the move 'the takeover'. The ball would be thrown in to him in the box, he'd hold it up and I'd come across him and take it off his feet. Sometimes it resulted in a penalty and on other occasions we managed to snatch a goal. We never practised it in training; it was done off the cuff and probably stemmed from the fact we had played a lot of football together from a young age and were almost able to read each other's minds. No matter how it came about it was very difficult for the opposition to stop.

John Robertson still has a mystique about him because of what he has achieved. I speak from the heart, sometimes without thinking, but Robbo is more guarded and that is something I think people are respected for. The only time we both got our knuckles wrapped was when we spoke out about Wallace Mercer's decision to sack Alex MacDonald. Because he was worth more than me in the transfer market I am sure Robbo got a bigger apology from Wallace when the dust had settled.

I also formed an unlikely alliance with Tosh McKinlay during his time at Tynecastle between 1989 and 1994, despite the fact we were like chalk and cheese. He was Celtic-daft, a Roman Catholic and didn't take a drink; I was Hearts-daft, a Protestant, liked a drink but just couldn't handle it! Despite being from the opposite side of the religious divide – as was Walter Kidd – I refused to let that get in the way of our friendship. Why should it? I'm delighted steps have been taken over the last few years to combat sectarianism, but it still amazes me how scouts at juvenile games in the Seventies and Eighties could live with themselves having to ask a football coach what school the kid they were watching went to and whether the young lad was from a Protestant or Catholic background.

I enjoyed Tosh's company, while my ex-wife Vicky became pretty close with his wife Yvonne. It shows that two people, despite having different lives and beliefs, can get on well. Tosh, despite being in direct opposition on that fateful day at Dens Park in 1986, is still a very good friend. He's got a wonderfully dry sense of humour and is one of these guys I won't see for a year but when he or I call up for a chat it's like we've never been out of each other's lives.

I think a lot of the guys I developed friendships with in football had the same outlook in life as the Gaffer. I had loads of respect for Jimmy Bone and Stewart MacLaren but the slightly older teammate I got on best with in the early years was Willie Johnston. What he achieved in his career was immense but he was, and still is, a gem.

Sandy Jardine was never someone I ever got that close to but he was another old head the youngsters were able to turn to for advice once Bud Johnston and Jimmy Bone moved on. He was the perfect foil for Alex MacDonald and set high standards on and off the pitch. Sandy also had a huge impact on Craig Levein's career while helping to nurture other young talent at the club. It was typical of his professionalism that he was voted SPFA player of the year in 1986 at the age of thirty-seven, a reward for keeping his body in excellent condition. He also became one of only a handful of British footballers to play more than a thousand times in the senior game, a milestone he celebrated at Hearts. Sandy's family held a small party for him on the day he reached this great milestone and all the players went up to his house in Liberton to acknowledge his proud achievement.

Sandy was the bad cop, or the more serious cop, in his partnership with Doddie, who was the bubblier of the two, at least that's how it was with me. If I got a dressing down it was from Sandy and not Alex; the Gaffer was the one who picked me up again. One of the many regrets I have from *that* season was that our failure to win the league probably cost Alex and Sandy the chance to become the management team at Rangers, where they had made their names as players. I felt they deserved the opportunity to manage on a bigger stage, although I was delighted they stayed on at Tynecastle.

It was 1975, a long time ago, when Sandy Jardine, along with Jim Brown, presented me with a winner's medal at Balgreen primary school and it's amazing to think I went on to play alongside him at Tynecastle. Sandy, like me, was a former pupil at Balgreen and Tynecastle High and I used to dream of emulating him and becoming a professional. My dream, for once, came true.

I remain good friends with another two massive Jambos, Scott Crabbe and Jimmy Sandison, and it's great they are still involved on match days with the club they love, carrying out ambassadorial duties in the Gorgie Suite. Both men invariably attend away matches with their kids, maroon scarves around their necks.

Gary Locke – the most straightforward lad I've ever had the pleasure to know – and I share an undivided love for our football club while Gary Naysmith provided me with one of my most humbling moments as a professional. Handed his first start for Hearts at the age of just seventeen due to a shortage of players – Neil Pointon, David Weir, Pasquale Bruno and Paul Ritchie had all been sent off at Ibrox the previous Saturday – he belied his tender years to produce a man-of-the-match performance against Celtic in our 1–0 victory in the Coca Cola Cup quarter-final (our emergency signing Andy Thorn was reportedly paid £5,000 for that one game). As I was leaving Tynecastle I noticed Gary standing at the corner of McLeod Street and Gorgie Road. Vicky and I offered to give him a lift back to Loanhead and as we were driving I noticed in the rear-view mirror that he had a big smile on his face.

'No wonder you're smiling mate,' I said to him, 'I thought you were outstanding tonight.'

'Yeah, it was fun, but I'm also happy because now I'll get to buy mum an expensive new fireplace,' he replied.

The young man went on to explain to us he thought there was an outside chance of him playing and had told his mum of his hopes when they were out shopping on the Sunday. She had been looking at fireplaces and had her eye on two; one was cheap, the other more expensive. Gary had promised her that if he was selected to play against Celtic and pocketed a win bonus he would buy her the more expensive fireplace. Here was a youngster who had made his first start for Hearts just hours before, beaten Celtic after extra-time and won the man-of-the-match award yet Gary Naysmith was more excited about getting home to tell his family he would be splashing out on a new fireplace. It's no surprise to me that despite representing his country on thirty-eight occasions and playing at the highest level in England, Gary has never changed as a person; he still puts other people first. He is the perfect example of how a professional footballer should conduct himself and an ideal role model for youngsters.

As far as other teammates are concerned Henry Smith was a bit of a loner, in the nicest possible sense, simply because he got on well with most of us and decided against being part of any dressing-room factions. He still holds the record for the most number of accents used in one sentence without even knowing he's doing it!

Two other teammates at Hearts, Craig Levein and John Colquhoun were, and still are, very close to each other but unfortunately the same cannot be said of Craig and me. There are some people in life you get on with and others you don't and I would put Levein into the latter category. You have to work with people but you don't have to be their best friend. Personality clashes occur in every walk of life but I must stress that any problems – which were reasonably infrequent during our time as teammates – never affected us on the pitch. But away from the football club we chose to spend time in the company of others.

The years since our playing days have not brought Craig Levein and I any closer; in fact we no longer speak. One or two things have happened down the years that have caused our relationship to deteriorate and I believe it is highly unlikely we will ever be on speaking terms again. I won't lose any sleep over it and I am certain that he won't either. I have never been someone who lacks an opinion although I don't intentionally try to stir the shit; I am passionate, especially when it comes to Hearts. I am sure there are more than a few people out there who have taken offence at some of my remarks. One of them was Craig Levein, following my response to his comments at the press conference prior to the Edinburgh derby of October 2001.

He had apparently said to the media when discussing the upcoming match at Easter Road that 'it was worth three points like every other game' and he saw no reason why his players should try any harder against Hibernian. He expected full commitment from his team in every game and argued that if they were able to give more when facing their local rivals then why couldn't they put in that same effort every week. I can understand his reasoning with regards to commitment but I did not echo his sentiments about the Edinburgh derby being just another game and pretty much said so the following day during a radio commentary (Hibernian beat Hearts 2–1). I said Craig Levein was out of order for suggesting the fixture 'was just another three points'. Somebody was obviously listening on Craig's behalf and told him the details of my remarks. Let's just say my former teammate wasn't best pleased with me . . . .

It has always been my belief that unless Hearts are striving to win things on a regular basis then the four most important matches of the season are the Edinburgh derbies. Craig Levein had a similar mentality to Sandy Jardine in that it was the same three points awarded for a victory against Hibernian as it was for a win against Partick Thistle or St Mirren. Although factually correct, that was the outlook of people who were not born into a football club and had to acquire their affection for it.

Maybe I attached too much importance to games against Hibs during my playing career but for me they were special occasions and deserved to be treated as such. I think any Hearts player who has been in a dressing room, either at Tynecastle or Easter Road, and has just savoured victory in an Edinburgh derby will concur. Whether it was being part of the two long unbeaten records in the Eighties and Nineties, experiencing the joy of Wayne Foster slamming the ball between Jim Leighton's legs, the three sensational matches against Hibernian in season 2002/03 or going to their home and spoiling their CIS Cup-winning party, games against our local rivals are always extra special. Craig Levein has his thoughts; I have mine.

* * *

Sunday, 8 September 2002

There were not many people who outlasted my stay with Hearts but one person who did so was our wonderful physiotherapist Mr Alan Rae, a real gentleman with a dry sense of humour and a quick wit. Alan began life at Hearts on a part-time basis, juggling his job at the Edinburgh Royal Infirmary with helping out at Tynecastle before joining the club full-time in the mid-Eighties and staying there until packing up his sponge and retiring in the summer of 2005. Not many players spend ten years at the same club these days, meaning that testimonials are now rare events. I was fortunate enough to have mine in 1991, when Everton provided the opposition at Tynecastle, but there is no such reward for long-serving members of the backroom staff. To put this anomaly right the Federation of Hearts Supporters Clubs came up with the idea of rewarding Alan Rae for his sterling service with a lunch in his honour in the Gorgie Suite. I was delighted to contribute to the occasion by purchasing a table at the lunch, while Craig Levein was one of the special guests invited to dine alongside Alan at the top table. The afternoon was a huge success with plenty of money raised for the guest of honour and credit for that must go to the Federation. The drink flowed freely throughout the afternoon, rather too freely at my table, given my inability to handle more than a single glass of lemonade. That was to lead to a problem.

Having drunk not wisely but too well I approached the top table and offered a handshake to Craig Levein in a bid to let bygones be bygones. We were never going to be best mates but I wanted to offer an olive branch. My clear impression was that Craig ignored my handshake, which I thought was rude; in fact it made my blood boil. It also told me he wasn't interested in mending bridges, which, of course, is his prerogative. If the roles were reversed I'm not saying I would have shaken his hand but I'm sure I would have at least acknowledged his presence. With hindsight maybe I was to blame for putting us both in an awkward situation. Had I been sober there is no way I would have approached him so once again my inability to handle more than two shandies got me into a fine mess. But I didn't lose any sleep over what happened; it is simply a case of learning from your mistakes and moving on.

There was just under a year between the Edinburgh-derby comments and the Alan Rae appreciation lunch and it took a further eighteen months before our paths crossed again. It came at the end of April 2004, less than six weeks after the Federations of Hearts Supporter Clubs and the Heart of Midlothian Supporters Trust launched the Save Our Hearts campaign. A journalist from the *Edinburgh Evening News* had approached me looking to write a story about my involvement in the campaign. As well as discussing the part I had to play I also took the opportunity provided to use the article as a vehicle to try and remove Chris Robinson from the club. I called on supporters not to buy season tickets while Robinson remained in office as chief executive; some may see this as disloyal but I will never regret those comments. Robinson, in my view, was taking the club to oblivion so why should fans buy into his plans?

I've been asked many times if I thought what I said in the *Evening News* was naïve and reckless, as Craig Levein later claimed. But the people who really knew me, and knew how big a part the club played in my life, understood why I had taken this stance. The disappointing thing for me on this occasion was that Craig Levein was also well aware of my feelings for Hearts but, in discussion with the powers that be at Tynecastle I'm sure, a decision was taken severely to criticise my article. The following day – during a press conference prior to a league match against Dundee United at Tannadice – Levein told journalists:

> I was incensed to read that Gary Mackay had effectively been encouraging people not to buy season tickets. In my time here, the players that have pulled on a jersey have done nothing but their best and it's been difficult to tell some of those guys that we can't afford to keep them. If fans don't buy season tickets, it will come out of the football budget and I might have to tell more players that we can't renew their contracts or ask them to take wage cuts so it's a disgraceful and reckless comment to make because it's only me and the players who'll be hurt by this. Gary has done a lot of talking recently and a lot of it has been representative of what the supporters think. My fear is that people will think this is too.

Levein then claimed in the press conference that the manner in which fans had protested against the chief executive had, until that point, been successful because it had not affected the playing staff. 'There's been a significant change in board policy as a result of the demonstrations and that, to me, is a significant victory,' he insisted. Fair enough, he was entitled to his opinion, but the 'significant victory' he was referring to didn't change the fact that Robinson remained in charge.

His final broadside to the assembled media (who had turned up expecting to preview the Dundee United match but ended up going away with headlines of a different sort) related to Graeme Weir, his striker but also my client, and how the youngster may have lost out in the long run because of my tactics. 'I'd like to take Gary Mackay into the office when I have to tell a young player that they aren't getting a new contract at Hearts because of the money situation,' Levein said. 'Gary was a player himself one time and he had a family and a mortgage to pay. That's why it's disgraceful that he is doing something like this which could, in all likelihood, affect my budget.'

Continuing to lay it on thick he added:

> How is he going to feel if he comes to me next year asking for more money for Graeme Weir and I have to tell him that we're going to have to free him? How will he explain that to the player and his

family? I don't know what I would think if I was Weir. He is represented by Gary and his contract is up next year. If I have to tell Graham: 'I'm sorry son, you aren't getting a new deal because season-ticket sales are down,' then how is that looking after your client? We aren't playing games here; we're talking about people's livelihoods. I've had to sit in the office over the last two years telling people they can't get new contracts and I can't understand why, as an ex-player and manager, he would choose to say something like this. It's a non-sense, and it's now up to Gary to make amends for his comments.

All credit to Craig Levein. He played his part to perfection when given a platform and ensured the newspapers had a back-page headline the following morning. I had my say and he had his. In my view he knew my comments were not designed to have an adverse affect on Graham Weir but used the opportunity to milk the situation for all it was worth and probably had the last laugh if the outcome was judged on column inches in the press.

We are two completely different people, I accept that, but have no problem with it. Shortly after Craig was appointed manager of Hearts he branded some of the players 'thieves' for picking up their wages following a dismal performance against Aberdeen at Pittodrie in January 2001. He also promised to make their lives 'as miserable as hell' after cancelling their mid-season holiday. Craig chose to adopt an outspoken approach at the start of his tenure but that was his choice and doesn't make it wrong, although it's not something I would necessarily have done.

That's another difference between us. Those comments were probably thought out before being delivered; he is after all a studious and meticulous individual. I, on the other hand, don't normally think before I open my mouth and prefer to speak from the heart. I have no regrets that the relationship deteriorated.

* * *

Finally, I thought it would be fun to jot down a 'Best XI' from those Hearts players I was fortunate to share the pitch with since making my debut in 1980 and also a 'Best XI' from those players I watched as a supporter prior to joining the club as a player.

Best XI (I played with): 4–3–3 formation

There were several former teammates who were close to inclusion in my team, but at the end of the day these are the eleven guys I played alongside between 1980 and 1997 who have been selected for 'Mackay's Marvels'.

1 Gilles Rousset

A very talented goalkeeper who recovered from his mistake in the 1996 Scottish Cup final to produce a man-of-the-match performance against the same opposition when Hearts beat Rangers in the final at Parkhead in 1998. Away from football, one of the nicest guys you could meet.

2 Walter Kidd

A resilient full-back who gave his all in every game he played and was also someone not to be messed with. A true friend then; a true friend now.

3 Tosh McKinlay

Unfortunately for Tosh it took a move to Celtic for him to receive international recognition with Scotland when everyone at Hearts knew he should have been called up while playing at Tynecastle. His delivery into the box from the left was unsurpassed. A top lad.

4 Craig Levein

A top, top player with Hearts who deservedly played for Scotland at the World Cup in Italy in 1990. He would undoubtedly have won many more caps for his country and most probably have gone on to bigger and better things had he not suffered two serious injuries.

5 Sandy Jardine (captain)

Achieved so much in the game before he came to Hearts yet remained an outstanding player, a huge influence and a superb example to all the youngsters at Tynecastle. A true gentleman.

6 Kenny Black

Great left peg, great fitness, great competitor and a great football brain. Regularly covered to allow Tosh to make runs forward and provide delivery into the box. Also retains one or two secrets about me that he maintains will never be aired in public . . .

7 Steve Fulton

Technically as good a footballer as I played with. I remember one day after lunch at Tynecastle that one of the youngsters got up having left some food on his plate. The lad hadn't even left the room when Baggio devoured the remaining morsels, having already eaten all of his lunch. He seemed surprised when I questioned him, and replied 'You mean you don't do that as well when you're in the house? I eat all the kids' food so the wife doesn't feel bad about her cooking!' An outstanding player.

8 Colin Cameron

At his prime the best box-to-box player in Scotland – always seemed to be in the right place at the right time, with an uncanny ability to snatch vital goals. He was bought from Raith Rovers and handled the transition to a bigger club with aplomb.

9 Sandy Clark

If I was only able to select one man alongside me in the trenches it would have to be Sandy. Had an unbelievable ability to fend off defenders and also got his fair share of goals. He played a huge part in my football development, and that of Robbo's.

10 John Robertson

Robbo had a wonderful knack as a goal scorer. Although one or two of his managers said he didn't work hard enough there are very few players a boss would develop his attacking formation around. Robbo was one of the select few. His goals were so important to Hearts. The best footballer I ever played with.

11 John Colquhoun

Got his fair share of goals for a wide man and also possessed an excellent delivery into the box, which Sandy undoubtedly benefited from on a number of occasions. He was quick, sharp and had a good football brain.

Manager: Alex MacDonald, the Gaffer

Best XI (I watched): 4–3–3 formation

1 Jim Cruickshank

The best in a long history of excellent Hearts goalkeepers. He wasn't the tallest keeper around but made up for his lack of inches with reflexes that were second-to-none.

2 Walter Kidd

Watched him from an early age . . .

3 Gary Naysmith

A top youngster whom, I am pleased to say, fulfilled his potential. Came into the side as a teenager and didn't look out of place, winning a man-of-the-match accolade against Celtic in one of his first appearances in maroon. He deserves everything that has come his way.

4 Steven Pressley (captain)

An outstanding leader of men.

5 David Weir

Simply indestructible and indestructibly simple.

6 Eamonn Bannon

Another teenage hero of mine. He departed for Chelsea because that was the only way to keep the club afloat at the time.

7 Drew Busby

A hard bastard.

8 Ralph Callachan

Why did he sign for them? Like Eamonn he had to move on (to Newcastle) for financial reasons. I was just about able to cope with him leaving Hearts but that wasn't the case when he returned north and signed for the team on the other side of the city. A superb player with immense technical ability.

9 Rudi Skacel

A constant goal threat when playing for George Burley. Who knows what he would have gone on to achieve at Tynecastle had Burley remained in charge.

10 Donald Ford

A member of the Scotland World Cup squad in 1974, in which he was in the company of greatness. That says it all about Donald; he was selected as part of a group of forwards that included Denis Law, Kenny Dalglish and Joe Jordan.

11 Roald Jensen

My first hero. Played with enthusiasm and was always willing to take on defenders. An old-fashioned dribbler and crowd pleaser, of which there are sadly too few in the modern game.

Manager: George Burley; he brought so much to the club in such a short space of time.

12

Leaving Hearts

'All good things must come to an end'

Having paid their money to buy Hearts from Wallace Mercer in 1994, Les Deans and Chris Robinson were entitled to make their own decisions. One of their first acts, in June of that year, was to get rid of a good friend of mine as manager and replace him with Tommy McLean. Sandy Clark and I have always had an excellent relationship and I felt he was doing a good job; he had handled the transition from player to manager as well as anyone I've ever known and was respected by the players, which is half the battle. He is as open and honest as the day is long and he knew all there was to know about the club, having been not only a player but also a youth coach. Despite the fact that we finished seventh in the league in 1993/94 I feel that if Sandy had been given a bit more time he could have given the club the success it so richly deserved.

While it's never nice when a mate loses his job, the new men at the helm, perhaps understandably, wanted their own manager. It was a decision supposedly made for the right reasons, but, with hindsight, wasn't well thought out and nearly proved catastrophic. First division Airdrie – with the Gaffer in charge of their side – knocked us out of the Scottish Cup at the semi-final stage in April 1995 while a dreadful league campaign was only rescued by our victory against Motherwell at Tynecastle on the final day of the season the following month. If we'd lost that match we would have finished second bottom and been faced with a two-leg playoff with first division Dunfermline Athletic to preserve our top-flight status.

That game against Motherwell was, in my opinion, my best performance in a Hearts jersey but it almost never happened. I'd been on the bench against Hibernian the previous week (after both my integrity and professionalism were quite ridiculously questioned, as discussed elsewhere in this book) and was not selected to play a prominent part in any of three practice matches at training on the Tuesday. I was under the impression I was to be a substitute once again, this time for the biggest match of the season. Ignoring protocol, I went to see assistant boss Eamonn Bannon and told him that Tommy McLean would be making a huge mistake by not including either Gary Locke (who was also selected in the weaker of the two sides in the practice matches) or me in the starting line-up. I explained that we were the two biggest Jambos at the football club, and, having grown up supporting the team, we knew exactly how important the fixture was. For whatever reason, whether it was my rant or not, I was included in the side (although Lockie remained on the bench). Brian Hamilton and John Robertson were on target for us that day and the rest is history.

When I spoke to the press after the match I said it was great for both manager Tommy McLean and the board that we had preserved our Premier League status and that it would have been a financial disaster if the club had been relegated. But those comments nearly cost me my friendship with Sandy Clark. I was caught up in the emotion and was simply delighted we were staying in the Premier League but Sandy felt I had betrayed him with those words and I suppose he was right. Here was me waxing lyrical about Tommy McLean and Chris Robinson; the former had replaced my friend as manager and had not initially selected me to start against Motherwell, while the latter was an important factor in Sandy getting the sack.

I can understand why Sandy was in the huff with me but he was man enough to give me a call and arrange a meeting so that we could talk face-to-face. As a result of him confronting me with his thoughts, like any decent man should, a situation that could have spiralled out of control and led to the end of a valued friendship was nipped in the bud and we are now as close as ever. I was thirty at the time, an experienced professional, but the way that issue was handled taught me a valuable lesson and proved that you're never too old to learn.

* * *

Tommy McLean's time as manager of Hearts was pretty nondescript. In charge for just one full season – 1994/95 – he won sixteen of his forty-three games at the helm and led us to a disappointing sixth place, only two points above second-bottom Aberdeen in the play-off position. I never really had much of a problem with Tommy although I would have liked to have started more than twenty-one of the thirty-four games I played in. However, I was very grateful to him shortly after he arrived. He saw what I was earning in comparison with the rest of the squad and wanted to give me more money. Due to financial constraints it was impossible for him simply to bump up my salary. However, he arranged an afternoon job for me in the commercial department, working with the now sadly departed Brian Whittaker. We dealt with local businesses and supporters clubs, while helping to arrange kids' parties and the like. It was his way of recognising my long service and it meant an extra £12,500 per annum. While I was still by no means the highest earner at the club it brought me closer to the top guys. I will always be grateful to Tommy for going to such lengths to enhance my salary.

People were genuinely surprised that McLean was not successful at Hearts. After all, he had been a top player and had proved an excellent manager at Motherwell, where, despite working to a shoestring budget, he won the Scottish Cup in 1991. He was of course famously dour, as was his assistant Eamonn Bannon, and in consequence interaction with the players was far from easy. Nevertheless this was not an insurmountable obstacle and, in my view, the turning point for the manager came one Monday night in February 1995 after we had beaten Rangers 4-2 at Tynecastle in a Scottish Cup tie after throwing away a two-goal lead. It was around the time our league form started to dip, something the manager was deeply concerned about and it may have contributed to his reaction in the dressing room. When he came in he severely criticised our performance, despite the fact that we had just reached a cup quarter-final by defeating one of the Old Firm. I felt he was out of order and I am sure that many of my teammates took the same view. In fact I am convinced that incident changed the course of our season. We ended up fighting a grim relegation battle and of course lost out to Airdrie in the Scottish Cup semi-final.

After the defeat by Airdrie the club took a decision to bring in a sports psychologist. His brief was to speak to the players, both collectively and individually. I am sure it was done with the best of intentions and was designed to boost our confidence. But the initiative backfired, despite the fact that the players genuinely wanted it to succeed. We even put forward two options to ensure that it did: the players and the management team both had to be present; or it had to be the players only who were present, with a guarantee that our views were not taken back to the management. But even though we were given a promise that the interviews would be completely confidential there was still a nagging doubt in our minds. The truth is we no longer trusted management; we suspected that our views would be reported back no matter what guarantees had been given. For this reason the psychologist episode only served to heighten tension in the dressing room and the period until the end of the season was a distinctly unhappy experience. It is perhaps no surprise that results deteriorated.

Having said that I enjoyed my sessions with the psychologist, which were conducted on a one-to-one basis. I found them stimulating and highly revealing. And I am pretty sure that nothing got reported back to the powers-that-be.

* * *

Jim Jefferies's track record in management prior to getting the Hearts job in the summer of 1995 was phenomenal, especially at Falkirk. He won 98 of 237 games in charge in nearly five years for a 41 per cent win ratio, extremely impressive when you consider three of those five seasons were in the Premier League. He also led the Bairns to fifth place in the top division (above Hearts) in 1994/95. It was no surprise, therefore, when the club identified him as an ideal successor to Tommy McLean. It was time for a change and, having got rid of McLean, there was a feeling that the Falkirk boss – and former Hearts captain – was the man to take the club forward. The pursuit of Jefferies, however, was anything but orthodox.

In July 1995 I was part of a large, twenty-four-man squad that had travelled north to the Highlands for a couple of pre-season friendlies, culminating in a fixture against Montrose at Links Park on the Sunday on the way back down the road. We were staying in Cove, near Aberdeen, and the squad was evenly split for matches against Peterhead (Friday) and Elgin City (Saturday) on consecutive evenings on the final weekend of the month. I was chosen to play against Elgin so, in essence, had Friday night to myself. At least I thought I did until I was asked for a favour by the club. I was given a phone number and asked to call Jim Jefferies; my brief was to put pressure on him to leave his job as manager of Falkirk and come to Hearts.

After making the call I was not particularly happy with myself. I was now part of something that did not feel right – a player being used to tempt another club's manager to resign from his job and come to Tynecastle. I can understand why I was asked to do it. Jim and I knew each other well; we had been teammates at Hearts in the early Eighties and he had tried to sign me for Falkirk on a couple of occasions. We had been in communication for about twelve months because I feared my career with the team I supported as a boy was coming to an end under Tommy McLean, although nothing ever came of it and I stayed put. When I did get the opportunity to work with Jim again it was not under the circumstances I expected.

Jim's first proper game in charge was the friendly against Newcastle at Tynecastle in August 1995, although he had travelled down to Derby for the pre-season match at the Baseball Ground four days earlier. Watching from the main stand (with Eamonn Bannon in the dugout) as we quickly conceded three first-half goals, to say he was not best pleased was an understatement and he came down to the dressing room at half-time to give us a piece of his mind. We ended up drawing the match three-all but I think he had seen enough to give him serious food for thought.

I was still working in the commercial department in the afternoons with Brian but within six weeks of taking over Jefferies pulled me into his office and said he didn't want me doing that any more. He was not keen on me being as close to the administrative and financial side of the business. I can understand that now but I found it hard to accept at the time; all I was thinking about was what would happen to my additional income. Jim was aware my part-time job was worth an additional £12,500 per year to me but he agreed to add additional appearance money of £250 per game to make up for it.

I went through a patchy spell of form in the early part of his tenure and Jim decided to bring in Paul Smith to ensure more competition for places in midfield. My attempts at holding down a spot in the top team were not exactly helped when I was sent off at Easter Road for stamping on Gareth Evans in Jim's first Edinburgh derby as manager of Hearts. We were 2–1 down at the time but Robbo rescued me again with an equaliser in stoppage time to earn us a point. I was annoyed at myself for getting the red card because it's bad enough playing poorly when you're trying to impress a new manager, never mind getting your marching orders for an over-active right boot!

In the week leading up to the first Edinburgh derby of the season at Tynecastle – in November 1995 – I was selected to play in a strong reserve team against Kilmarnock at a Junior ground in Ayrshire. It featured the likes of Jim Hamilton, Colin Cramb and David Hagen. I was chosen to start the match at right back, in direct opposition to a speedy young winger by the name of Alex Burke. I felt I did reasonably well and produced a standard of performance that you don't always get in a reserve game as you get older. However, the fact I was playing for the second string in the week of an Edinburgh derby suggested to me I would not be starting against our Capital rivals and would be lucky to find a place on the bench.

As fate would have it, however, Paul Smith had a problem with his back that week and took very little part in training. While aware of his injury, I got the impression that the longer the week went on without anything being said about me playing then the less chance I had of featuring. However, on my arrival at Tynecastle on the day of the match assistant boss Billy Brown pulled me aside and said, 'I've pushed as hard as I can and I've managed to get you back in the team.' I was vying for a starting jersey with Brian Hamilton and, when Paul was ruled out on the morning of the match, I was selected to play instead of Brian, but as a defensive midfielder. I had never played that position in my life.

'Just make sure you do what we're asking you to do and you'll be fine,' said Billy. 'Don't panic. Keep the ball moving at all times, from side-to-side if you have to, and try your best to break up any opposition attack.' This, for me, was a completely new game plan. I started my career as an attacking midfielder and I'd been used in behind the strikers when Scotland won the European under-eighteen championships in Finland. Joe Jordan tried to convert me into a wing back and now my attacking instinct was being curtailed in favour of a more defensive approach. That afternoon it took me a while to adapt to sitting deep, while John Millar pushed on, but I was pleased with my overall contribution to our 2–1 win.

It's funny to think that Jim Jefferies was looking for me to come and play for him at Falkirk only eight months previously and then within a short space of time he was the new manager at the club I wanted to be at. The problem was my form hadn't convinced him I was a long-term option for his midfield. Paul Smith moved on – he was a Hearts supporter like me and we actually went to matches together when we were younger – but I think his presence at the club pushed me to raise my standards for a spell. However, despite seeing off his challenge, I started to fear for my place when Jim signed Stefano Salvatore, a player more comfortable in the holding role than me. When I look back now I realise that I was right. The writing was on the wall. I just didn't know it at the time.

* * *

All the silverware I won as a kid is at my mum and dad's house. It would have been great to add to the collection of winner's trophies after turning professional, but, alas, it was not to be. It was looking like two Scottish Cup runners-up medals, from 1986 and 1996, was going to be all I had to show from my time with Hearts. I was able to add a League Cup runners-up medal following a dramatic wintry afternoon at Parkhead in November 1996, the last opportunity I had to win silverware in a maroon jersey. It looked liked being a familiar tale for me in finals when an early double strike from Ally McCoist gave Rangers a two-goal lead after just twenty-seven minutes. However, Steve Fulton managed to pull one back for us just before the break. It was the ideal time to reply and the half-time team talk by Jim Jefferies suddenly became far more positive. He kept telling us we could get back into the match as long as we had belief. We went out on to the field of play for the second half refreshed, re-energised and ready.

The manager's positive attitude soon paid off. John Robertson equalised on the hour mark and I honestly believed there was now only going to be one winner. I felt I would finally get the chance to taste victory in a cup final after sixteen years' service to Hearts. We were on level terms for only five minutes.

From where I was standing in the middle of the park there looked to be a clear foul on John Robertson on the touchline nearest the main stand but linesman Alan Freeland, standing right in front of the incident, disagreed and kept his flag down. Rangers produced a lightning-quick break up the park from which Paul Gascoigne scored to put them back in front; he added another two minutes later, and, despite a late consolation goal from Davie Weir and a man-of-the-match performance from Neil McCann, another cup final was to end in personal disappointment. I believe I was destined never to win a major trophy playing for the team I loved.

Coca Cola Cup final: Sunday, 24 November 1996
Celtic Park:
Hearts 3–4 Rangers

Hearts: Rousset; Weir, Pointon, Bruno, Ritchie; Cameron, Mackay, Fulton, McCann; Paille (Beckford), Robertson

Rangers: Goram; Cleland (Robertson), Moore, Gough, Petric, Bjorklund; Miller, Albertz, Gascoigne, Laudrup; McCoist

* * *

Contract negotiations with Hearts were always pretty straightforward throughout my time at Tynecastle. My deal was up during the summer of 1996 and Jim Jefferies asked for a chat. He explained that at my age, thirty-two, it would be difficult for him to offer more than a one-year extension because he didn't think I would be able to play as regularly as before. I accepted what he had to say and, as usual, I inked the deal without too much fuss. Unlike the current structure at Tynecastle, the manager was then responsible for all contract matters while Billy Brown took 90 per cent of the training, usually under Jim's watchful eye. It was after training one morning in January 1997 that I first got an inkling there might be a career for me at Tynecastle after hanging up my boots.

We were sitting beside each other at lunch, and, since I wasn't playing as regularly as I would have liked, the manager mentioned a possible opportunity to coach at youth level following the departure of Paul Hegarty. Nothing concrete, it was simply a possibility. I told him I would jump at the chance. Around that time I was starting to think about what I would do when my playing days were over and coaching was high on the agenda. We spoke again two or three weeks later but it was never mentioned again. Whether it was my fault for not following up the initial chat with Jim, or because he could have had a memory like a sieve, I don't know. Perhaps I read too much into that initial conversation but the least I could have done was to try and find out if he was serious.

I never did see out those final twelve months with Hearts and I never did get the chance to combine the end of my playing career at Tynecastle with the start of my coaching career. John McGlynn was later appointed to take charge of the youngsters. The rest, as they say, is history.

* * *

Preparation for the match against Celtic at Parkhead on Saturday, 1 March 1997 was the same as for most other away games. The squad met up at Tynecastle at 12.15 p.m., normal for a match in the west, and arrived in the east end of Glasgow ninety minutes later. Upon arrival Jim Jefferies announced the team and I was delighted to be given a starting jersey after six consecutive games as a substitute:

Rousset; Ritchie, Weir, Naysmith, McPherson; Locke, Mackay, Salvatori, Severin; McCann, Robertson

We had beaten Celtic at Hampden Park (their temporary home for a season due to reconstruction at Parkhead) less than two years previously and travelled west optimistic of a repeat result. It was not to be as goals from Jorge Cadete and Paolo di Canio secured a 2–0 win for the home side. I received a yellow card to compound my misery. As it turned out a caution was the least of my worries. I left Celtic Park that evening completely oblivious to the fact that, at the age of thirty-two, I had just played my 640th and final competitive match for Hearts.

Was I forced out or did I choose to leave? I think it was a bit of both. The arrival of Stefano Salvatori from Atalanta hadn't helped my cause and there was no guarantee of regular action when I had to compete for a place with younger guys like Steve Fulton, Colin Cameron and Salvatori. I played in most of the matches between the start of that season and the turn of the year but my appearances became more fleeting, and usually from the bench, when Stefano returned from injury at the start of February 1997 after being out of action for more than three months. If I'd been at any other team I would have chapped on the manager's door after six consecutive matches as a substitute and asked for an explanation, especially when we only won two of them (against Kilmarnock and Raith Rovers – my last ever appearance at Tynecastle). But, with hindsight, maybe there was an inward acceptance that my seventeen-year association with the club was coming to an end and I simply didn't want confirmation of that fact from Jim Jefferies.

Looking back I probably thought I could go on playing forever, but, in reality, my form had dipped and I was failing to maintain the standard of performance that I had produced earlier in my career. My stubbornness was understandable; I had played so many games for the club and found it difficult to accept that my standards were slipping. After training hard all week and being desperate to start matches there were younger, fitter guys coming in to fill my role and that should have told me the writing was on the wall.

There's never an easy way to end a relationship that lasts for such a long time but my departure was probably best for both parties. Given my feelings for the club I would not have wanted to be offered a new deal purely on sentimental grounds. I've always been close to Jim Jefferies, and have the utmost respect for the man, and I knew he wouldn't stand in my way or be awkward to deal with. It didn't take long to complete my £10,000 transfer to Airdrie, three or four days at most, and that ensured there wasn't too much room for sentiment on my part. Of course I found it difficult to accept my association with the club I loved was coming to an end but at least I didn't have too much time to dwell on it. Jim and Billy Brown had come to a decision that my legs had gone as far as playing regularly at Premier League level was concerned and, although I didn't agree with them at the time, they were spot on. Alex MacDonald also realised I wasn't as sharp as he remembered when I joined Airdrie; he felt I wasn't even up to the standard required to play regularly in the first division. I can only put that down to playing so many games and my body finally telling me it had had enough. I always tried my hardest during training with Airdrie, but, unfortunately for me, there were quicker, sharper and hungrier young bucks on the playing staff and that took its toll on my career. I managed to start thirty matches for Airdrie in two seasons before I realised it was best to take a step back and let the youngsters take over. It was time for a changing of the guard.

* * *

I was never going to leave Heart of Midlothian Football Club with a smile on my face but I have to admit to further disappointment on two counts when I walked out the front door for the final time on Thursday, 13 March 1997. Not getting the chance to begin my coaching career at Tynecastle was one (who knows, that opportunity may never have materialised even if I had stayed); the second was the decision not to give me the £10,000 transfer fee as an ex-gratia payment for my long service. The latter, especially, left a sour taste in my mouth for a period of time although I did end up getting the money after Vicky arranged a meeting with Jim Jefferies and successfully pleaded my case. (That same amount of money was later to be my financial input into the Save Our Hearts campaign.) I suppose it was embarrassing having my wife sort things out when I left, instead of me doing it, but at the time I couldn't accept what I know now: that my legs had gone and I was no longer good enough to play for Hearts. You could say I took the huff. It goes without saying I would rather have been part of the squad when the Scottish Cup was brought back to Gorgie in May 1998 for the first time in thirty-six years but as usual my timing was lousy; my old body gave out at just the wrong time.

Football, however, is not a charity. You don't pay someone a salary just because they've given seventeen years' service. I realised that but didn't like it. Now I fully respect the decision taken by Jim Jefferies and Billy Brown. In fact I still have a very good working relationship with both men through my agency business and I have represented them at various times since then and hope to do so in the future.

I should say more about Jim Jefferies, who is, after all, one of the most significant figures in the club's history. But his place in the pantheon of Hearts greats is not due to his ability on the pitch: he was an honest, workmanlike defender-cum-midfielder who always gave of his best. It was only when he moved into management that he really came into his own. He brought many of the qualities he had displayed as a player to the role: hard work, honesty, commitment, complemented by a thorough knowledge of the game. In addition players always know where they stand with Jim; he is forthright and tells it like it is without flannel, as I had discovered. He is also lucky to have Billy Brown alongside him in the dugout, someone he can trust completely. It was no surprise to me when the duo guided Hearts to the Scottish Cup final in 1996, just a year after we had been embroiled in a relegation dogfight. Although Rangers beat us 5–1 that day they were at their absolute peak, with the likes of Laudrup, Gascoigne and Gough playing out of their skins. It was a massive leaning curve for everyone involved and we did much better against them just a few months later in the League Cup final, when we lost a close match by the odd goal in seven.

13

One Day in May

'The best things come to those who wait . . .
and wait . . . and wait!'

I have never had a problem getting up in the morning, even at weekends. I prefer to be up and about doing things rather than spending additional time in my bed. The same cannot be said about my son, Nicholas. There was normally only one reason for him surfacing before eleven on a Saturday morning; that was when Hearts were playing at Pittodrie and the supporter's bus was leaving at some ungodly hour. But there was another, rather more auspicious, occasion for which he put in an early appearance: it was shortly after seven o'clock on Saturday, 16 May 1998. I heard noises coming from his room; he was up and we weren't playing at Aberdeen. That was when I knew it was going to be anything but a normal day.

I arranged with the club to get fifty tickets for the Scottish Cup final against Rangers at Celtic Park. I promised my mates I would organise a bus from the Wheatsheaf pub in Balgreen Road and told them I would take care of the tickets. Most of them were season-ticket holders and obtaining a handful of additional briefs wasn't a problem. A fifty-two-seater bus was hired and was scheduled to depart for Glasgow at ten. The Wheatsheaf was opening early, especially for us; it would give our happy band an hour-and-a-half to eat, drink and be merry before setting off on a journey that would either see us return triumphant or in tears. I had no idea that I would be coming back to Edinburgh later that day with triumphant tears!

It was a massive day for everyone connected with Hearts and it was also a big day for me. I was attending my first Scottish Cup final as a fan since the match against Rangers at Hampden in 1976. My younger son Ryan accompanied me throughout the day while his older brother Nicholas made his own travel arrangements. It was a real family day out and it was great to see so many of my friends and their children when we arrived at the Wheatsheaf as the day began in earnest at 8.30 a.m.

A full Scottish breakfast washed down with three lager shandies calmed the nerves slightly but it was impossible not to get caught up in the atmosphere. All around us the kids were getting their faces painted maroon; I was just praying the paint would not be smudged by tears at quarter to five. It was a day on which mixed emotions were guaranteed and even those started early when I was asked by a friend of mine, Tony Cole, if I had a spare ticket. They were like gold dust and initially I had to disappoint him. But the disappointment was short-lived as a Hearts supporter later asked me if I could find a home for the ticket of his friend, who was unable to attend. I was just delighted to be in a position to help out given how much the game meant to our fans.

Despite our different football allegiances, Tosh McKinlay and I have been good mates since he moved to Tynecastle in December 1989. It wasn't often we wanted the same team to win but this was a day when we happened to agree; he left his Hoops scarf in the drawer for a few hours and replaced it with a maroon one. Tosh played a big part in helping me out with pre-match drinking facilities for the boys and girls and had booked the Bower bar in Rutherglen for our party of fifty. The bus journey through to Glasgow was booze-filled and boisterous and on arrival we found out we were sharing the venue with another busload from the Tower bar in Livingston. I always bump into familiar faces when I'm in the company of Hearts supporters and this time was no exception: one of the first faces I saw at the bar was St Johnstone striker, and Jambo fanatic, Roddy Grant. He was clearly the worse for wear. I was getting that way – strong stuff those lager shandies – and the more I had to drink the more I got a bizarre sensation, feeling, call it what you will, that it was going to be Hearts' day. Rangers were coming to the end of their great period of dominance; it was the end of an era at Ibrox and something told me we were going to spoil their party. After all I had been through in my career I just felt something special was about to happen. Tosh popped into the pub shortly before our departure to wish us well for the day ahead – a lovely touch from a lovely guy.

It was a gorgeous afternoon in Glasgow so we decided to walk from Rutherglen to Parkhead to soak up the sun. Ryan's constant singing was in keeping with the rest of the day but we had to give him some support as we approached London Road, where we were met by hundreds of Rangers supporters disembarking from buses and straining their vocal chords. There was never a hint of trouble and the two sets of fans mingled happily in a colourful sea of maroon, blue and white. By this time there were thousands of people heading for the stadium but I still managed to meet Walter Kidd, Eamonn Bannon, Scott Crabbe and Neil Berry, each of us with some terrible memories of cup semi-finals and finals. It seemed ironic we were all at Parkhead that day as supporters, having failed to win anything with Hearts during our time as players. I wondered if they, like me, were slightly envious at being on the outside looking in.

We entered the stadium half an hour before kick-off and our seats were in an excellent position, opposite the main stand just a few rows from the front. Being a good friend of Gilles Rousset I roared over to him during the warm-up to wish him all the best and he acknowledged me with thumbs up. I'm not sure about other supporters but I've always found it very difficult to enjoy a cup final. It should be the pinnacle of your season, a time to savour the atmosphere and let the occasion take care of itself but with Hearts that has never been possible.

We couldn't have asked for a better start: Stevie Fulton was fouled inside the box within the first sixty seconds. Colin Cameron was calmness personified, scoring the penalty with his first touch of the match. Given his history of scoring against Hearts, the half-time introduction of Ally McCoist for Stale Stensaas probably sent a shiver done the spine of many followers of the Boys in Maroon but I was actually pleased he was sent on ahead of Ian Durrant, who I thought was more of a danger. We had an ideal vantage point to witness Stephane Adam score our second but I don't think I could go through the last ten minutes of that match again after Rangers reduced the deficit to one goal.

From where I was sitting it looked as though Mr McCoist had won a penalty in the last ten minutes. I was convinced if Rangers scored a second they would go on to win the game and I don't think I have ever been as relieved when referee Willie Young had awarded a free-kick, which came to nothing. There was no fourth official in those days to signal how long was left, so the last few minutes felt like a lifetime. The whistles from the Hearts supporters desperate for the game to end seemed to last forever, before finally being replaced by cheers. We had done it. Heart of Midlothian had won the Scottish Cup for the first time in forty-two years.

Scottish Cup final: 16 May 1998

Celtic Park

Hearts 2 Rangers 1

Hearts: Rousset; McPherson, Ritchie, Weir, Naysmith; Salvatori, McCann, Fulton, Cameron, Flogel; Adam (Hamilton 78)

Rangers: Goram; Porrini, Stensaas (McCoist 45), Gough, Amoruso; Bjorklund, Gattuso, Ferguson, McCall (Durrant 68); Durie, Laudrup

Attendance: 48,946

There were tears in my eyes when Gary Locke and Stevie Fulton were presented with the Cup. There was also a tinge of jealousy. I had spent seventeen years at the football club with nothing to show for my efforts. I remember thinking back to the previous final against Rangers at Parkhead – in the Coca Cola Cup in 1996 – and I genuinely thought when the score was tied at two-each that we would go on to win the match and I would become the first captain of Hearts to lift a trophy since the League Cup win in 1962. It was not to be then and it was not to be in 1998 but I didn't let that spoil my afternoon. Of course I would have loved to have been on the pitch with the rest of the players, showing off the silverware to the supporters, but I was fortunate to have the next best thing when Gilles, having remembered where I was sitting, brought Stephane and the Cup over to celebrate. I tried to get onto the perimeter of the pitch, and was helped over by a steward, but was stopped in my tracks by a policewoman before I could vault the wall at the front of the stand. She informed me that my actions could set a precedent for others fans, and, although I was disappointed, she was right.

I couldn't get on to the pitch but was delighted that our two French heroes were able to come to the front of the stand. Carla, the daughter of one of our party, Jimmy Dunn, was fortunate enough to get a kiss from Stephane and that not only made her day but also her father's. Jimmy's dad had told him about the Scottish Cup win against Celtic in 1956 with monotonous regularity and Jimmy always said he was determined that one of his daughters would be with him the day Hearts finally brought the Cup back to Gorgie.

It's never dull being a Hearts fan but one thing it doesn't do is to teach you what to do on the back of winning silverware. It's something you can't prepare for. You would have thought the journey back to Edinburgh would have been even more booze-filled and boisterous than the one made in the opposite direction a few hours before, especially having won the Scottish Cup for the first time in most of our lifetimes, but that wasn't the case. Maybe it was the combination of an early start, constant alcohol, an energy-sapping ninety (plus) minutes and warm sunshine but the trip home was a quiet affair. Or maybe it just took time for the result to sink in.

The club was kind enough to invite me to their private party that evening in the Gorgie suite. I duly attended with my wife, Vicky, and got chatting to Paul Hegarty and his wife Linda but it didn't take long before I felt alienated. I had sobered up by this point and felt slightly uncomfortable, as if I was gatecrashing a party, even though I had been invited. While still a Hearts supporter, I was an Airdrie player and I had been to many of these gatherings in the past as a loser. The time had come for winners to gather together and celebrate and I couldn't bring myself to stay any longer than an hour. I was ecstatic for everyone involved but I was an outsider looking in and didn't feel part of the inner sanctum. It was time to leave and to give the people who had achieved time and space to enjoy their night. Before I departed I made sure I said thanks to those I knew well for restoring the pride of the Hearts supporters.

I'm sure I would have been made welcome at many bars and pubs in Gorgie that night but the time was right to head home. I had been in the pub since half-past eight that morning and had been on an emotional roller-coaster for a full thirteen-and-a-half hours. I was shattered.

Many Hearts supporters have said that the celebrations on the Sunday afternoon were on a par with the dramatic events in Glasgow the previous day. I'll never be able to compare the two because of a pre-arranged trip south. I had organised a visit to Old Trafford for Calder boys club to give the kids a wee treat at the end of their season. Once more, a touch of irony. Here was me heading to the home of the biggest club in the world (and one of the teams I could have joined at the start of my career) but it was a club that had, unusually, won nothing that season. So the tour of Old Trafford included viewing an empty trophy cabinet, while I had left behind one of the biggest street parties Edinburgh had ever seen. One or two of my boys called off on the Sunday morning, despite having paid for the trip, because their parents had decided to take them into town to witness the open-top-bus procession through the streets of the Capital, but I had made a commitment to the rest of the squad and I had to go to Manchester. In any case not all of my players were even Hearts supporters!

Perhaps it wasn't a bad thing I was three hundred miles away. I was jealous enough at Parkhead as it was and I would probably have ruined the day for those in my company if I had been in Edinburgh. It wasn't until we were coming back up the road on the Sunday evening and stopped at a motorway service station that I saw pictures of the parade on television. It was huge. Some estimates put the numbers of well-wishers on the streets of Edinburgh at 500,000. I felt proud for the club and the city, but also envy and more than a touch of sadness. After a long wait my team had won the Cup and I had not been a part of it.

It was at that moment I realised how distant I had become from the inner core of Heart of Midlothian Football Club.

14

A Footballer's Lifestyle

'If you don't appreciate it, you don't deserve it.'

Terry Josephson – motivational author

I have tried to be as honest as possible throughout this book but the most important thing was being honest with myself. I've enjoyed looking back at my career, I've been able to smile at the amusing tales from nearly seventeen years at Tynecastle and I've even shed tears when recalling the more emotional moments. But this is the one chapter that has given me sleepless nights. I don't mind admitting there were even times when I was ready to pull the plug on the whole project rather than having to write about the mess I have made of my personal life at various times. Everybody makes mistakes, although I seem to have made more than my fair share. If I was to have my time again there are many things I would do differently. However, the damage has been done. To those people I've hurt, I am truly sorry.

* * *

I've decided to deal with my private life at the end of this chapter; before doing so I wish to try and explain what it was like to be a professional footballer in the Eighties and Nineties.

I was very happy with every single contract I signed at Hearts. I put pen-to-paper at Tynecastle on 16 June 1980 – around the same time as Davie Bowman, Stuart Gauld and Ian Westwater and a few months before John Robertson – and I have no idea how my salary compared with theirs. Whether I was on more, less or the same money as them didn't bother me then and it doesn't concern me now. My father negotiated the finer details of my initial deal – a two-year apprenticeship with a one-year professional contract – but I agreed every other contract during my career without the need for representation. I earned £50 per week in my first year at Tynecastle, £10 more the following year and £70 in year three. That was in addition to a £3,000 signing-on fee, of which £1,250 was paid up front; the same sum was given to me just before Christmas in my first year while the final instalment of £500 was paid in the summer at the end of my first twelve months with the club. I was so grateful to dad I was doing cartwheels. To leave school at sixteen and become a professional player with money in my pocket was a dream come true. Even after tax I was still walking out with £37 in the first year and I felt like a millionaire, although I must admit with the clothes I wore no-one would have known.

The money I was earning at such a young age allowed me to enjoy my teenage years with friends. It meant I was able to fund a summer break to Santa Susanna in north-east Spain in 1981 with schoolmates Gary Birrell and Kenny Munro, my first holiday abroad without the parents. Sadly a good friend of ours, Gordon 'Fish' Marr, who was to be the fourth person in our group, was unable to afford it after being released by Hearts a few months before. That was one of the first things I learned as a professional: football is not always kind.

Apprentices in all walks of life get paid very little compared with their later earning potential, but there is little doubt that youngsters at football clubs more than earn their measly salary. We came into Tynecastle every morning at least an hour before the professionals, laid out their gear, which we had washed and dried the day before, cleaned the training equipment if required, then made sure any outstanding duties were seen to before getting ready for training in the away changing room. Once training was over we had our daily Mars Bar and can of Coca Cola, purchased from the back of Jim Docherty's car; then it was back to work washing the pros' kit and cleaning their boots for the next session. Worst of all was scrubbing the communal bath after more than twenty grubby bodies had used it. When I think back to the amount of dirt and scum that floated on top of that water I'm convinced the players would have needed another wash when they got home. It all had to be cleaned, however, and we weren't allowed to leave the changing room for our next chores until the bath was in pristine condition, ready for another day of muck and grime.

I remember one Tuesday how jealous we first-year professionals were when young Mr Bowman was excused his duties. We were keen to know the reason, but when we found out we wished we hadn't asked. Aged just sixteen years and four months, Davie told us he'd been included in the first-team squad for the midweek Anglo-Scottish Cup tie at Airdrie the following day and, as a result, was allowed to go home and rest ahead of the big game. (Bow played for Hearts in an East of Scotland Shield tie against Berwick in October 1979 when he was only fifteen, but that match was not recognised as a real first-team fixture so it doesn't count.)

The first time I ever had the privilege of skipping my chores was on the day of my seventeenth birthday: 23 January 1981. I was to make my first start for Hearts in a Scottish Cup tie against Greenock Morton the following day at Cappielow. Facing a team containing a host of decent players – the likes of Roy Baines, Andy Ritchie, Jim Holmes, Jim Tolmie and Bobby Thomson – we came away with a very creditable goalless draw. I kept my place for the replay the following Wednesday, but we were beaten 3–1 at Tynecastle and I watched with admiration as Ritchie pulled the strings in midfield and was a deserving man-of-the-match recipient.

Complaints aside, my apprenticeship is something I will always look back on fondly. The camaraderie, the cleaning, the jokes, the piss-taking and even the weeding of the terracing – the Gorgie Road end was constantly overrun by weeds and regularly required us on our hands and knees with the help of only a trowel – made us far more respectful of our positions when we became professionals.

* * *

I could have made more money out of football, of that there is no doubt. However, I was perfectly happy with every contract offered to me by Hearts because it meant I could live the life I was accustomed to, in the city I loved, surrounded by the people I cared for. Every deal was negotiated without the services of an agent; on more than one occasion I came to an agreement with Wallace Mercer and Pilmar Smith over lunch at Rafaeli's Restaurant (now known as Sygn) in the West End. When Joe Jordan arrived at the club he dealt with contracts himself and was very easy to deal with.

I mentioned at the start of this book that the highest basic salary I earned while playing for Hearts was £39,000 per annum. I guessed that made me one of the lowest-paid experienced players at the club, but, as I've said many times before on these pages, I did not play the game simply for cash. I was lucky to be involved in the squad when hefty bonuses were paid out – £1,000 was not uncommon for a victory against Hibernian, Rangers or Celtic – but it was usually the case that European bonuses were the best of all. For example there was the day that Mike Galloway scored a vital away goal in Mostar in round three of the UEFA Cup in December 1988, in front of only a handful of Hearts fans inside the extremely intimidating Velez stadium. I turned to Kenny Black and said: 'That's the £3,000 in the tail for Christmas presents' and we both chuckled. That goal, following our 3–0 win at Tynecastle in the first leg, secured our place in the quarter-final.

Bonuses were paid out in Europe if we qualified for the next round so despite managing a sensational 1–0 victory against Bayern Munich at Tynecastle at the end of February 1989 we failed to pick up a penny after losing the second leg 2–0 in Germany, thus crashing out of the tournament. We were on £5,000 per man to secure our place in the last four but stunning strikes from Klaus Augenthaler and Erland Johnsen in Munich put paid to that, although, having won the first leg, I'm sure every Hearts player would have forsaken the hefty bonus if it meant going through.

Wallace Mercer got it spot on, perhaps even taking a leaf out of Jim McLean's book at Dundee United; we were well rewarded if we achieved. I may have been on a relatively low basic wage compared with others at the club but I did more than all right from win bonuses. However, I would have swapped them all from the various cup runs if it meant actually winning the trophy.

I always considered myself well paid for doing a job I loved, but I've never been someone who splashed the cash with gay abandon. Our kids went to state schools; Ryan and Nicholas both attended St Cuthbert's primary before moving on to St Augustine's. Nor did I ever get that excited by flash cars; I was more than happy to swap my Ford Orion for a Sierra before moving up to a Rover from Alexander's at Fountainbridge.

Vicky and I started off in a two-bedroom flat in Harrison Road before moving to a three-bedroom terraced house in Tyler's Acre Avenue (in the same street as Wayne Foster). I moved house once more during my playing days and that was to Dovecot Park just off the Lanark Road, a property that ultimately became a four-bed detached.

The money I earned also allowed me to take the family to Florida on a couple of occasions as well as to Cyprus and Portugal. These trips were funded in part by the likes of Paul Kane, Mickey Weir and Gordon Hunter, because I used to save money from the regular win bonuses we earned for beating Hibernian. The holidays were a big part of my life; they were the only real way I was able to escape after giving so much to Hearts, off and on the park. But I now realise that two-week period with my family – the longest time I would be with them 24/7 throughout the year – wasn't enough to sustain a healthy marriage.

I was fortunate that I never had any real bother from Hibs supporters; the fact I never hid my allegiance to Hearts probably helped. There were one or two occasions, usually in the latter part of a Saturday evening, when someone would pull me up in a pub and claim a relative of theirs was a better player than I was. I remember one in particular, when I was out with a few

of the boys in the Rutland. This lad – I think his name was Willie Herd –
came up to me and said I couldn't lace his brother's boots. To this day I'm
not sure if he said that to provoke a reaction or if that was what he really
believed. Everybody is entitled to his, or her, opinion and I told him there
would be no argument from me if that was what he believed. When you
confront someone in a pub you have to be prepared to fight, and that was
never my forte.

In his autobiography *Back From The Brink* Paul McGrath gives details
of a pub culture at Manchester United in the mid-Eighties involving the so-
called Gang of Five: McGrath, Bryan Robson, Norman Whiteside, Kevin
Moran and Gordon McQueen, although Alex Ferguson quickly put a stop
to that when he took over. A lot of the lads at Hearts liked a casual drink
but I never experienced a similar culture in our changing room. Once a
month, usually on a Tuesday, a group of us would maybe head into town if
we were off the following day, while Montpelliers was a popular haunt for
a few of the boys after playing on a Saturday. But if you want McGrath-like
tales then I'm afraid I'll disappoint you.

* * *

There is a myth that each of us has a destiny and even if that is true I think it's
unlikely I am destined to be a manager. I enjoy coaching my under-fourteens
on a Sunday and have fun doing media work with the likes of Hearts.tv, Talk
107, Setanta and the BBC. I get a kick out of my involvement with the
Heart of Midlothian Education and Community Trust and the annual Coca
Cola training for kids in schools across Scotland. I'm kept busy before and
after games at Tynecastle in my role as a matchday ambassador in the
Gorgie Suite, alongside Jambo fanatics Scott Crabbe and Jimmy Sandison.
My agency business – Kickstart 2000 – takes up most of the rest of my time
and to be honest that doesn't leave much free space in my diary.

I don't know what the future has in store but one thing I am keen to ensure
is that my association, however tenuous, continues with Heart of Midlothian
Football Club for the rest of my working life. I'm perfectly happy with the
way things are just now – the commentary and ambassadorial duties on a
matchday – but if there's ever an opportunity of more involvement then I'd
jump at the chance. Trust me: I won't be hard to deal with.

* * *

I consider myself a very loyal person. I'm still close to a few schoolmates –
Bread, Alex McGregor, Alan McPherson, Kenny Munro and Gary Birrell –

and we still meet up as a group two or three times a year even though our lives have taken us in different directions. Bread and I played in the same school football team at Balgreen primary while Alex (father of Rangers keeper Allan McGregor) and I were teammates for the Edinburgh primary-school select, in which he vied for the goalkeeper's jersey with Gordon Marshall. I played against Alan, Kenny and Gary in primary seven when they were at Stenhouse primary before all six of us moved on to Tynecastle High School. We've all been through different, and at times difficult, situations in our private lives but have always been there for each other when the going got tough and we still have that bond. It's impossible to underestimate the impact of those friendships.

We were actually at a Hearts game against Rangers at Ibrox in January 2007; Alan took the rest of the boys to the match (a dull goalless draw) while I carried out my normal duties doing co-commentary for the Hearts website. Although he stayed in Glasgow Allan McGregor came back through to Edinburgh with the rest of us for a night out even taking part – along with his father – in some horrendous dancing at The Jamhouse on Queen Street before heading west to go back home. That spoke volumes to me not just about the relationship he had with his dad but also with us. Speaking of laughs there are no lines drawn in the sand when we are together. Abuse is dished out about attire, looks and spots on faces, and it's delivered with both barrels. It's been that way for forty years and I hope it continues for forty more.

I've also built up friendships over the years, mainly through football, with Billy Ramsay, Colin Sime, Ken Stott, Iain Macleod, George Foulkes, Gerry Kennedy and Gordon Lockerbie, among many others, although the last two mentioned have both passed away. Rest in peace lads.

I also consider myself very loyal to Hearts. I always have been and always will be, but that blind loyalty had severe consequences. It contributed in part to the breakdown of my marriage. I wasn't loyal enough to the most important people in my life, my family, and while they supported me throughout my career that support was not reciprocated. I always put myself first, whether it was preparing for matches without taking their thoughts, feelings or pre-arranged plans into consideration. If we won I would go out for a couple of drinks with the boys to celebrate, when I should have been spending quality time with the people who loved me the most and for the right reasons.

It's easy to sit back now and analyse where it went wrong. I was completely oblivious at the time as to how my actions, and more importantly my selfish behaviour, were affecting my family. I wish it had been so apparent to me back then and maybe I could have done something about it. Or maybe not . . . .

I am not proud of a lot of things I have done but this chapter is not about trying to seek redemption, nor is it about looking for sympathy or making excuses. I have made mistakes and I am the one who has to live with the consequences.

* * *

Vicky and I got married at the Braid Hills Hotel on 29 June 1988 and it was a memorable day. I was twenty-four and we had been dating for a couple of years. We have two sons, Nicholas and Ryan, who have been brought up in the proper manner to follow Heart of Midlothian, and we had some wonderful times together as a family. My career as a footballer allowed us to go on summer holidays to some fantastic destinations, including Cyprus, as well as visiting one of the most idyllic places on this planet: Key West in Florida. It was my reward for all the hard work during the season and the family's reward for putting up with me. Unfortunately, at the time, my self-ishness made me think these holidays only came about because I was the earner, not realising the main reason I was earning was due to the secure family home that was being provided by my wife and kids.

I know people in all walks of life who have experienced marital problems and there were difficult times in our marriage to go along with the good times. I should have put as much time and effort into my marriage as Vicky did because I realise now when looking at other relationships, successful or not, that the only way any male–female combination can work is if both partners give of their best. I can now admit to having many flaws during my married life, one of which was putting Heart of Midlothian before my marriage on a number of occasions. That flaw has only become evident with hindsight and I now realise my head was so far up my own arse I thought the world revolved around me.

We like to think of Edinburgh as a city, which of course it is, but it has all the intimate qualities of a big town and those playing for Hearts and Hibs quickly become highly recognisable faces. I'm not saying I regretted putting myself forward for charity events and personal appearances to pro-mote both the football club and myself but when you are doing these things it is very easy to believe you are a single man. I should have been spending a lot more time with my wife and children.

I was a local boy made good, playing for his local team. However, it doesn't matter if you're sixteen or thirty-six; nobody teaches you how to handle fame and (relative) fortune and that is a problem. I think that all young players should be given guidance on how to handle what is coming their way: the money, the media demands, the often critical attention of the public. And, most importantly, the need to keep your feet planted firmly on the ground, something that I often failed to do.

It frustrates me greatly when I look back at the effort I put into both my career and my friendships yet failed to put that same effort into my marriage, the most important of the three. The naivety of a grown man, if you like. It is said that 53 per cent of marriages in the United Kingdom end in divorce and I'm pretty sure a fair percentage are due to infidelity. That's not a pleasant statistic but neither is the fact that my marriage also became a statistic and it's up to me to deal with that. The reason for it breaking down in 2003, after fifteen years, was because of me. It was due to my behaviour, which I am not proud of, and certain actions. I have nobody to blame but myself. My behaviour caused embarrassment to my wife and two boys. It hurt them and that is something I will live with for the rest of my life. The damage has been done and no amount of apologising will rectify those errors. I know what I have done wrong. I do not wish to elaborate any further.

15

Illness

'The best health service in the world.'

Kickstart 2000, the football agency I set up with Bert Logan in August of that year, was two months old. Our business focused on the representation of professional sportsmen and women but in its embryonic stage also incorporated a consultancy arm. Bert or I would attend matches on behalf of clubs, either to scout a player or provide a dossier on a specific team. Livingston was one of our first clients and I was happy to help out two old friends, Jim Leishman and Davie Hay. That part of the job was enjoyable for a former footballer and could also, at times, be pretty glamorous. I flew to France one day to keep tabs on a striker called Jean-Claude Darcheville at Lorient and ended up coming back raving about a left midfielder called Ulrich Le Pen. At that time those were the kind of players Livingston were hoping to attract to West Lothian but their interest soon waned when they heard how much the French side was looking for in transfer fees. Not long after I watched Le Pen he was on his way to Ipswich Town after George Burley paid £1.4 million for his services.

21 October 2000

It was not always that glamorous and one day Jim Leishman asked me if I could head down to Somerset Park and compile a dossier on both Ayr United and Alloa Athletic. Livingston were due to play Alloa the following week, then Ayr, and Jim saw it as an ideal opportunity to kill two birds with one stone. After being sacked as manager of Airdrie United I also picked up a bit of weekend work with Radio Forth as summariser on Hearts matches.

I had a free Saturday that week because of the Edinburgh derby at Easter Road on the Sunday so it gave me the opportunity to witness two games in twenty-four hours. Neither Jim Leishman nor Davie Hay could attend the match at Somerset Park as their team was in action against Caledonian Thistle in Inverness so I gladly accepted the chance to watch a bit of first-division football, the first I had seen that season since losing my job at New Broomfield in the summer.

I travelled along the M8 and down the A77 with Scott McFarlane, a friend of mine and a coach with Hibernian Boys Club. Midway through the first half I turned sharply after seeing someone I knew heading for his seat. At that point the lights went out. The next thing I knew I was in the capable hands of two paramedics, one male and one female, and they were strapping me into a portable chair. They carried me downstairs into the waiting ambulance, which then proceeded to the main hospital in Ayr, where I spent the night. At the time I had no idea what had happened and the whole experience knocked me for six.

The doctors at the hospital were unable to diagnose the condition so they filed a report to give to my GP. Upon my return to Edinburgh my own doctor, after reading the report, made an appointment for me at the Western General in Edinburgh where I was placed in the capable hands of Professor Grant. He proceeded to carry out an intensive range of tests after which he said everything pointed to me being epileptic. The condition, however, would only be confirmed if I had another fit.

March 2002

There's no such thing as a glamorous place to suffer a seizure but if there were I wouldn't have picked ramshackle Somerset Park for my first and the salubrious surroundings of Pilrig Park for my second. It was a Sunday morning fifteen months after my initial fit and I was walking from the pavilion towards the pitch to prepare for a game involving Calder Boys Club under-tens, whom I trained. My mobile rang; I can't remember who was calling, but I told them I would return their call at the end of the match. Just seconds after ending the conversation I said to John Weir, a fellow coach, that I could feel a build up of pressure against my brain and it felt like waves were swirling through my head. Once again the next thing I remembered was waking up in an ambulance receiving oxygen and on my way to hospital. I was headed for the Western General in Edinburgh and another consultation with Professor Grant. I also remember being concerned for my boys and the opposition; it is not easy for kids of such tender years having to witness someone having a seizure.

As it was my second fit Professor Grant carried out twice as many tests and I had to undergo a computerised axial tomography scan, also known as a CAT scan. The professor asked John to give a detailed report of how I appeared immediately before the seizure. After receiving the results of the tests and the scan he diagnosed me as an epileptic and told me I would have to take tablets called Tegretol three times a day for the rest of my life. Despite the horror of blacking out twice I was relieved that it was treatable with medication.

* * *

This is the transcript of an article by Dr Keith Hopcroft that appeared in *The Scotsman* on Tuesday, 28 May 2002:

THE most surprising aspect of the news that former Hearts and Scotland footballer Gary Mackay has epilepsy is that people are surprised. Because epilepsy is common, affecting about one per cent of the population. And it can occur in anyone: young, old, healthy and infirm. Though no longer as stigmatising as it once was, epilepsy remains a poorly understood illness. And with good reason: it comes in various guises, has many different causes and can be difficult to diagnose.

Epilepsy is defined as a tendency to repeated seizures. A seizure – the modern word for 'fit' – is a sudden discharge of brain activity, somewhat like a short circuit in electronics. The result can be dramatic, such as the well-known type of fit causing a blackout and shaking limbs. But it can be more subtle – for example, a minor twitching of one side of the body, or a blinking, glassy stare for a few seconds, especially in children.

But one fit does not necessarily mean epilepsy. One in twenty of us will experience a seizure at some time. The occurrence can only be labelled 'epilepsy' when it is a recurring phenomenon, so doctors 'delay' the diagnosis with good reason.

What causes it? Usually nothing: in 60 per cent of people there is no underlying problem, although there may be a family history of epilepsy. In these cases, many things can trigger a fit, such as alcohol, stress, tiredness and, very occasionally, flashing lights. In the other 40 per cent, the seizures are caused by some other illness, such as a stroke or brain tumour, this likelihood tending to increase the older the patient is when seizures start.

Medication is usually very effective. Traditionally, there has been a trade-off between keeping the seizures under control and suffering side-effects from medication. But with newer drugs, many patients can anticipate a fit-free, side-effect-free future.

I wouldn't wish epilepsy on anyone, but if any good came out of my diagnosis it was greater public awareness of the condition. I was completely oblivious to the fact that more than fifty million people worldwide have epilepsy and seizures can happen to anyone, even the fittest professional sportsmen.

Exactly five months after Dr Hopcroft's article appeared in *The Scotsman* I was at Easter Road watching a League Cup tie between Hibernian and Rangers when defender Alen Orman collapsed in a heap on the pitch approaching the end of the first half. The sight of the player shaking uncontrollably brought back bad memories but that was the first time I had witnessed someone else having a fit. It wasn't a nice thing to see, and I'm sure that it wasn't a nice experience for the lad either, but he appeared to recover pretty quickly. It surprised me that he was passed fit by doctors to start the Premier League match against Aberdeen at Pittodrie three days later but it transpired it had only taken him a matter of minutes to recover from seizure. It took me quite a bit longer to get back to normal after my attacks, but everyone is different.

Alen later revealed he had been living with epilepsy for more than a year prior to the match against Rangers and had been seeing three consultant neurologists on a regular basis. They had given him the all-clear to continue his career. It would have been easy for him to quit football there and then but he refused to let his condition get the better of him and for that he must be commended. It would have been easy to throw in the towel in case he suffered another seizure during a match but he was strong enough to continue and was rewarded in 2005, when, having joined Swiss side FC Thun, he played in the Champions League and performed admirably against the likes of Freddie Ljungberg, Robert Pires and Jose Antonio Reyes. He even received a kick to the face from Robin van Persie after the final whistle, but, given all he'd been through, I'm sure that was the least of his worries.

* * *

23 January 2003

There are a few things I have done in my life that make me proud; one was officially opening the Enlighten Holistic Centre in Edinburgh. Enlighten is a registered charity that helps to tackle epilepsy and I felt honoured when I was asked to become a patron, along with the Earl & Countess of Dalkeith, former Scotland rugby captain Tom Smith, opera singer Miranda Keys and pianist Marta Lunati. It was also a great privilege to be asked to open the special relaxation centre in the West End in special memory of thirty-three-year-old bank worker Patricia Duff, who died following a seizure in September 2002. Patricia had lived with epilepsy for twenty years and her family and friends helped raise £2,000 at her funeral, including donations from her employer Lloyds TSB and Colinton bowling club, where her dad was a member. The money was given to the centre in her memory.

Epilepsy affects one in every two hundred people in Britain and is the most common neurological condition, with stress being a factor in many cases. For some people it can be controlled so they can live with it, but it can also devastate your life. I appear to be one of the fortunate ones for whom medication can control the condition but I realise others are not so lucky. It therefore gives me great pleasure to help Enlighten whenever I can in its mission to widen opportunities for people affected by epilepsy and to raise awareness of epilepsy issues in all sectors of the community. I got a lot out of football and it's time to give something back.

16

Save Our Hearts

'Fighting the good fight'

Football clubs evolve and change. They always have and they always will. The departure of Wallace Mercer from Tynecastle in June 1994 was the end of an era for Hearts while the arrival of Les Deans and Chris Robinson signalled the start of a fresh one. I always had a lot of time for Robinson. Sally Robinson, that is. She was the finance director for the new regime prior to the appointment of Stewart Fraser and, among other things, was responsible for much of the day-to-day running of the club. I got on very well with her, something that cannot be said of my relationship with her namesake.

* * *

Apart from his decision to get rid of Sandy Clark as manager I did not have much of a problem with Chris Robinson during the early stages of his tenure. There was of course the incident in the summer of 1995 when the club asked me to contact Jim Jefferies about the vacant manager's post, which should have pleased everyone at Tynecastle because we secured the services of an excellent manager. And then there was the time Les Deans asked me if I could be present at the opening of a brand-new set of mobile floodlights in Balerno as a favour to Robinson. I gladly gave up my time to attend and Chris and his wife were very grateful.

Those two examples aside, there weren't too many other times when I viewed Chris Robinson in a positive light. When I left Hearts in March 1997 he wanted Airdrie to pay £10,000. I was disappointed at not getting that cash for the service I'd given the club over seventeen years, but he was adamant. I had good and bad spells during my playing career and while I was far from the greatest player to pull on a maroon jersey no one could have accused me of not giving my all. Although I had no legal entitlement to the money in terms of my contract I always tried to portray the football club in a positive light and felt I was worthy of a one-off, ex-gratia payment for the loyalty I had shown. (As I explained earlier in these pages my ex-wife Vicky went to see Jim Jefferies and got me the money.)

The straw that broke the camel's back in my relationship with Chris Robinson stemmed from an incident in October 2000. I had been to see the club's administration manager, Colin Sked. At that time Hearts were looking for more ex-players to act as matchday ambassadors in the Gorgie Suite. The club also wanted to found a former-players club and Colin saw me as the ideal person to liaise with colleagues, having helped put together a squad to compete against Rangers, Dundee United and Celtic in the Scottish Masters at Braehead a few weeks previously. I had recently set up my agency business but had no problem taking a little time out to help the club.

During a previous discussion Colin had given me a list of twenty-five names and asked if I could get addresses and phone numbers for them. After collating the information I phoned him and, at his request, went to see him at Tynecastle. The meeting went well, the names and numbers of the seventeen players I had been able to contact were exchanged and I made my way out of the commercial offices towards reception. My path took me directly past Chris Robinson. The look on his face told me he was less than happy to see me on the premises. He had no idea why I was there; nor did he realise I was helping his club out. But his look, I thought, made it clear he didn't want me anywhere near the property. His actions left me incandescent with rage and I remember shouting at him, 'that is a disgraceful way to look at anybody'. He ignored me and walked on. My raised voice was enough to create a scene and it didn't take long for the club's communications manager, Dougie Dalgleish, a good friend of mine, to come rushing out of his office to see what was going on.

If I had been at Tynecastle that day trying to get something *from* Hearts then Robinson may have had a point about a non-employee being allowed into the inner sanctum of the club's offices. The fact is I was trying to help Colin Sked, one of his employees, so to say the incident left a bad taste in my mouth would be a severe understatement. From that moment on my dislike for Robinson reached new levels. Although I could not have known it at the time our chance meeting at Tynecastle was the first link in a chain of events that led to the formation of Save Our Hearts. That incident intensified my lack of respect for the man but those feelings paled into insignificance when he subsequently changed both the name of the football club and the club badge.

In my eyes he was quickly becoming Public Enemy Number One.

* * *

Shortly after the arrival of Craig Levein as manager of Hearts in December 2000, Robinson released details of plans to create a multi-million-pound, all-seated stadium with a capacity of 30,000 in the west of Edinburgh to replace Tynecastle. This state-of-the-art complex, to be located between the Braehead quarry and Turnhouse golf club, would have had a roof over it to keep everybody nice and dry when those big, bad rain showers arrived. He called it his 'Towards 2005 Initiative'. What a surprise those plans came to nothing and failed to get off the ground. In my book it was a waste of money, something the club could ill-afford at that time. I may have been an outsider looking in but I was well aware that Hearts were in no position to spend money without getting a return on the investment. Therefore, the board's decision in 2001 to reject a reputed £4.5 million cash injection from a consortium, which included his former business partner Les Deans after the pair had fallen out, was baffling. The reason given by the club was that the offer was not in the best interests of Hearts. My suspicion, based on what I heard from various sources, is that it would have led to a much-reduced role for Robinson at Tynecastle, although I have no definite proof of this.

Needless-to-say the decision to reject such a large cash injection did not go down too well with most supporters. One man held too much power as far as they were concerned – a case of Robinson and his followers – and even former chairman Wallace Mercer had a go at the chief executive and the board at the AGM in 2002, accusing them of mismanagement. By this stage a lucrative television deal with Sky had fallen through after Celtic director Dermot Desmond held fresh negotiations with Nationwide League clubs down south amid claims he was seeking a move to English football. The satellite broadcaster had opened negotiations with SPL chief executive Roger Mitchell after the league's plans for its own subscription-based channel was vetoed by the Old Firm. The lack of a lucrative television deal – the BBC ended up obtaining cut-price rights to broadcast top-flight matches – left many clubs with an uneasy financial future. Motherwell was forced into administration, signalling the start of the downsizing of Scottish football. Things were also getting worse at Tynecastle: the club's debt had been rising at an alarming rate, and, in my view, one man had been allowed to gain too much control over the way Heart of Midlothian was being run. Something had to be done.

I was approached by the secretary of the Federation of Hearts Supporters Clubs, John Borthwick, in November 2002 and asked if I would accompany him to a meeting at the Grosvenor hotel in Edinburgh. He'd been asked to attend by three fellow supporters who had grave concerns about the state of the club, both on and off the field. The purpose of the meeting was to determine if it was viable for various fans groups to come together and form a single organisation in a bid to purchase a shareholding in Hearts. It was our way of bringing about change and giving us a say in the running of the club. It also sowed the seeds for the formation of Save Our Hearts, which eventually got up and running sixteen months later, although the path was not without potholes.

I'll always remember when the Federation were coming together with the Supporters Trust to set up Save Our Hearts a prominent Hearts supporter, Robin Beith, said to me one Friday evening in the Orwell Lodge in Edinburgh there was no way we would ever win our battle. Robin was quick to point out that Robinson had changed the club badge and even the name – from Heart of Midlothian Football Club to Hearts FC – without much opposition, so, in his opinion, we had no chance of succeeding. One of the biggest Hearts fans I knew had thrown in the towel before the fight had even started and, while that was difficult to take, his words were used as a stimulant when things weren't going well.

Another dagger through our heart was the announcement by Chris Robinson at the start of January 2004 that the club had secured an agreement in principle with the SRU for Hearts to play at Murrayfield from the start of season 2004/05. Tynecastle was to be put on the market in a bid to alleviate the club's huge debts following several years of what many commentators viewed as financial mismanagement. This manoeuvre by Robinson and the board was designed to generate much-needed revenue and put Hearts back on an even financial footing. But it seemed to me that it did nothing to address the concerns of those thousands of fans who wanted to stay at Tynecastle; it was simply a way of raising much-needed capital to combat the club's financial problems. In protest I requested the return of the Scotland top I wore when I scored against Bulgaria, which had been on show in the executive lounge. I also produced a 'Robinson Must Go' placard, which I displayed both before and after I made the half-time draw at a Scottish Cup tie against Celtic. I was determined to show my solidarity with the fans, most of whom, so far as I could judge, believed it was wrong to move from Tynecastle on purely economic grounds.

This was the scenario we dreaded but it also meant the planning had to stop. Save Our Hearts had to be transformed from a promising idea on a bit of paper to the formation of a group of supporters hell-bent on rescuing what was quickly becoming a situation with dire consequences. It was time to let our actions do the talking.

Marches were arranged through Gorgie, fundraising events were organised and our campaign received a huge boost when Peter McGrail agreed to donate an extra £50,000 every time the group raised another £250,000. I also put in £10,000, the exact sum of money I (eventually) received from Hearts when I left Tynecastle to join Airdrie. It was the least I could have done having never achieved anything tangible either as an individual with Hearts or as part of a team on the park. I had an unfailing belief that what the board was doing was wrong and would have been hugely damaging, maybe even fatal, to our club. I put my heart and soul into the campaign to stop them, but what I put in was nothing compared to what so many other individuals contributed who didn't have a background of having played for the club. They became an inspiration to me with their devoted support to the football team on the pitch and to our cause off it.

* * *

My immediate reaction when I heard about the document *Not Fit for Purpose* was that it could have related to the views of many supporters with regard to Chris Robinson's stewardship of Heart of Midlothian Football Club, rather than the title of a dossier he dissected during a sixty-seven-minute slideshow presentation at the annual general meeting in the Gorgie Suite near the end of January 2004. It was designed to inform shareholders why the board believed the club had to move away from Gorgie to a new stadium. It had two main strands. The first was that Tynecastle could not generate the commercial income a club of the size of Hearts needed while the second concerned the length of the pitch, which was too short for European games and could not be lengthened without massive costs being incurred. Interestingly, the document made only a fleeting reference to the club's massive debt, noting that 'the move to nearby Murrayfield can also be carried out against a background of significant debt reduction'.

I was present at that AGM in the Gorgie Suite but had to walk out before the end. From the perspective of a lifelong Hearts fan I just thought that Robinson's arguments were fundamentally flawed: despite Tynecastle's shortcomings it would have still been preferable for the club to stay in Gorgie. I decided it was better for me to leave than to listen to any more. Pretty pictures of Murrayfield with its entire top tier bedecked in maroon, slides showing 'Welcome to Murrayfield: Home of Hearts FC' and claims that the cost of renting the stadium would be almost as much on a one-off basis as it would be for an entire season. I simply had to walk otherwise I would have said something that I would later have regretted. I also wouldn't have done myself any favours by speaking out at that time and didn't want a reaction. There were a few other shareholder-fans who felt they were better standing outside so as not to create a scene. Robinson appeared to me that evening as a desperate man in a desperate situation. I came to the conclusion that one person embarrassing himself in front of a packed room was more than enough for one night.

Following the publication of *Tynecastle: Not Fit for Purpose* I took it upon myself to do some research rather than just accept Robinson's analysis of the situation. I had been involved in the fundraising for the original 500 Club back in the mid-Nineties to help pay for the new stands and those supporters had shown loyalty to the club by ploughing money in when it was desperately required. Now with the proposals to leave Tynecastle I felt they were being urinated upon from a great height. Yes there were problems with Tynecastle in its existing state but with the help of the man who helped design the three new stands, architect Jim Clydesdale, I came to the conclusion that the problems outlined by Robinson were not nearly severe enough to justify leaving Tynecastle. For example, Jim reckoned the pitch issue could be resolved with additional expenditure of just £100,000.

In my opinion Chris Robinson was putting his own spin on the situation and in so doing was attempting to convince thousands of my fellow Hearts supporters that the proposed move would be beneficial to our club. I also thought he was trying to push through plans that would paper over the cracks of the deteriorating financial situation; under his stewardship the debt increased from around £5 million to a figure in the region of £20 million, a quite staggering sum for a club of our size.

* * *

Like everybody on this earth there are people I like and others I dislike. Hate is a very strong word and it's one I use very infrequently. When I was younger I had a naïve hatred of Hibernian Football Club. As I grew older I got to know their chairman, Kenny McLean senior – a man who just oozed class – and he was even involved in helping set up events during my testimonial year. Kenny epitomised the class that has been evident in the Easter Road boardroom for a long time. I would add the names of Tom O'Malley, Rod Petrie and Kenny McLean to that list; unfortunately, class is a priceless commodity that we at Hearts seem to have missed out on at times.

Chris Robinson is the only person I hate. According to evolutionary psychologists, hate is a rational reaction to people whose interests consistently conflict with one's own. That would only be true in this case if I had

had a similar desire to move Heart of Midlothian Football Club away from its spiritual home and he had beaten me to it. Save Our Hearts became a passion for me because I firmly believed that the board's plans would have ended in the destruction of our great club. Even if the plans had been hatched by Les Deans I would have told him he was wrong, but that scenario wouldn't have had the extra edge it had because of my personal feelings about Robinson. The irony is that his brother Raymond, a Hearts supporter, is such a lovely person.

* * *

Save Our Hearts had been on the go for exactly a month and a day before one of its defining moments arose, and it had nothing directly to do with our organisation. I felt the resignation of Hearts chairman Doug Smith on 5 April 2004 was a huge embarrassment to Chris Robinson and that it left the chief executive even more isolated. To his credit, Doug had always been willing to take on board the views of supporters and now, despite his position as chairman, he realised that pushing through a move to Murrayfield would have dire consequences and, admirably, he fell on his sword.

Doug's departure signalled the arrival of Labour MP and fervent Hearts supporter George Foulkes as chairman. This was probably the most advantageous appointment any of the Save Our Hearts group could have wished for because, despite being isolated on the board, George helped us achieve our two main goals: staying at Tynecastle and removing Robinson from office. I was caught completely unaware when George was appointed because, just two days earlier, Iain Macleod, John Borthwick and I had attended a meeting with him in the centre of Edinburgh, during which we asked him to lend his support to our campaign. Ever the canny politician he had mentioned nothing to us about his new role.

When addressing the media moments after taking over as chairman, Foulkes immediately contradicted the long-held position of Robinson by advocating a year's delay in the move to Murrayfield. Although the Scottish Premier League had rubber-stamped the flit to the home of Scottish rugby there was still no legally binding agreement between Hearts and the Scottish Rugby Union lodged with the SPL, so George's motion to delay the move had come in the nick of time.

Around the same time that George Foulkes was starting work at Tynecastle a meeting was taking place elsewhere in Edinburgh. It had been brokered by the city's Deputy Lord Provost, Steve Cardownie, and it brought together former Hearts chairman Les Deans and Vladimir Romanov, a

Russian-born, Lithuanian multi-millionaire. It would have huge consequences for the future of the football club.

* * *

The summer of 2004 was a time for patience but also a fair bit of head-scratching. There had been no follow-up to the initial meeting between Deans and Romanov and that particular avenue appeared shut off until Les, frustrated at the lack of progress, asked George Foulkes to resurrect proceedings. Thankfully, George managed to fix up a meeting in the House of Commons with Vladimir Romanov (and Sergejus Fedotovas) and persuaded him to come back to the table. However, any deal remained a long way off and things got even worse on 18 August 2004 when Hearts reached a conditional agreement to sell Tynecastle to Cala Management Limited for £22 million. The sale had to be confirmed by a vote of shareholders at an extraordinary general meeting on 13 September.

This announcement was a body blow for everyone connected with Save Our Hearts but it intensified our efforts to be successful. While I hated Robinson with a passion my feelings for him paled into insignificance compared to my desire to save Tynecastle. There were people who disagreed with some of our methods, and I accept a few things we did were wrong, but they were a means to an end. There was never any chance that a hundred noisy fans shouting outside his office in St Andrew's Square at lunchtime would have forced Hearts director Brian Duffin – one of Robinson's main allies – to resign but we felt we had to make a point.

We even held a meeting in the Orwell Lodge in a bid to come up with fresh ideas to halt the sale although that didn't quite go according to plan. Needless-to-say the room that evening was full of angry Hearts supporters all passionate about the future of their club and a cry of 'why not just head up to his house and let him know we won't go away' was met with cheers. Not the most sensible suggestion in the world but there was no way anyone was going to stop us. A convoy of twelve cars – all tooting their horns and flashing their lights – drove up to Robinson's home in an exclusive area of Balerno. It didn't take a genius to work out his neighbours were not best pleased to see us. Nor was his wife. In fact, raging is how I would describe her. 'Get out, get out,' she bawled, 'he's not in.'

The EGM was held in the Gorgie Suite at Tynecastle. I've attended many football matches that failed to match the raucous atmosphere of that evening. The precautions taken were akin to those used to protect presidents and prime ministers: police stationed at either end of the hall and outside; three Hearts security officers positioned in front of the top table to protect

Robinson and his colleagues as they sat down; a heavy cordon of both security and Lothian and Borders' finest as the chief executive hurriedly made his way out of the arena via the side door beside the bar at the end of a wild night. The deed was done; the sale of the stadium was passed by a narrow majority although there was one good thing that emerged from the EGM. It was agreed that the deal to sell Tynecastle would not be concluded before 31 January 2005 after George Foulkes insisted on a five-month get-out period in the resolution to sell in order to let interested parties come up with alternatives. That was the catalyst for us to push on and give the chairman as much support as we could to attract new investment as he continued to fend off the imminent sale to property giants CALA. Once again he had come up with the goods.

Less than a week after the stormy scenes at the EGM two of Vladimir Romanov's representatives flew over to Scotland to attend Hearts' fixture at Dunfermline. However, they were mainly in Scotland to hold talks with the club's main shareholders – Leslie Deans, Chris Robinson, Robert McGrail and Scottish Media Group – and to discuss finance. Deans and Robinson appeared keen to sell a majority of their substantial shareholding to Romanov although SMG were not quite so willing and were much harder to convince. Despite the latter's lack of enthusiasm, there was suddenly a little light at the end of the tunnel as far as Save Our Hearts was concerned, although our job was far from complete.

* * *

Following Hearts is never dull but at least supporters get an opportunity to experience the full gamut of emotions. I've had plenty of unhappy moments both as a player and a supporter, but there have not been many better days than 30 September 2004. I was in Portugal to commentate on the UEFA Cup second leg tie between Braga and Hearts when, on the morning of the game, I received a phone call informing me that Chris Robinson had agreed in principle to sell his 19.6 per cent stake in the club to Vladimir Romanov (a deal that was concluded four months later). The subsequent two-all draw and progression to the group stage of the UEFA Cup that evening made it one of the happiest days of my life.

Granted I did not know much about Romanov and his background but I knew enough to reach the conclusion that even the Devil would have received a warm welcome from most of the Gorgie faithful if he'd secured a deal to buy out the old regime. The fact that George Foulkes was happy with the transfer of shares was good enough for me. It's impossible to understate the key role that George played and I hate to imagine the condition Heart of

Midlothian Football Club would be in today had it not been for his skills as chairman and mediator. The only regret I had about the deal was that Robinson walked away with money in his pocket. Trust me to find a negative from such a positive day!

There were many key dates as far as the Save Our Hearts campaign was concerned but I struggle to think of a more important one than 22 December 2004. By that stage Vladimir Romanov had obtained enough shares to be able to call another EGM – scheduled for 10 January 2005 – to vote on a proposal to halt the sale of Tynecastle to CALA Homes. In essence it meant the club would remain at its spiritual home as those in favour of Romanov's plan finally outnumbered the dissenting voters, due mainly to Les Deans and some other major shareholders agreeing to support Romanov's motion. Heart of Midlothian Football Club had been saved from a potentially fatal blow. Sometimes in life you have to fight for what you believe in and up until the formation of Save Our Hearts I had never campaigned for anything in my life. However, staying at Tynecastle was a cause well worth fighting for and there are so many people who deserve the utmost credit for the support they gave.

An announcement on the official Hearts website suggested the EGM could well be delayed by a couple of weeks because 'further clarification and formalisation of the proposals was required' according to club officials. However, Romanov forced the meeting to take place on its original date of 10 January and 70.2 per cent of votes cast were in favour of the proposal to scrap the sale of Tynecastle. While that was a joy, the best part of the meeting from my point of view was when Chris Robinson was obliged to vote with Vladimir Romanov under the initial agreement to sell his shares!

I got involved with Save Our Hearts to try and help prevent the sale of the stadium so once that goal had been achieved I felt the time was right to step down as the fans' figurehead and get back to normal life. Incidentally, everyone who put money into Save Our Hearts got it back, including myself with the £10,000. The money was the least of my concerns. The campaign had saved Tynecastle saved from the bulldozers, while the departure of Robinson was a bonus. Being able to say that we, the members of the organisation, had a part to play in both those events was, for me, priceless.

There was a bit of a sour taste left in my mouth a few weeks later when I was banned from making the half-time draw during the Tennent's Scottish Cup tie against Kilmarnock. George Foulkes had given me the go-ahead to make the draw on the pitch along with Donald Ford, despite my previous indiscretion pretty much a year to the day with my one-man protest on the pitch and my 'Robinson Must Go' banner. However, both Donald and I were denied access to the players' tunnel by a security guard who claimed he'd been told by the match commander, chief inspector Brian Muir of Lothian and Borders Police, that I should be barred from the park in the interests of public safety. Can you believe it? A wee lad from Gorgie who wouldn't hurt a fly, and couldn't fight his way out of a paper bag, was considered a danger to the public. I later found out that representatives of the Federation of Hearts Supporters' Clubs, who had invited Donald to be their guest for the day in the executive suite, were given assurances from the police that it was not their decision to ban me from the tunnel. Nothing like passing the buck!

* * *

'Good riddance as far as I'm concerned' was the quote I gave to journalists on 18 July 2005 when they asked for my opinion after Chris Robinson finally severed his ties with Heart of Midlothian Football Club. The next time I bumped into him was in a petrol station in Slateford in March 2007. He was on the phone at the time (to his wife I assume by the way he was talking) and I just felt total disgust towards the man. I looked at him but he never engaged in eye contact when he employed me so there was no chance he was going to do so in a garage forecourt. I'm not a fighter but I would make an exception for him.

His departure from Hearts in July 2005 was followed three months later by the decision of SMG to sever their ties with the club after Vladimir Romanov agreed to purchase the company's 19.9 per cent stake. SMG was a huge bugbear for us during the Save Our Hearts campaign, to such an extent that along with fellow members of the organisation I travelled through to Glasgow one afternoon to protest at their ongoing decision not to sell their shareholding. It was a great relief when they were no longer part of the equation. Around that time Romanov also purchased the 5.7 per cent stake held by Halifax Bank of Scotland on his way to amassing 55.5 per cent of the available shares and becoming the majority shareholder in Hearts.

We'd finally reached the end of the long and difficult road. Once again the football club had evolved and changed. The departure of Chris Robinson from Tynecastle in July 2005 was the end of an era for Hearts while the arrival of Vladimir Romanov signalled the start of a fresh one.

17

An Audience with Romanov

'First impressions count . . .'

Four million people live in Lithuania. Two million Lithuanians live else-where; 350,000 are currently in Britain, the highest number of immigrants from one country on our shores with the exception of the Poles. With that statistic in mind perhaps it's not that surprising that Vladimir Romanov identified the United Kingdom as an ideal place for an overseas business venture. It took a while before I came face-to-face with the man himself. My first indirect involvement with him came during a meeting with Sergejus Fedotovas – one of Mr Romanov's business advisors and a future director of Hearts – at the Caledonian Hotel in Edinburgh. It was September 2004, just before Hearts shares changed hands from Chris Robinson to the fourth-richest person in Lithuania.

I make no apologies for using my position as a former player to get maximum exposure for Save Our Hearts. I was one of the higher-profile members of a group whose aim was to force change at the football club and ensure matches continued to be played at Tynecastle. Vladimir Romanov also wanted change, but for different reasons. My stance intrigued Sergejus and he was keen to find out what all the fuss was about. I didn't realise it at the time but my actions as a media 'whore' for the benefit of the SOH campaign had somehow got onto the radar in Lithuania.

Sergejus Fedotovas is a very private individual and says little in public without being prompted, but when he does talk it's usually worth listening to. He was the one who informed me about the number of Lithuanian immigrants in the United Kingdom and he made me aware of that statistic when telling me about Vladimir Romanov's reasons for wanting to invest in Heart of Midlothian. Romanov had, of course, done his homework and had meticulously researched the history and traditions of the football club. In addition, according to Sergejus, he was acutely aware of Edinburgh's reputation as a global financial centre. He had not yet purchased a single Hearts share but had already envisaged Scotland's capital city as an ideal location for a future branch of UKIO Bank, a plan that has since come to fruition with premises on Castle Street plus the multi-million pound acquisition of the former Royal Bank of Scotland headquarters in St Andrew Square.

Sergejus made no secret of the fact that Vladimir was a businessman first and a football fan second, but he did state categorically that success on the pitch was the key. It was explained to me that Romanov was well aware there was no point trying to run before he could walk; he meant that it would be pointless opening banks only to find there were no customers queuing up to open accounts or to borrow money. He was hoping the publicity generated in Scotland, courtesy of a successful football team, would open doors for his bank. He was also hoping to be the saviour of Hearts. All in all it was not a bad way to make a first impression.

Sergejus Fedotovas had put Vladimir Romanov's cards on the table, now he was keen to find out why I wanted to remove the chief executive. Did I simply have a personal vendetta against Chris Robinson or did I genuinely want the club to go forward? We were checking each other out and finding out just how authentic the other party was. The discussion was purposely kept confidential and it remained that way. Neither the press nor the broadcast media got a sniff. Sergejus and I shook hands at the end of our meeting and went our separate ways. It would be another two-and-a-half years before our paths crossed again.

* * *

Since that first meeting I have always thought that Sergejus Fedotovas would be the sensible one at any gathering. The calm type who would sort things out without a commotion; the ideal mediator. For that reason I always hoped he would be at Tynecastle in a hands-on role, but that never really materialised. He became a name for Hearts supporters to associate with rather than a face they could identify. Of course that wasn't the case when Sergejus was appointed acting chief executive on completion of the transaction that took Romanov's shareholding in Hearts to 29.9 per cent on 1 February 2005. He was based mainly at Tynecastle until the appointment of Phil Anderton as chief executive. Following Phil's arrival, and the subsequent departure of Fedotovas, I can only recall a few occasions in which Sergejus was either seen in Edinburgh or heard from. Therefore, when the opportunity presented itself to go to Lithuania in June 2007 to meet him and many others from the UBIG stable to celebrate Mr Romanov's sixtieth birthday it was an offer I could not turn down. It would give me the chance to reacquaint myself with Sergejus and to get his views on the progress of Hearts in the two-and-a-half years since we first met. More importantly, and I mean that with no disrespect to Fedotovas, I would also get the opportunity to spend quality time with the man behind the headlines: Vladimir Romanov.

I made the trip to Lithuania with a good friend of mine from Newcastle, Iain Macleod, who, like me, was a member of Save Our Hearts. Romanov's people were looking for a couple of prominent Hearts supporters to travel to the Baltic nation. This was part of a strategy, hatched in Lithuania, to get supporters to realise that he is an integral part of the club and not just a mystery figure who appears at Tynecastle from time to time. It was a privilege to be asked to represent the wider body of Hearts supporters and I used the opportunity to see exactly what part Heart of Midlothian Football Club plays in our owner's life.

I was made aware prior to departure that I would be granted the exclusive company of Mr Romanov for a couple of hours on the Tuesday at his office in Kaunas. Prior to that there was his birthday party in the headquarters of his bank, also in Kaunas. We were staying in the Lithuanian capital, Vilnius, so it meant a trip of about forty-five miles on the Monday evening, then back to our hotel in Vilnius at its conclusion and the reverse journey early the next morning to meet him again. Despite having so much money and so many acquaintances, the birthday celebration was decidedly low key and limited to a gathering of family, friends and close allies. The evening, however, was an eye-opener.

Iain and I were sitting at a table for three at the party and there was one spare seat. It was earmarked for Vladimir's English-speaking personal assistant, Diana, but she spent a lot of time in the early part of the evening rushing about with her clipboard making sure everything was running to schedule. The celebration was due to last three hours and once she was satisfied that everything was in order she sat down beside us and had a drink. She asked Iain if he was Gary Mackay; with hindsight, I wish he had said yes. When it was pointed out that I was the person she was looking for Diana proceeded to ask me if I had my speech ready. This was news to me. She informed me that everyone with a birthday gift for Mr Romanov had to make a speech after presenting it to him and I was due up on stage shortly. My language was choice to say the least so if you are reading this Diana please accept my sincere apologies! I hoped Iain would come up with an excuse that would get me out of the public speaking. With inspiration sorely lacking from that quarter I asked Diana where the toilets were. Politely, she suggested that I was joking but I told her I had to go there and then. She informed me that she would change the running order, so there was no excuse. In the end I succumbed to her charm.

What do you get the proverbial man-who-has-everything for his sixtieth birthday? The fourth-richest man in Lithuania could surely afford to buy anything he wanted so the decision was not an easy one. The Scotch whisky idea was quickly ruled out after Charlie Mann showed us a thirty-one-year-old bottle of Highland Park prior to leaving Scotland. We plumped for a Hearts kilt and sporran, a Scottish quaich and the complete works of Robert Burns. The latter was Iain's idea after speaking to Sergejus during a memorial service at Contalmaison and finding out about Mr Romanov's love of poetry in general, and Burns in particular. Vladimir had even written his own poem on a wreath to commemorate those who perished at the Battle of the Somme.

Just before it was my turn to get up and present the guest of honour with his gifts we witnessed a rather rotund gentleman at the table in front of us doing likewise. Instead of going straight up to Vladimir he made for the corner of the room, where he produced a metal trolley, on top of which was a gigantic, marble chess set with pieces around four inches high. If he got any change from £10,000 he would have been lucky. By comparison our gifts seemed so inadequate. Mr Romanov, who was sitting right it front of a large orchestra, shook the man by the hand and thanked him after listening to his speech. It had gone like clockwork; in fact the same thing had happened with every guest, with two assistants on hand to collect the gifts and put them to one side. Now it was my turn.

At this point Vladimir was aware that Iain and I were Hearts supporters from Scotland but apart from that didn't know us from Adam. I collected our gifts from the table, walked over and proceeded to make a speech telling him how delighted the supporters were when he took over our club and saved us from an uncertain future. I explained that we were well accustomed to a roller-coaster ride following the team and that it was never dull being a Hearts fan. This was translated for his benefit and then he smiled warmly and shook my hand. At that point I handed over our gifts and his eyes lit up when he saw the kilt. By complete contrast with the other presents he had received, which were handed straight to his two assistants, he promptly placed the kilt on the back of his chair and removed the sporran before wearing it over his suit. It stayed there for the remainder of the evening and it was even suggested to me at a later date that the kilt also got an outing later that night but for the eyes of Mrs Romanov only . . . .

It was a privilege to attend such an intimate celebration, and, although we were unable to understand much of what was being said, it was nice to see the respect that a lot of people, both from Lithuania and other nations, have for the owner of our club. To then get the chance the following day to spend a couple of hours with Vladimir Romanov was an opportunity afforded to few top businessmen, never mind two Hearts supporters, so we headed back to Vilnius tired but excited about what was in store.

* * *

The road between Vilnius and Kaunas is not long – about the distance between Edinburgh and Glasgow – but the traffic at peak times is congested, similar to the M8, so it was decided that Charlie Mann, Iain and I were to be picked up at 8.30 a.m. in order to get us to Kaunas for ten. The journey would normally take around fifty minutes but that could be doubled in heavy traffic. A maroon BMW 7 Series – including the numbers 007 as part of its registration plate – pulled up at our hotel right on schedule. There were also two submariners from the UK, Jim McMaster from Scotland and Englishman Dave Barlow, heading east to meet Mr Romanov so they followed in a taxi.

To the best of my knowledge there has never been a prominent Eastern European in Formula One but if Bernie Ecclestone was ever looking for one then I can heartily recommend our driver that day. 'Maniac' is the best word to describe him and I'm just glad there were no speed cameras on the road otherwise the constant flashing bulbs would have given the impression of a discotheque through the blacked-out windows. In fairness he got us to our destination, probably a lot quicker than he should have, and we arrived at Vladimir's Romanov's offices just over an hour after setting off. Upon arrival we met journalist Will Stewart and his partner Svetlana, who informed us that she would be translating when we met Mr Romanov.

The UBIG offices are located on the fifteenth and top floor of an imposing building. As we made our way along the corridor we were aware of posters and newspaper cuttings relating to Hearts. There were a handful dotted about the place but they paled into insignificance when we approached Romanov's office area and witnessed a huge maroon-and-white mural with paper cuttings identifying the positive events that had occurred since he gained control of the club.

Within his own personal office, which is dominated by a huge wooden table and eight seats, there are several more pictures of Tynecastle in addition to numerous bits of memorabilia relating to submarines and submariners. This said to me that Hearts is not just a toy to this gentleman but plays a huge part in the UBIG operation. There were more club-related pictures at the top end of his room as well as drawings of the new national stadium in Kaunas. At the other end there was a giant television, a DVD player and a white board. There were names scribbled in black pen; the Kaunas players who were playing against Zalgiris Vilnius the following evening.

Svetlana introduced us to Vladimir Romanov and he remembered me from the night before, intimating that I had given him the kilt and sporran. She explained that Iain had been part of the Save Our Hearts organisation and that I was the record appearance holder for 'his' famous club. He had not been made aware of my history – he had only been told I was the representative for Christophe Berra and Lee Wallace – and I could see the warmth that emanated from him when Svetlana told him how many games I had played and that I had represented my country on four occasions. He immediately paid more attention to what she was saying and seemed very keen to find out more. Using broken English, eye contact and hand gestures – and with Svetlana's help – we discussed our club and joked about memorable incidents from the past. I asked him if he had used his beautiful table to perfect the art of climbing on top of wooden structures, similar to when he climbed on the ledge at the front of the director's box at Tynecastle to celebrate after we had beaten Aberdeen to secure a Champions League spot. He replied that he would have jumped from the window sill outside if we had not qualified.

By now I was much more relaxed and was enjoying the company of a man with a great interest in my Hearts career. I had only been in his office for a matter of minutes yet it felt like we had known each other for a long time. If we had been old acquaintances I could have understood what happened next, but he surprised me when he walked up to the whiteboard, wiped off the names of the Kaunas players and gestured for me to join him. He told me to put my Hearts team on the board. I wondered if I was being tested but I proceeded to write nine names:

Gordon; Karapidis, Zaliukas, Berra, Wallace; Mikoliunas, Kingston, *space*, Driver; Velicka, *space*.

I left two blank spaces, left-centre midfield and a striker, as I felt those were the two positions that needed strengthening, before giving him the marker back. The first thing he did was put a question mark above the name of Craig Gordon. This was very interesting. Was that because the future of the player was uncertain at that time, long before he moved on to Sunderland for £9 million? I never did find out. He then filled in the blanks with Ruben Palazuelos in central midfield alongside Laryea Kingston and Mauricio Pinilla in attack with Andrius Velicka. He scribbled 2009 beside Christophe Berra and 2011 alongside Lee Wallace; I was informed those were the years he expected both my clients to be at the top of their game and worth the most money. And he also wrote a few additional names for certain positions. Pascal Mendy joined Christos Karipidis at right-back, he included FBK Kaunas player Mindaugas Baguzis in central defence and moved Marius Zaliukas forward into midfield while adding Ricardas Beniusis as an additional striker. It was a surprise that he was sharing all this with me having only met me for the first time the day before. I certainly hadn't travelled to Lithuania thinking I would be involved in squad selection.

I'm not sure if Mr Romanov agreed with the nine players I selected but the fact he didn't rub any of them out suggests we were at least in partial agreement. He even asked, in a jovial manner, why I didn't want to be the manager. I told him that it was the only job I would do for nothing and I couldn't afford to do so at that point! I admit to being critical of interference from above in the past but this was enlightening and provided me with hope that he does welcome input after all, although how much influence others would have is open to conjecture.

After getting the chance to pretend I was Rolf Harris at the white board, we then moved over to the big wooden table for a more in-depth chat about Hearts. We spoke about various events that had taken place since he had become involved at Tynecastle. He brought George Burley's name, albeit briefly, into the conversation and also mentioned George Foulkes and Phil Anderton but didn't say too much about them or give any reasons as to why they were now employed elsewhere. It came across that he was not too disappointed the trio were no longer at the club but what he thinks of them as individuals will not alter my opinion: George Foulkes remains a close friend, George Burley remains a top manager and I am not surprised that he was appointed Scotland coach in 2008. As for Phil Anderton he is a top bloke who was very easy to deal with during his brief spell in Gorgie. The football club has moved on since George Burley but there will always be regret in my mind, and possibly even in the mind of Vladimir Romanov, about his departure and what might have been.

The performances by Hearts in August and September 2005 were the best I have ever witnessed from any Hearts team, whether as a player or fan, but Romanov believed it was right to remove Burley. I didn't agree with his decision then and I still don't but there must have been good reasons for it. I would have loved to have heard his side of the story but as we were discussing the future, not the past, I felt it wasn't the right time to ask Vladimir if he would make that same decision again. Be assured I will ask one day.

We also spoke about youth development – a topic close to my heart – while I touched on the money Hearts had brought in from the sale of Paul Hartley, Rudi Skacel and Andy Webster. Those three players had not been brought through the ranks but had been bought and sold for a decent profit, something that doesn't happen very often in the present climate. Mr Romanov said he was more than happy to give decent youngsters an opportunity to make a name for themselves. Then, once he deemed them to be at the peak of their form – Berra in 2009 and Wallace in 2011, for example – he would sell them on to generate maximum revenue. I was informed by one of the interpreters that Vladimir took great pleasure in identifying players he could bring to the club for a modest fee before being sold for a much greater sum; in for £100,000 and out for £1 million were the hypothetical figures quoted. He speculates to accumulate, like the buccaneering businessman he is.

When the conversation moved on Vladimir produced paperwork with statistics that related to the health and wellbeing of the players at FBK Kaunas. It was the most thorough collection of data I had ever seen, and each folder related to specific individuals. I drew parallels with what I had witnessed when Lokomotiv Moscow put Garry O'Connor through the most intense medical I had ever witnessed. The Eastern European mentality is to leave no stone unturned. I asked how the data had been collated and was informed that various Russian methods were used to test the players, at which point Vladimir told Svetlana to ask me if I'd like to be put through one of the tests. When I asked who was to carry it out I was told it would be a woman called Rima . . . .

When I was a player I was a nosy bugger and loved to know everything that was going on. These days I never ask my players about the goings on at their clubs and only find out if they volunteer the information. So I had only heard of Rima because her visit to Scotland had been widely reported in the media. She had been flown in from Lithuania by Romanov, along with other New Age therapists, to assist with the diagnosis of injuries. It was said she tapped golden sticks on body parts to determine fitness levels while one of her colleagues used his hands to manipulate energy fields in the back and was known to Hearts players as Pyjama Man, because of the striped medical kit he wore at Riccarton. Thus was born the infamous 'Rima and Pyjama Man' headline. I had never been told if she was a twenty-one-year-old blonde stunner standing six-foot-two, or, as it transpired, a smaller and much less attractive but very warm individual in her mid-forties. I had not travelled thousands of miles only to reject an opportunity like that so I agreed to be tested and we made our way to her office, where our group was warmly welcomed.

The room was full of coloured charts detailing the mental and physical wellbeing of FBK Kaunas and MTZ-Ripo players. I was standing beside a machine where the person being tested puts five fingers into the holes provided so that the tip of each finger occupies the relevant space. The computer then takes a reading. I'm not in the same physical condition as Goncalves, Berra and Kingston – and probably wasn't even when I was playing – so there was apprehension on my part. However, although slightly nervous, I thought in for a penny in for a pound and went through with it. The test results appeared pretty much instantaneously on the computer and I was shown what they meant. She was talking about my stomach and the fact it didn't have enough bacteria. That may have been due to the excess alcohol from the previous evening but was more likely related to a recent tummy upset. She also identified two other problems, one in my neck and the other in my back. Both were correct and the results proved to be highly accurate. I was then persuaded to try out another piece of equipment that Rima claimed would give more precise details about the problems in my neck and back. Her golden rod! I expected it to be the size of an elderly gentleman's walking stick but it turned out to be the length of a pen, only slightly thicker. It had a flat head and was shaped like the implement guys use to shave nose hair or trim their eyebrows. I was then invited to remove my top. Never being particularly shy as a player I agreed to this without much encouragement, even though I had reached the age of forty-three and the six-pack was not what it used to be.

Rima then proceeded to run the golden rod around the top half of my body, making sure she pressed down on my nerve ends so that the red light on the instrument was illuminated when problem areas were identified. She claimed to be able to tell by the feedback from the rod exactly where there either was, or had been, discomfort. Now maybe she just got lucky or maybe I wanted to believe what she was telling me but the first thing she identified was a problem at the top of my spine to the left, near my neck. She said there was an unusual area of thickness. As it happens, ten days previously I was unable to go to the gym because of that same problem. Having been told there was an issue with my back, it was then explained to me there was an area between the fourth and fifth vertebrae that was causing concern and I should get it checked out upon my return to Scotland. I was then told there was a problem with blood circulation in my right leg and was asked if I had ever suffered a serious injury. I broke my ankle playing for Hearts.

From being initially sceptical I was very impressed by the accuracy of her prognosis. Maybe it was easier for me as a middle-aged man to embrace a situation that was quite funny for most of those watching, but it was also enlightening. If those methods can help the physical condition of a player then I can understand why Vladimir Romanov is keen to use them. On the other hand I can also understand why British footballers would find such methods difficult to embrace; we are very firmly set in our ways. But the tests are for the benefit of players, and, after experiencing them, I think they should be approached with an open mind.

* * *

We were only meant to spend two hours in the company of Vladimir Romanov but it was nearly three hours before we sat down for lunch and at no time did he either get restless or insist he should be elsewhere. I was later told he ditched as many as ten appointments that morning to spend time with us – Iain, Charlie and myself plus the two submariners Jim and Dave – and he genuinely seemed to be enjoying himself. Here was a man who had an empire to run but that morning decided he would rather spend his precious time with people who shared similar interests instead of in routine business meetings.

I've been fortunate to meet a lot of people in my life who have had the destiny of others in their hands; heart surgeons, for example. I have also met people who have power because of their wealth but not all of them are kind-hearted and not all of them empathised with this Gorgie boy in the way that Vladimir Romanov did. I was really taken by the man and the warmth he exuded. They are two completely different people from two completely different walks of life but I see a number of similarities between Mr Romanov and the Gaffer: direct eye contact, warmth, a firm handshake that belies men of their limited physical stature.

After lunch Mr Romanov asked what my schedule was for the rest of the day. I informed him I was travelling back to the airport in Vilnius with Iain and Charlie; we had our cases with us. Without prompting he asked if we wanted to stay in Lithuania a while longer and attend the FBK Kaunas match in Vilnius with him the following evening. Charlie and Iain had prior commitments and had to decline but I was delighted to accept, as anyone with a passion for Hearts would have done, because it allowed me to witness at first hand the team that a lot of our players originated from as well as seeing the standard of football in Lithuania. More importantly it allowed me to spend more time in Mr Romanov's company. Vladimir seemed pleased that I accepted his offer and told me me his personal secretary would alter my plane tickets and book another two nights for me at my hotel, all at his expense.

He also invited me to join him and the Kaunas coach, Angel Cervenkov, later that afternoon to watch a DVD of the 9–1 win against Zalgiris Vilnius the previous week. While Charlie and Iain headed back to the airport to catch their flights home I got the opportunity to run the rule over the performances of the Kaunas players in that Baltic League match with the owner and the coach. We also watched Ricardas Beniusis – one of the names Mr Romanov had put up on the white board earlier – score four goals, all in the second half.

I spent several hours in Mr Romanov's company that day in an extremely interesting environment. I saw many examples of how thorough he is in the running of his three football organisations. I didn't consider what I had witnessed as much of a problem when it came to interference in team affairs. But it is the case that mistakes have been made on both sides, particularly with the reporting of the Rima situation. I wonder if an explanation was given to the Hearts players before they were asked to comply; it might have made a big difference. It's pretty clear there are cultural differences but with a bit of give and take I am sure that a happy medium can be found. I can relate to the finger tests, having experienced them, although I can understand why Scottish players would have poured scorn on the idea when it was initially suggested. The golden rod has received plenty of stick but I felt it was spot on. I appreciate I was standing there looking like a pregnant Behemoth, while Rima pinpointed regions of my back, but I will remember the few hours spent in a new environment for a long time to come.

* * *

I had been made aware the previous evening by Angel Cervenkov that the league match between FBK and Zalgiris would be much more evenly contested than the Baltic League tie the previous week when FBK ran out 9–1 winners. It transpires the Baltic League is a competition taken about as seriously by Eastern Europeans as we take the East of Scotland Shield. I expected the result to be a lot closer after the Vilnius players were hammered in the local media but, having seen the previous match on DVD, I was convinced there was no way any team – especially one as average as Zalgiris – would be able to turn an eight-goal deficit into a victory in less than seven days. I couldn't have been more wrong.

It was evident Zalgiris were in no mood to suffer another reverse at the hands of FBK and the longer the game went on the more tetchy it became, resulting in the quality diminishing rapidly. The only goal of the game was scored by Zalgiris, although FBK captain – and four-goal hero the previous week – Ricardas Beniusis missed a penalty near the end of the game that would have earned Kaunas a draw. The best player on the pitch that day was Rafael Ledesma, the Brazilian left-winger for Kaunas, but he was a million miles away from being good enough for the national team. There are quite a few Brazilians of a similar standard playing their football in Lithuania but unless they have an EU passport it would be virtually impossible for them to move to Britain.

There were players from FBK who, given time, could develop their skills further and I had perhaps seen them on a bad day. Valdas Ivanauskas and Vladimir Romanov would watch those players most weeks and be aware of any potential, although there was no one who could have stepped directly into the Hearts side. Following a brief discussion with Mr Romanov I was invited to watch another match later that evening, between FC Vetra and Ekranes. I was pleased I made the effort to attend and of the four teams I watched I thought Vetra were the most impressive. Their line-up included the likes of former Dunfermline defender Andrius Skerla, a decent player in his time, although once again the standard of football was on a par with the top half of the Scottish second division or possibly the lower half of division one. I thanked Vladimir Romanov for his hospitality and when I shook him by the hand I said, 'here's to a good season for Heart of Midlothian' and his reply, through Svetlana, was 'yes, I hope so too, and not just this season'.

The trip to Lithuania filled me with a renewed belief that, if I am honest, had begun to wane at the end of season 2006/07. I had said to Vladimir in his office the previous day that the football club is far more important that any one individual; it had survived for 133 years and I wanted it to be around for the next 133 years. The likes of Alfie Conn, Willie Bauld, Jimmy Wardhaugh, Dave Mackay, Alex Young, Donald Ford, Wallace Mercer, John Robertson and George Burley will be remembered forever but Heart of Midlothian will always bounce back from the loss of individuals. I am desperate for more names to be added to that list, to see new heroes emerging for future generations and I just wanted to make Mr Romanov further aware that he had not simply purchased a business but a football club that is a way of life for so many people. I was born with a passion for Heart of Midlothian, he inherited his with the purchase of shares and I was always slightly concerned he was not fully aware just how much the football club means to supporters. Those concerns were mostly eradicated after seeing him in his own environment, the place where he is most comfortable, and witnessing a maroon-and-white shrine. I'm sure the cynics would argue that knowing we were on the way his aides spruced up the office to give the impression of someone who cares more than he actually does. But anyone going to those lengths must have some feelings for Hearts.

* * *

I have been accused of changing my opinion about Vladimir Romanov as often as the weather but please let me defend myself. I remain a believer because, to date, he has made it possible for the club to remain at Tynecastle. However, it is clear not only to me but also to anyone taking an interest in Heart of Midlothian Football Club that crucial mistakes have been made since he came to power. Instead of the eight managers we've had since the start of season 2005/06 that figure could quite easily have been just one, George Burley, and who knows what would have been achieved had that been the case.

I believe Hearts would have won the league had George remained as manager, simply because of the momentum that was building. Others might disagree, but I believe he was the right man to deliver the championship and had a team good enough to hold off Rangers and Celtic. Players responded to George and there is no doubt that the amazing start Hearts made that season was due to the way he motivated them. Having witnessed that kind of response to the Gaffer and the belief he instilled in us, parallels can certainly be drawn. We had genuine flair in our team – John Colquhoun in particular provided an abundance of skill out wide – but Burley wanted flair middle to front at all times and his team was a joy to watch. When he left it was no surprise that many of the players lost form and focus. When you lose a manager players believe in as strongly as they believed in George there will always be a negative reaction, especially from those he signed, like Skacel, Brellier and Bednar. It was thanks to the more experienced guys, like Steven Pressley, who had such strong feelings for the club, that Hearts were still able to finish second and to win the Scottish Cup, despite upheaval off-the-field.

I'm delighted George has been given the Scotland job and if he can transmit on a bigger stage what he did at Hearts then we can look forward to competing in the finals of major championships. The only possible negative factor is that he won't get the chance to work with players on a daily basis, something he's been used to in previous jobs.

As far as Graham Rix is concerned his was an appointment I could never fathom. In the first place he wasn't the household name promised after Burley left. And, secondly, a blind man could have foreseen the negative publicity that would attach itself to the club given Rix's conviction. Nevertheless everyone deserves a second chance in life, and I also happen to believe that Hearts supporters should get behind the man in the dugout no matter their personal feelings towards him. I thought Rix handled himself in a dignified manner during his brief period as head coach. Having to work with the owner of a club who wanted to be involved in every decision would not have been easy for anyone but Rix was in no position to argue. Looking back there are certain similarities between his time at Hearts and also that of Joe Jordan – both men found themselves virtually replacing the irreplaceable in Alex MacDonald and George Burley. What George was able to get out of that group of players over a limited period of time was always going to be extremely difficult to replicate. Graham Rix tried manfully but the shadow of Vladimir Romanov and Valdas Ivanauskas was too much for him.

In between George and Graham – and on many other occasions during his time at the football club both when Vladimir Romanov was in charge and also before that – I felt John McGlynn almost single-handedly held the club together before deciding that Starks Park in Kirkcaldy was a relative sanctuary compared with the uncertainty at Tynecastle. When I look back to when he started it's always difficult for me to forget that I could have been doing that job. However, John worked tirelessly for the club and thoroughly deserved his move into management in November 2006. It's very rare to find someone willing to graft season in season out for hours on end and be happy to do so without any plaudits, but that pretty much sums John up. People go on about legends, but unsung heroes are just as important and that phrase describes him perfectly.

Valdas Ivanauskas achieved. As simple as that. He will go down in history as the manager of a Hearts team that won the Scottish Cup for the second time in a ten-year period and the man who secured qualification for the Champions League. No one can ever take that away from him. We spoke a few times about various players from Lithuania; his judgement of a player and my judgement were usually different but football is all about opinions. Some you get right and some you get wrong. All I will say is that Valdas was fortunate that he had someone like John McGlynn by his side.

I think the less said about Eduard Malofeev's twenty-three days in charge, the better. That man should never have been allowed near the position of head coach at Hearts, even for such a short period. He may have been a good coach in the early Eighties, leading Dinamo Minsk to the championship in the Soviet top league in 1982, but surely someone should have told Vladimir Romanov that Malofeev's insistence on deploying those same antiquated tactics some twenty-five years later was an accident waiting to happen.

I never had much involvement with Anatoly Korobochka, and, while he seems like a nice man, I think the sporting-director role he was tasked with by Mr Romanov was questionable. Was there any real need for such an appointment? I can understand Vladimir wanting a Russian-speaker involved, someone who would be able to report back, but I think the level of influence afforded to Korobochka was wrong.

Stephen Frail did a decent job in extremely difficult circumstances. A former teammate of mine at Tynecastle, Shaggy was a very good footballer and I am convinced he would have gone on to represent Scotland had it not been for a serious knee injury sustained during the 1–1 draw against Dundee United at Tannadice in March 1995. Following his appointment as caretaker boss at the start of January 2008 he brought much-needed stability to the football club.

Another crucial Vladimir Romanov mistake was his insistence on being involved in team-selection matters for far too long. I was as surprised as anyone when Steven Pressley, Paul Hartley and Craig Gordon – who soon became known as 'The Riccarton Three' – sabotaged a pre-match press conference in October 2006 in order for Elvis to read the following pre-prepared statement:

> This statement is no reflection on Eduard [Malofeev] who, from my initial impressions, seems a very honest and diligent man. I would like to wish Valdas a speedy recovery, but whether he returns or not is almost incidental in relation to the problems associated with this football club. I have tried, along with the coaching staff and certain colleagues, to implement the correct values and disciplines but it has become an impossible task. There is only so much a coaching staff, a captain and certain colleagues can do without the full backing, direction and coherence of the manager and those running the football club. While publicly I have expressed the need for unity, behind the scenes I have made my concerns abundantly clear. The last two years have been very testing for the players – together we have faced a number of challenges and worked hard at retaining some degree of unity. However, due to the circumstances morale, understandably, is not good and there is significant unrest within the dressing room.

With the appointment of Csaba Laszlo it now looks as though Mr Romanov has wisely decided to take a step back, but it should never have reached the stage when any Hearts player considered speaking out about what was going on behind the scenes, let alone in front of the media.

I have huge respect for what those three players did. They were in a poisonous working environment, in part due to the meddling of the owner, and they had the guts to do something about it, knowing full well that by speaking out against their paymaster there may have been severe consequences. I think they took a stance and a half because as players all you really want to do is train then play, then train then play. That became impossible as the club was starting to resemble a soap opera and they felt the situation would get even worse if they didn't say something. They showed class, something that was much needed at Tynecastle, and is sadly missed now.

If I had been in the same position I would have done something similar. Tolerating a situation like that is basically to accept it. If I think there is a problem I try and nip it in the bud before it gets a chance to grow arms and legs. That's what those three players did and for that they should be applauded. Had it been me as one of the three, however, I very much doubt I would have either ended up at Celtic (Hartley and Pressley) or headed south to the English Premiership in a multi-million pound move. Knowing my luck I would have been farmed out to Bonnybridge Juniors and never been seen nor heard from again!

* * *

I have questioned many decisions taken by Vladimir Romanov since he arrived in Scotland, and will continue to do so. I am particularly concerned about the level of debt the club is carrying: £36 million according to the accounts published in March 2008. This is equivalent to three times the club's turnover and is a huge burden, even if much of it is owed to parent company UBIG. The board's intention is to reduce losses by focusing on Scottish players and younger players and this is a step I welcome, even if it makes Hearts less competitive in the short-to-medium term. On a more positive note the plans to redevelop Tynecastle are ambitious and could give us the revenue we need to compete at the highest level. But we have been promised much in the past by the owner – regular involvement in the Champions League for example – and I remain sceptical.

As I said to Romanov in his boardroom, if I am occasionally critical it's because I want Hearts to be around 133 years from now. If he allows that to happen by structuring the club correctly then we can look forward to a prosperous future for ourselves, our children and our grandchildren. Supporters want success and can excuse most things if there is an end product. The bigger picture will always be the long-term future of Heart of Midlothian Football Club. On balance, I think we're in a better position under the stewardship of Mr Romanov – Champions League qualification for the first time and our second Scottish Cup win since 1956 were both achieved with the Lithuanian at the helm. It's clear that he did something right, even though his methods are sometimes questionable.

He demands loyalty from his staff and that was apparent from the way UBIG personnel behaved in his presence. There was togetherness in the company, with everyone pushing in the same direction. That, for me, spoke volumes and I can understand why he demands that from his staff at the football club as well. Having spent valuable time in Lithuania I am now more open to the way Vladimir Romanov works and I have no doubt he wants Hearts to be successful. You don't start in business where he did – on the bottom rung of the ladder in a repressive communist dictatorship – and get to where he is now without having an immense desire to succeed along with considerable grit and determination. If he can replicate the success of his other business interests at Hearts then the future is bright for everyone of a maroon persuasion.

I'm sure it will be as long as he leaves the football side of things to the football people and lets the business people take care of the business.

18

Agent Mackay

'Football agents are not all bad . . . but the truth is that even if one of my best friends became an agent tomorrow I would find it difficult to have the same trust in him.'

Gordon Strachan – *My Life in Football* (2006)

I like Gordon Strachan and have a lot of time for him. Even after that statement. He's entitled to his opinion and has probably had more than one bad experience with – as I like to call us – representatives. At least he is honest enough to give some of us the benefit of the doubt before going on to slaughter the rest.

My foray into the world of football agency/representation came about when I'd gone from player to assistant manager to being in charge of Airdrieonians. Some managers just seem to have that *je ne sais quoi*, a knack of knowing what to do and when to do it and they make the management game look easy but unfortunately that wasn't the case when I replaced Alex MacDonald as Airdrie boss in August 1999. I was thirty-five and considered management to be the next step. It was an opportunity I simply had to take but, with hindsight, one I wasn't ready for. I had to deal with off-the-field issues that some managers who have been in the game for forty years may never have experienced, but I never successfully got to grips with the job specification.

My spell in charge at the Shyberry Excelsior Stadium was brief, 354 days to be exact, after which I was sacked for winning only eight out of forty-one matches. It was no surprise to me – although it was a major per-sonal disappointment – when I was dismissed, having guided the team to a second-bottom finish in the first division. Maybe I should have realised what life was going to be like when I took charge of the side for the first time as a caretaker boss and we were beaten 3–0 by Hibernian at Easter Road. I was a manager for less than a year but experienced more traumatic events in that short period of time than anyone deserves. Take your pick from the following. Poor form on the park and financial struggles off it, leading to administration. The possibility of the formation of Lanarkshire United, and a football club in Airdrie lost forever. Liquidation on 14 June 2000. I was in the wrong place at the wrong time.

Being involved at a club that released twenty-seven players on the say-so of the liquidators in a bid to half the escalating debt was horrible, and I would not wish that experience on my worst enemy. Trying to explain to players with a decade of service that they no longer had a future was awful, but that was still easier than witnessing the tears after explaining our predicament to the younger lads. I had only been a manager for ten months yet that brief spell in charge provided me with a steeper learning curve than any of my nineteen years as a player. Being a professional footballer is a doddle by comparison. You train. You go home. You play. You go home. That's not the case as a manager; you are the focal point and the person responsible for up to forty players. I'd never been party to situations like that because life as a player always went smoothly. I signed contracts at Hearts without much negotiation while even as a player with Airdrie everything was agreed without much fuss. Administration gave me an insight into the business side of football, while the actions of a particular agent led me to the conclusion that recommendations by players' representatives are not always in the best interest of their clients.

When provisional liquidators KPMG were appointed at the beginning of February 2000 every player was told they had to choose one of two alter-natives. They could either accept a deal entitling them to half their salary while remaining at the club until the end of the season then take a chance on what would happen after that or they could leave it up to KPMG and me to identify which guys we wanted to keep and which ones we would let go. There was a strong core of experienced players at the club – Jimmy Sandison, David Farrell, Gareth Evans, Allan Moore, Paul Jack and Sandy Stewart – and, after consultation with their teammates, they decided to accept half salary. One for all and all for one. They believed it was in the best interests of the club to keep things together for as long as possible and to help the younger lads: the likes of twenty-one year-old Eddie Forrest; Austin McCann, who was a year younger; and Alex Neil, who had just turned nineteen. That's what

I call team spirit. The club was losing around £10,000 per week and time was not on our side, but the decision of the players to accept the wage reduction was not only admirable but also curried favour with the provisional liquidators. But it wasn't long before a spanner was thrown into the works.

Two days after KPMG's appointment I was working away in my office when there was a knock on the door. It was Austin McCann and Eddie Forrest. They had come to tell me that their representative, Ian Redford, a top player in his time, had advised them not to accept the deal. I immediately informed the pair they would be putting themselves in a very awkward situation. I was keen to know the reasons for his advice, so, with the two young lads still in my office, I phoned Ian to arrange a meeting.

I made sure my assistant, Walter Kidd, was present at the meeting as I felt it was important to have backup and I'm glad I did. Redford was adamant that the boys would not accept half salary. Now I've been on the pitch and witnessed Walter get angry, but I've never seen him as animated as he was that day. I'll never forget the scene; a normally mild-mannered individual suddenly rearing up from his chair with veins sticking out of his head and having a right go at the man opposite. 'You're just making these kids lambs to the slaughter,' he bellowed at Ian in front of Austin and Eddie. Walter continued, 'You're not the one having to go into the changing room and explain the decision but the two boys will have to do that. Are you still convinced your advice is in the best interest of your clients?'

It was also pointed out to Ian that the experienced guys in the squad were the ones taking the biggest hit, but they were doing so in a bid to try and keep the team together and prevent redundancies. After much persuading, the boys accepted the status quo and the meeting proved to be extremely worthwhile for both the club and the players, especially because of what happened in the following few months.

Alex Neil and Austin McCann, along with Eddie Forrest, were the only three players retained by the club when KPMG was forced to release twenty-seven others in June 2000 to continue the cost-cutting measures. The squad included a lot of experienced older players who did not have much of a sell-on value but those three had potential so were kept on to raise much-needed funds in the form of transfer fees. It wasn't long before Clyde chairman Ronnie McDonald got in touch to tell me he wanted to sign Austin and Alex and was prepared to offer £30,000 for the pair. The bid was rejected following dialogue with KPMG, who felt the offer was inadequate. Barnsley, though, were more successful a few days later and a bid of £25,000 was accepted for Alex Neil at the start of July. It turned out to be the last piece of significant business I was involved in as manager; I lost my job two weeks later.

Austin, meanwhile, remained at the club until the turn of the year but the wait was worthwhile as he got his dream move to the Premier League with Hearts in return for Airdrie – now under the stewardship of Steve Archibald – getting a payment in the region of around £30,000.

Hindsight is a wonderful commodity although even with that benefit it's still impossible to predict what would have happened to Eddie Forrest and Austin McCann if they had followed the guidance of their representative. I didn't know it at the time but that whole episode – especially the meeting in my office – had a huge bearing on how I conducted myself in the agency business. I felt the advice given was selfish and erroneous and it left a bad taste in my mouth. Sometimes in football, and in life, I believe you have to consider the bigger picture.

The decision to relieve me of my duties at Airdrie brought to an end an association with professional football that stretched back twenty years (give or take nineteen days). I was suddenly at a loose end. Here was a thirty-six-year-old man who had spent the first six years of his life dreaming of being a footballer, the next ten years playing and preparing for the life of a foot-baller and the other twenty years living the life of a footballer before going on to manage footballers. So it will not come as a surprise to learn that I had nothing lined up when I left Airdrie. To give myself time to clear my head I decided a sabbatical would be just what the doctor ordered. That, however, lasted precisely six weeks, at which time there was another knock on the door. I was relieved that, on this occasion, it was not Austin McCann and Eddie Forrest but a good friend of mine, Bert Logan. He came to my house in Dovecot Park in Edinburgh to discuss the possibility of setting up a company, a football agency. This was something we had discussed flippantly on a couple of occasions – usually over a couple of shandies (for me) or a glass of wine (for him) – but this time he came to the house armed with paper-work. He meant business. Discussions went well, one thing led to another and I told him I was convinced we would be able to give better advice to our clients than some agents I had dealt with in the past. That sunny August afternoon will go down as the day Kickstart 2000 got up and running.

* * *

The FIFA website lists around fifty licensed agents in Scotland alone, many of whom have been in business for a lot longer than Bert and me. We knew from the outset we had our work cut out, although one thing in our favour was our strong work ethic. Although finding new clients was the main aim, our business also included a consultancy arm; as I explained earlier I undertook many trips, both at home and abroad, either to report on future opponents for client clubs or to scout a player for them.

By the end of our first season with Kickstart 2000 I had attended around 150 matches in just twelve months, in addition to watching Hearts on a Saturday. I took in under-eighteen games, reserve matches, youth fixtures, schoolboy internationals, anything to increase my client base. There were even occasions on a Tuesday when I would attend three matches – at 1 p.m., 3 p.m. and 7 p.m. – seeing a fair bit of all the reserve games before chatting with players afterwards. It took a while to get established and networking in the early days was the main way to obtain business. Word of mouth was also helpful while my previous relationship with Lee Makel and Gary Locke at Hearts helped me get a step on the ladder and my first two clients.

With most top players already represented, it didn't take a genius to work out that starting at the other end of the spectrum with talented kids was the way forward. One of the first things I did was to identify the good youngsters at Hearts and Hibernian and keep a watchful eye on them, checking out which ones were already represented and which ones were not. Several kids at Hearts impressed me, although there were two in particular I was interested in signing up.

Having watched him on a number of occasions I approached a lad who was just sixteen by the name of Christophe Berra – I also spoke with his mother and father – to see if he would be interested in signing up with my company. However, he felt he did not require representation at that stage. However, I was delighted when, the following year, Christophe decided it was time to employ an advisor and remembered our chat. With the blessing of his mum and dad, he was one of the first players to sign up with Kickstart 2000, after Locke and Makel. I've been delighted to represent Christophe ever since, helping him ink a five-year deal with Hearts in July 2006. It was very pleasing for me when he was appointed club captain in August 2007 at the age of just twenty-two, following the departure of Craig Gordon to Sunderland. It is also a bonus that, due to my commitments to Hearts.tv, I am able to witness most of his performances and if he calls for a chat I am able to talk about the game having witnessed it from the press box.

The other lad I was interested in signing up was someone I was aware of since he was ten years old. My son, Ryan, played against Lee Wallace on a number of occasions in the youth ranks; Ryan turned out for Hibernian Boys Club while Lee pulled on the maroon of Hearts BC. From an early age Lee performed regularly as a left-winger, and it was only later that he was deployed at left back. With Christophe waiting twelve months before joining my company, Lee, therefore, was signing number three after Locke and Makel. Once again I was delighted when young Mr Wallace signed a five-year deal with Hearts in August 2006, just a few weeks after Christophe made the same commitment. I am convinced both players have a successful career ahead of them.

Meanwhile the ability of three players with connections to Hibernian stuck out like a sore thumb in the early years: Derek Riordan and Garry O'Connor plus one other who provided me with my first regret as an agent. I attended a Scotland Schoolboys fixture at Broadwood one evening and was mightily impressed by the kid deployed in left-midfield for Scotland. He was magnificent. The fifth-year pupil playing a starring role that night was a lad by the name of Scott Brown. I made a big mistake. I should have tried to develop a relationship with him after the game – even just a chat – but for whatever reason I didn't.

The situation with Derek and Garry was different as both were already represented. Garry O'Connor was from Port Seton, a part of the world particularly well known to Bert Logan. One day Bert called to tell me that he'd been speaking to one of Garry's uncles, who had informed him that the striker did not have the best relationship with his agent, Jim McArthur. I kept abreast of the situation and when Garry eventually decided to leave Jim I was delighted when he signed up with Kickstart 2000. It wasn't long afterwards – less than a fortnight in fact – when I was attending a match at Olivebank in Musselburgh that I met Jim and, naturally, he was annoyed at what we'd done. He said he was disappointed in me, claiming I had poached his client. I didn't know it then but I was fated to have the same experience.

* * *

It's funny how things sometimes work out. In January 2006 Lokomotiv Moscow offered Derek Riordan a life-changing opportunity. He had impressed them during the second leg of the UEFA Cup tie between Dnipro and Hibernian in the Ukraine four months previously and former Celtic defender Rudi Vata, working as an agent on behalf of the Russian side, asked if Riordan was interested in making the move. He turned it down. Garry O'Connor had also caught their eye and they turned their attention to him after Riordan's decision to stay put. They were prepared to offer him a very similar deal; a deal that would change his life forever.

I was commentating for Hearts.tv at the Scottish Cup fourth-round tie against Aberdeen at Tynecastle at the start of February before carrying out my ambassadorial duties for the club in the Gorgie Suite. After leaving the stadium I switched on my mobile phone to find several new text messages, plus details of missed calls from Hibernian chairman Rod Petrie, Garry's mum Judy and Garry himself. Hibernian were also in Scottish Cup action earlier that afternoon, against Rangers at Ibrox, and my immediate concern was that Mr O'Connor – in my view a lad with a tendency occasionally to press the self-destruct button – was in trouble. There was an early kick-off in Govan so I was already aware that Garry had scored the opening goal in a surprise 3–0 win for Hibernian but I was not aware of any other news from Ibrox. Why else would these three people phone me on a match day? The possibility of a transfer was the last thing on my mind. I immediately phoned Judy and she brought me up-to-date with the interest from Russia, although that was all she knew at that time.

I informed Judy that I would speak to Rod Petrie if she could discuss the situation with Garry. Rod told me that his board had accepted a bid for the player, although he stressed they would not push him out the door. From what he could gather following brief correspondence with Rudi Vata the weekly salary on offer was ten times what Garry was earning at Easter Road. In addition there was a five-year contract on the table. I explained to Rod that I would discuss the situation with Garry that same evening. In previous correspondence, Petrie had always made it clear that Hibs would never stand in Garry's way if a life-changing opportunity came along. It was time to give the blonde-haired striker the good news!

All my previous plans were immediately shelved and I drove to Garry's house in Longniddry; his girlfriend Lisa, his son Josh and his mother and father, Lawrence and Judy, were with him. I told him what had been offered and Garry was understandably excited by the sums involved. For the next twenty minutes we went over the finer details as well as discussing the pitfalls. We also spoke about the positives of a five-year contract on that salary and the impact it would have. I told Garry and his family that it was vitally important to consider all the eventualities before making a decision. I was well aware that I was talking to a young person, and I knew the only thing that would have been going through Garry's mind was the opportunity to increase his income ten-fold. That would also have been uppermost in my mind as a youngster. However, I pointed out that money was not the only consideration and advised him to sleep on it. Without hesitation he told me he wanted to move to Russia. He was adamant. His mind was not for changing.

As I left Garry's house I made one phone call – the most important one in my mind – and that was to Tony Mowbray. Tony is one of the humblest people I have ever come across in professional football and I told him it was only fair that he should be kept in the loop. I passed on Gary's thanks for all the help he'd given him and suggested that he would understand the reasons why his player wanted to move to Lokomotiv. Tony was appreciative of the phone call.

By the time I arrived at Rod Petrie's house in East Lothian he had obtained the full facts and figures of the proposed deal following further consultation with Rudi Vata, who in turn had been liaising with officials from Lokomotiv Moscow, and Rod had printed them off for me to look through. The key details were as discussed and that night the wheels were put in motion. One thing I had not bargained for was the long, drawn-out saga that followed before Garry eventually put pen to paper thirty-one days later, on 7 March. It wasn't long before I found out there were four agents involved in the deal. I was looking after the interests of the player; Rudi Vata was dealing with Hibs on behalf of Lokomotiv Moscow; a Serbian agent was acting on behalf of Lokomotiv coach Slaboliub Muslin, himself a Serb, while a fourth representative from Paris had also found his way into the tangled web. However, that scenario was simplicity itself by comparison with Garry's medical.

Having spent seventeen or so years as a player at Tynecastle, the only intense medical testing I had to undergo was prior to joining Hearts in 1980. For some reason – possibly time constraints – they were not necessary when I moved to Airdrie in March 1997. So my experience of the treatment room was limited to Alan Rae's cupboard (only kidding Alan) at Tynie and not much else. There's a different mentality and way of life in Russia and knowing what I now know they have more than a fair claim to wrestle the 'efficient' tag from our friends in Germany. Lokomotiv Moscow were preparing to shell out £1.6 million for a player and pay him a hefty salary so, quite rightly, they left nothing to chance.

Neither Garry nor I had any inclination of what lay ahead in Munich as we left Edinburgh airport on the last day of February 2006. It was perhaps just as well because had Garry known what was in store then he might have changed his mind. We were told our itinerary would be made available on arrival but there was no time to settle into our hotel before the testing began. They were the most rigorous examinations I have ever witnessed. Garry was required to visit three separate clinics in Munich; he saw four different doctors over two days and underwent a battery of tests, none of which were witnessed by anyone from Lokomotiv. The Russians had selected the best people and they were happy to trust the experts. At the end of two exhausting days for Garry we made our way back home while the test results were collated and sent to Moscow.

Munich in March is a bit like Edinburgh, pretty cold. Neither city, however, experiences temperatures on a par with Moscow at that time of year. Garry was fortunate that the Russian season did not start until mid-March so there was no requirement for him to travel to Russia and experience the plunging temperatures prior to completing his move. All he had to do was relax on the flight back to Scotland. I would have liked to have relaxed as well but spent the first part of the journey in fits of giggles after a little faux pas from my travelling companion. Upon boarding our flight we were both handed a copy of the *Daily Mail*. It didn't take long before the weather was the topic of conversation and Garry remarked that he'd seen the map and that it was minus twelve in Moscow. That was quickly followed by an audible 'wow' as he proclaimed it was minus twenty in Mont Real. He had just renamed the second-largest city in Canada and the largest city in the province of Quebec! Needless-to-say this immediately lightened the mood after those two gruelling days in Munich.

Not long after returning home we got the news that Lokomotiv were satisfied with the results from the medical tests and on 7 March 2006 Garry O'Connor finally completed his move, putting pen-to-paper on a five-year contract worth around £4 million, before flying out to Spain to meet his new coach, Slavoljub Muslin, and his new teammates, at their pre-season base in Marbella.

It was a lucrative move for Garry, a super deal for Hibs and a very significant piece of business for Kickstart 2000, earning our company a more-than-decent five-figure sum. Some people may think that excessive, but they should consider the time and effort Bert and I put in to Garry's development. He was the most high-profile client on our books and it was our reward for years of hard graft. For most agents earning money is the end product of a lot of hard work and so there was no guilt on my behalf about that deal, which, as well as the revenue it generated, raised the profile of our business. I should also add that negotiations with Hibernian were always handled in a very professional manner, with mutual respect between Rod Petrie and me. I look forward to our paths crossing again many times in the future.

* * *

Being selected to represent my country on four occasions will always rank as one of the highlights of my career. Bulgaria, Luxemburg, Saudi Arabia and Malta are not exactly giants of the global game but my three substitute appearances and one start meant as much to me as playing against the likes of Brazil, Argentina, Italy or France. I wouldn't say appearing for your country these days is less important, but it does irk me when even the slightest niggle is enough for certain individuals to withdraw from international squads. In fact I didn't know whether to laugh or cry in the summer of 2007 when Blackburn winger David Bentley pulled out of the England squad for the European under-twenty-one championships in Holland, citing fatigue.

I have always enjoyed watching Scotland and was sitting at home on

Sunday, 8 October 2006 viewing a re-run of the fabulous victory against France the previous day at Hampden. Work commitments meant I was unable to be in attendance so I sat in front of the television to savour a repeat showing of a fantastic result for our country. The boys were a credit to the nation and it will take a very special experience to eclipse that afternoon. With Kenny Miller suspended I can fully understand that Garry O'Connor was frustrated at not being selected ahead of James McFadden as the lone striker, but I was delighted when Garry was eventually introduced to the action. It was his ninth international cap. I tried to call him on his mobile following the match but it went straight to the answer machine so I sent him a congratulatory text. Unbeknown to me at the time, however, that was to be the last correspondence I was to have with him for forty-eight hours.

Garry spent most of his time in Russia so there were a few occasions when we couldn't make contact. When that was the case my link with him was through his mother Judy. As an agent I like to think I look after my clients; I have never been someone who has pestered his players but I'm always available if they need to speak to me. There were times when I would call Garry directly, times when he'd contact me and other occasions when I'd liaise directly with Judy, whom I found a very stable and capable individual. My discussions with her were relatively infrequent, usually limited to the days leading up to games as well as immediately after matches. Correspondence on a Sunday was very unusual.

The phone rang. It was 5.45.

'Hi Gary; it's Judy. He's not going.'

Seven little words; one big problem.

What followed left me stunned. I immediately asked what she meant and was told that Garry had said that he was not going to be on the flight to Ukraine with the rest of the squad. I informed her that was not an option. He had to go. I asked her to confirm what time the players were meeting and she told me they had been due to report to Hampden for a training session at four o'clock that day, nearly two hours earlier. She said there was no point in me trying to call Garry as he was refusing to speak to anyone. Phoning Garry was not an option but I had to get in touch with the SFA and explain what had happened. Trying to speak to Walter Smith or any other member of the coaching staff was futile as they were involved in the training session so I decided to give Andy Mitchell – head of communications at the SFA – a call. 'He's not turned up for training,' were Andy's first words to me. 'No shit, Sherlock,' would have been my response had we not have been in such a delicate situation. I informed him of the news passed on to me by Judy and told him that the player would not be joining up with the squad. I also told Andy that I had no idea where Garry was. The message was passed on to a very angry Walter Smith, who then excluded him from the travelling party.

As is normally the case after major matches at Hampden Park the players vacate the national stadium via the mixed zone in the basement, allowing members of the media the chance to speak to them. I was aware of some of Garry's comments to the press after the France match, when he intimated his desire to leave Lokomotiv for the sake of his homesick family. He also claimed the Russian side was sympathetic about his predicament. I was well aware that he had failed to settle in Russia so this was not news to me. In my opinion it was unlikely those reasons were related to his non-appearance at Hampden.

I was finally able to make contact with Garry on the Monday although I didn't get far in my attempts to find out why he had made such a decision. He told me he just didn't want to go. He was finding things very difficult in Russia and simply did not have a sufficient desire to be part of the squad that was heading for the Ukraine. I found this difficult to comprehend although I understood his personal circumstances and was fairly sympathetic about his predicament. My opinion was that Garry believed it was unlikely he would be involved in Kiev, especially with Kenny Miller returning from suspension, and had decided to have an extra day or two with his family before heading back to Russia. If that was the case he had not thought through the consequences.

I had to calm a situation that could quickly have escalated out of control. He had upset Walter, Lokomotiv Moscow were wondering what was happening and the Tartan Army had been let down by one of their own. I explained to Garry that it was in his best interests to get back to Moscow as soon as possible because his employers would not be happy with him taking two days' holiday. As far as his Scotland future was concerned I took the view that making an apology was the best course of action. I took it upon myself to make a statement on his behalf of Garry. I had a duty to represent him and felt this was the best course of action:

> I apologise to the SFA, Walter Smith and his staff for my non-appearance for the flight to Kiev for this week's international. At the earliest opportunity I hope to meet with Walter Smith, face-to-face, to explain my reasons. On my return to Moscow I will be concentrating on doing my very best for Lokomotiv while hoping my Scotland team-mates continue their great start to this campaign.

Not exactly Shakespeare, I'm sure you'll agree, but it was a means to an end, despite containing a distinct lack of information. The damage had been done and it was up to me to make sure that damage did not become irreparable.

I tried to cajole Garry into ensuring that the door that was his international future remained slightly ajar. I reiterated to him that such a scenario was only possible if he agreed to a face-to-face meeting with Walter Smith to explain his reasons. I'm still waiting for his response.

* * *

I think it's highly unlikely Garry O'Connor will ever explain the reasons for his failure to travel to Kiev and also what made him decide not to attend that Sunday-afternoon training session. Stories came out in the press about his sister Kerry, a lovely girl, being a recovering drug addict, who allegedly attempted to commit suicide less than two weeks before the match against France. If that was the reason for his absence then I understand totally.

One of my other main concerns for Garry was that, in my opinion, he wasn't keeping great company when he was back in Scotland. If you are sixteen or seventeen and being easily led that, to me, is understandable. However, when you reach the age of twenty-three or twenty-four I just think you should know better. Having an idea where Garry is in his life today, I know that he is now a more mature and grounded individual, who is working hard to realise his obvious potential.

There was no sign of an apology forthcoming as we entered November and his situation had been put on the back burner as far as the media were concerned. I then appeared as a guest on *The Press Box*, on Setanta, on Thursday, 23 November. I had agreed to take part in the television programme to plug a book I had contributed to – *Believe! Hearts: From Turmoil to Triumph at Tynecastle* – and also to talk about the situation in Gorgie. Inadvertently, the topic of conversation came round to Garry O'Connor's international future and, as his representative, I was asked for my views. I told the presenter, Rob Maclean, exactly what I had said to Garry but the papers the following day picked up on my quotes, made a mountain out of a molehill and I was done up like the proverbial kipper.

Quotes from the interview were splashed across back pages:

Garry has to realise he is almost twenty-four. He is a young man now and the only person who can correct this situation is Garry O'Connor.

He has to contact the Scotland manager, explain the reasons why he did not make the international gathering and see how Walter responds to that.

It is not Walter Smith's decision and it is not up to him to chase Garry. I can only advise Garry and I have told him the way he has to go. It is up to him to make that move.

I immediately had to explain to Judy O'Connor what had happened and requested that she convey my explanation to Garry. I said nothing on Setanta that I hadn't already said to the player but the newspapers had been left with very few scraps during the intervening period, so, understandably, they went overboard when they had something definite to go on.

On Garry's return to Scotland at the end of the Russian season in December 2006 I asked him to meet with Walter Smith and offer a long-overdue apology. Garry agreed so I gave him Walter's phone number. Knowing the type of person Walter is – rightly respected throughout the world of football – I was of the opinion that he would think more of Garry if the player broached the subject without using the good offices of his agent. For various reasons, that meeting never took place. As a representative you can only give a client the benefit of your experience. How Walter would have reacted during a meeting with Garry is something only he would know, but he never had that decision to make.

* * *

The decision of Rangers chairman David Murray to part company with manager Paul le Guen and the subsequent return of Walter Smith to Ibrox in January 2007 sent shockwaves throughout Scottish football. From my perspective I knew it was a golden opportunity for Garry, if he played his cards right. Just over a fortnight later Alex McLeish was confirmed as Walter Smith's replacement and the seeds were about to be sewn for Garry O'Connor's return to international football.

Garry is someone who opens up more when he is comfortable with people. He had a relationship with Alex and Andy Watson at Easter Road and I made Garry aware that he should speak to Alex at the earliest possible opportunity. He agreed but this time I told Garry to let me make the necessary arrangements. I phoned Alex McLeish to enquire if an apology from Garry would be helpful. He agreed that it would and suggested I speak to Andy Watson to progress the matter. For me Andy was the ideal mediator; he and I were former teammates at Hearts while Garry got on very well with him during their time together at Hibs. He asked for Garry's number and made the call. Garry subsequently explained to me the details of the conversation with Andy and intimated he was happy that an apology was the best way to resurrect his international career. There was one snag, however. He wanted me to make the apology on his behalf. After all we had been through I had no problem complying with his request. I wanted him back in the international fold because I knew it would help him get a move back to Britain; a move he desperately wanted.

Having made Garry aware of our plans, Bert and I sat down with two pencils and two blank bits of paper and, on Thursday, 15 February 2007, came up with the following:

> I unreservedly wish to offer my apologies for what can only be described as letting everyone down. My only defence is that there were extenuating circumstances in my life at the time that I have great difficulty in talking about. On reflection, I realise this is no excuse for my behaviour, and should I be given a second chance I intend to grab it. I have contacted the present management team to make them aware of my desire to play for my country again, if selected.

That written apology was then submitted to the SFA for the attention of Alex McLeish, with a phone call to the management team informing them the documentation was on its way. I also made clear to Alex and Andy by phone that it was Garry's decision to make the apology, he was in the right frame of mind to do so and neither his parents nor I had forced it upon him. There is no doubt that Garry was very lucky when Alex McLeish replaced Walter Smith as Scotland manager. I don't believe he would ever have apologised to Walter and so his international career could easily have ended at that point.

Garry O'Connor is no different to any other sportsperson. In my view they want to talk to the press when things are going well but very few, me included, are keen to speak when things are tough. That's why I made the apology on his behalf, then read out the statement to an impromptu media gathering at the Caledonian hotel in Edinburgh. It was uncomfortable for me, and I had done nothing wrong, but it was our duty to a valued client. It was also something that had to be done to help Garry get a move to the Premiership. Of course it would have been better if the apology had been immediate but that didn't happen. It then became a case of finding the right way of taking the situation forward. Throughout the whole saga I found it impossible to get annoyed with Garry O'Connor. He's a super big lad, although in my eyes one with a fair bit of growing up to do.

* * *

It was the start of a new year. The beginning of January 2007 and our client, both directly and indirectly, had made us aware that he was looking for a move back to the United Kingdom before the transfer window closed at the end of the month. It was our job to fulfil his request and so I flew to Portugal for talks with the director of football and the new chairman of Lokomotiv Moscow to negotiate a suitable fee for their player. I was informed that nothing less than 3.9 million euros would be acceptable and my efforts to negotiate a lower price proved futile. I informed them that the fee was prohibitive not least because Garry had not being playing regularly due to injury. In addition he did not have the opportunity to impress on the international stage following his Ukrainian vanishing act. My plea fell on deaf ears.

On my return home I spoke with representatives of two Premiership clubs, Wigan and Fulham, plus two in the Championship: Eric Black at Birmingham City and Garry's old boss, Tony Mowbray, at West Bromwich Albion. I made all four clubs aware of the fee being sought by Lokomotiv Moscow but none of them were prepared to meet it. Eric Black was honest with me and said that Birmingham manager Steve Bruce was not prepared to take the gamble. A couple of the teams enquired about the possibility of a loan deal until the end of the season but the Muscovites ruled that out. All that combined to ensure at least another few months of football with a Russian flavour for our client and, although he never admitted it, our failure to get him a move was, I believe, the straw that broke the camel's back in our relationship.

There had always been regular communication between us. But it didn't take long for that to change and I found it very difficult to contact him, with nearly all correspondence going through his mother. About three weeks after returning from Portugal I said to Bert that I could smell a rat. We had been unable to find Garry a new club and my gut feeling was that he had been tapped by another agent. When we did speak he was very evasive and his telephone manner suggested the end of our relationship was nigh. If Garry's mindset was to move on then that was something I was comfortable with. It was the right time to get out because I think the relationship had run its course. A lot of my time had been taken up dealing with Garry's business affairs, and the time had come for me to focus on the other footballers in our stable.

Our contracts all have a six-month get-out clause, which can be activated by either party following payment of outstanding funds. We had a decision to make. We could either terminate the contract with immediate effect or activate the clause and force Garry O'Connor to remain with us for another six months. After discussing the situation we opted for the former and sent him a letter agreeing to the termination of his contract with Kickstart 2000 in return for him settling his management fee. That was duly paid. Our correspondence also contained a note wishing him all the best for the future and I stand by the sentiments in that letter.

I can put my hand on my heart and say I gave solid, professional advice to Garry O'Connor from the day he agreed to be part of our stable until the day our relationship ended. I later received a three-line letter, sent by his mother and signed by Garry, thanking us for our help and wishing us all the best. The main disappointment was that our professional relationship wasn't closed in the way I would have liked, despite the fact that the contractual procedures were handled correctly by both parties. I feel sad that Garry did not feel capable of informing me, either over the phone or face-to-face, of a decision I knew was coming. I accept we were paid well as his representatives but I also thought we were friends and friends are surely entitled to that much. There was also a bad taste in my mouth when Judy told me that I couldn't get through to Garry because the phones were playing up. I felt she was being economical with the truth on his behalf although I have no definite proof of that.

If we had invoked the six-month clause I still think Garry O'Connor would have moved to Birmingham City. I don't think that his new representative, Rudi Vata, did anything that we would not have done. Even Alex McLeish said we were looking after the player well and I am sure Garry would agree with these sentiments. However, the player obviously thought Vata's history as a recruiting agent for Lokomotiv Moscow and his long-standing relationship with the Russians would be more beneficial. I tried, but failed, to get Garry a move during the January transfer window. In my defence it's a lot easier to do a deal if players are doing the business on the pitch. There is no better platform than the international arena and Garry's short absence may have played a part in managers being unwilling to take a risk in January 2007.

All credit to him though; he put his unrest in Russia behind him, got his head down and worked hard to turn around his fortunes, culminating in two goal-scoring appearances on the international stage. Having made his apology and got back into the Scotland set-up through a quirk of fate, a bit of luck, his own ability or all three, Garry O'Connor put himself in a position to get to the English Premiership without the help of any representative.

I have no regrets about getting involved with Garry O'Connor and I wish him all the best in his career. If we bump into each other again – when I'm coming out of Marks and Spencer as he's departing Harvey Nichols – I'd be happy to chat. We went as far as we could and it was never dull along the way. I lost out on another five-figure sum when he moved to Birmingham but that was something Bert and I were aware of when we terminated the deal. That's business and maybe Jim McArthur would say what goes around comes around.

Garry O'Connor was our highest profile client and got us a lot of publicity, both good and bad. Would he have got that move to the Premiership if we had still been representing him? I think so. Would he currently be playing for Scotland again without Kickstart apologising on his behalf? In my opinion: no.

19

A Final Thought

And now, the end is here
I've played for Hearts, a life's ambition.
Fans had no cares whichever players
Won silverware, my only mission.
'Twas not to be, but no debris
Tynecastle stayed, our goal achieved,
Our fight inspired, his plan backfired
We Saved Our Hearts, coz we Believed.

I'm glad I did it 'My Way'

Career Details

Hearts: July 1980 to March 1997

Played 640 competitive matches, starting 565 of those and coming on to the field of play as a substitute 75 times.

Including friendly and challenge matches as well as competitive games: played 737 times, starting 656 of those and coming on as a sub a further 81 times.

Scored 64 goals in competitive matches, including eight penalties: 45 in the league (32 at Tynecastle), 12 in the Scottish Cup (eight at Tynecastle), six in the League Cup (five at Tynecastle), one in Europe (against Slavia Prague at Tynecastle).

Including friendly and challenge matches as well as competitive games: scored 91 goals, including 10 penalties.

Competitive Appearances

1980/81	13 app (2 sub)	0 goals
1981/82	12 app (8 sub)	2 goals
1982/83	32 app (9 sub)	6 goals
1983/84	38 app (3 sub)	6 goals
1984/85	22 app (1sub)	6 goals
1985/86	37 app (2 sub)	8 goals
1986/87	39 app (7 sub)	9 goals
1987/88	47 app (1 sub)	8 goals
1988/89	42 app (2 sub)	4 goals
1989/90	34 app (3 sub)	1 goals
1990/91	32 app (4 sub)	4 goals
1991/92	47 app (2 sub)	2 goals
1992/93	47 app (1 sub)	4 goals
1993/94	40 app (2 sub)	1 goal
1994/95	26 app (14 sub)	2 goals
1995/96	29 app (5 sub)	2 goals
1996/97	28 app (9 sub)	1 goal
Total:	565 app (75 sub)	64 goals

Scotland: November 1987 to March 1988

Won four caps: against Bulgaria, Luxembourg, Saudi Arabia and Malta
Scored once: against Bulgaria in Sofia in November 1987.

1987/88   1 app (3 sub)   1 goal

UEFA European Championship qualifier

11 Nov 1987 versus Bulgaria: 1–0   Vasili Levski stadium, Sofia
(replaced Paul McStay, 46 min)

UEFA European Championship qualifier

2 Dec 1987 versus Luxembourg: 0–0   Stade de la Frontiere
(replaced Derek Whyte, 62 min)   Esch-sur-Alzette,
                                               Luxembourg

International challenge match

17 Feb 1988 versus Saudi Arabia: 2–2   Malaz stadium, Riyadh
(replaced Paul McStay, 63 min)

International challenge match

22 Mar 1988 versus Malta: 1–1   Ta'Qali stadium, Valletta
(first international start)

Airdrieonians: March 1997 to July 2000 (as player then manager)

Played 48 competitive matches, starting 38 of those and coming on to the
field of play as a substitute on 10 occasions.

Scored once: against Stirling Albion in April 1997.

Competitive appearances: by season

1996/7	7 app (1 sub)	1 goal
1997/8	27 app (3 sub)	0 goals
1998/9	4 app (6 sub)	0 goals
Total:	38 app (10sub)	1 goal

As manager of Airdrieonians: in charge for forty-one matches.
Won or drew eighteen. Lost twenty-three.

Index